WAR AND GRACE

*One Woman's Time
at the Trenches*

Desmond McDougall

OVERALL AREA OF F.A.N.Y. OPERATIONS
FRANCE AND BELGIUM
1914 - 1918

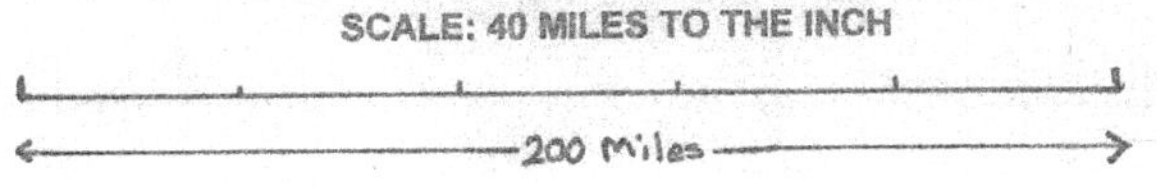

SCALE: 40 MILES TO THE INCH

Overall area of FANY operations

PROLOGUE

German Headquarters, Ghent, Belgium, October 1914

The Corporal of the Guard, utterly out of his depth, threw open the massive doors to the ante-room within. The usual hubbub ceased. Dead silence descended on the officers and men congregated there. All heads swung round, staring at her. One or two, mistaking her for a man, saluted without thinking.

"I saluted gravely back," Grace wrote later, *"and looked around for a likely interpreter."* Recovering himself, a very dapper ADC asked her business. She stated it quietly: *"I am English. I am a nurse. The English officer I have been nursing is dead. I want to return to England."*

A small group of officers gathered round her. All spoke perfect English. They made plain they could not permit her to return to England. She would go to Brussels, and from there she would almost certainly be sent to Germany.

Grace continued to press her point. She was a nurse. She would go to England to nurse English patients. Not to Germany to nurse Germans.

They couldn't understand it. An Englishwoman in British officers' khaki, with a Lieutenant's insignia. The discussion was brought abruptly to an end by a senior Colonel who strode up to the group. He was quite clear. She would present herself at these Headquarters at 9 o'clock the next day, when her papers would be prepared for her. She would then be sent to Germany via Brussels.

Savouring the drama of the situation to the end, Grace recalls:

"So, with many salutes we parted, and I swanked out through the courtyard filled with Germans, as if khaki had never before been so fittingly worn…"

CHAPTER 1
Family Background

It was 1936. Princes Street, Edinburgh was warm, sunny, busy. Mrs Grace McDougall, who had led the First Aid Nursing Yeomanry (FANY) with such distinction during the Great War, was taking tea on the balcony of a well-known café, with her three children. Across Princes Street on the Bandstand set in the Castle grounds, the Band of the Royal Scots was coming to the end of its programme.

There was a momentary silence. The Band rose to its feet. The rousing notes of the National Anthem rang out. The tea-drinkers took little notice, carried on their conversations to the clink of the teacups. All, that is, except Grace McDougall. Pushing back her chair, she stood up, straight, rigidly at attention.

With a flick of the eye, and a nod of the head, she indicated to her children that they must do likewise. They did so, reluctantly, and pink with embarrassment.

As the music rolled and swelled, one or two men at adjoining tables stood up. Others followed. Conversation ceased. Long before the final chords reverberated across Princes Street from the Bandstand, every man, woman and child on the balcony, and inside the cafe, were standing rigid, silent.

Grace sat down again, and an elderly man of marked military bearing approached the table. He looked down for a moment at Grace.

"Thank you for that," he said. "I wish there were more like you." He turned and walked smartly away.

There were few people who could have carried it off, especially a woman.

It was typical of Grace, determined, unashamedly patriotic, going her own way, never mind what people thought. The strong-minded courage of her own convictions had carried her through the stresses and horrors of the Great War, made her such an inspiring leader as Co-Commandant of the FANY, never taking no as an answer, pushing back the endless barriers that officialdom and prejudice put in her way; also, it has to be said, badly ruffling a few feathers in the process – not only within the Establishment, but among her FANY colleagues at Corps HQ, who were often left to pick up the pieces.

The first ever War Bride in khaki, after her marriage in January 1915 to Capt Ronald McDougall, Grace became known universally throughout the Corps, with respect, simply as 'Mrs Mac', still remembered and still in use today, a hundred years after she joined the FANY. To her close friends, she was always just 'Mac'.

Her memory, and the tradition of being stubborn and unflinching in the face of red tape – on one occasion she used the long-remembered phrase "red tape cuts no ice with me" – are carried forward with the Annual Award of 'Mrs Mac's Quaich', to the FANY who is deemed to have most lived up to that attitude in the past year.

Grace was born on June 3rd 1886, the fifth of six children. Her parents were both Highland Scots from west of Aberdeen. Her grandfather, Joseph Smith, a crofter at Woodend, Glen Tanar, was turned off his croft by the Laird in the 1830s. He moved to Dee Village, long since swallowed up by the expanding city of Aberdeen.

The reasons for his removal are lost in the mists of time. Grace's children remembered being told that it was to make room for sheep. More recent research has revealed an interesting piece in the 1896 issue of *'In Memoriam'*, a publication of important obituaries from Aberdeen and its immediate vicinity. It specifically mentions *"the farm at Woodend, on which the Mansion House of Sir William Cunliffe Brooks now stands"*. It seems there may well have been more to it than just sheep!

And just perhaps, her strong, inborn antagonism to arrogant misuse of Establishment power was an inherited instinct from that time. Who knows?

Grace's father, Charles, was a man of great charm and deep religious convictions, an Elder of Aberdeen Free Church. Much of his strength of character was certainly inherited by Grace, standing her in good stead in her role as Commandant of the FANY Corps in the war years ahead.

After serving his apprenticeship as a grocer, Charles opened his own business, and went from strength to strength as a businessman, becoming a partner and then owner of Gordon & Smith, a prestigious

High Class Grocers & Wine Merchants in Union Street. Considering that the 1841 Census listed him at the age of 14 as a 'Gardener', and his brothers as 'Labourers', he did remarkably well for himself.

He died in1896, when Grace was just 10 years old.

Grace's mother, Isabella, daughter of a slater, was a strong-minded woman of formidable character, who kept a firm hold on the children as they grew up, especially after the death of her husband. While she encouraged them in the pursuits and hobbies which interested them, she tried to instil a strong sense of responsibility to family and community.

Grace's siblings were varied in their interests. The eldest, Agnes, appears more domesticated than the others, staying with her mother until her premature death in a flu epidemic of 1915. Little is known of her.

The second sister, Isobel, studied medicine and became a doctor. She was a person who loved life, music and dancing, bringing a sense of fun into lives around her.

The next in line was Caroline, with a definite artistic bent, fond of art, painting, poetry, happy go lucky.

The first of the boys born was Charles Theodore (Charlie) who, together with his younger brother William (Billy), was to have a great influence on Grace's life. Charlie was three years older, Billy three years younger than Grace. Together they made a formidable trio, until both boys were killed in the Great War.

On the death of Charles Snr, the family's life changed once again. Isabella sold the thriving business, both boys being much too young to consider taking it over. The smallish house at 67 Dee Street was also sold, and Isabella moved to a virtual mansion, Ashley Lodge, in Great West Road.

Here they settled into a much more affluent lifestyle. Riding became the love of Grace's life. She developed into an extremely accomplished horse rider, along with her two brothers. The three of them, now almost inseparable, took up shooting and fencing. Grace excelled at both. In 1910 she became the first woman to win the Rifle Shooting Competition at the prestigious Richmond Rifle Club; as a fencer, she took part in matches not only in England, but in France and Germany as well, winning prizes and acclaim.

However, she still found time to take part in amateur dramatics, dressing up and writing, away from her brothers' influence. Although loving any time spent with them, she was as strong-minded as her mother, and made her own choices when she so desired.

But things were changing. As Grace moved into her teens around the turn of the century, the close-knit relationship with her two brothers drew to an end. Though still bound by their affection for each other, the paths of adulthood took them in different directions: Charlie to begin his full-time service with the 3rd Dragoon Guards; Billy travelling the world in search of adventure under the guise of studying the agriculture of different countries, finally leading a thousand-mile horseback expedition from Punta Arenas on the west coast of South America to Buenos Aires in the east.

While her brothers were away Grace spent a year at a Convent in Belgium, at her mother's suggestion, no doubt in the hope that the experience in that sort of environment would help to rein in her tomboyish energies, and lead her into more ladylike pursuits. She loved it, learned to speak French, which was to stand her in good stead later, but her adventurous spirit never diminished.

What she was really looking for was some real direction in her life, something she could grasp with both hands, direct her considerable energies and abilities into, and devote herself to wholeheartedly.

As December 1909 drew to a close, she found it!

An advertisement in The Times, seeking "young ladies of independent means to be trained in Horsemanship, Signalling, First Aid and Camp Cooking". It went on to detail age limits, and costs involved, subscriptions etc. But to Grace, all that was subsidiary to the main item to catch her attention. The word 'YEOMANRY'. That one word jumped out of the page at her, The First Aid Nursing Yeomanry Corps.

Grace herself wrote later: *"It was solely because of its title 'Yeomanry' that I sought out this Corps."*

What she didn't know then was that as fast as 1909 was fading away, so were the FANY Corps. In January 1910 Grace travelled to London to find out more, listened to the rose-tinted account of the Corps given by its founder, self-styled Captain Baker, decided it was for her, and signed up.

It was a momentous decision, and was to have a huge impact, not only on Grace's life, but on the FANY Corps itself. Teetering as it was on the cusp of oblivion, Grace seized it with both hands, pulled it back from the edge, built and moulded it into a lasting, outstanding Corps of intrepid, fearless and dedicated women.

The Smith Family

Ashley Lodge

67 Dee Street

Gordon and Smith

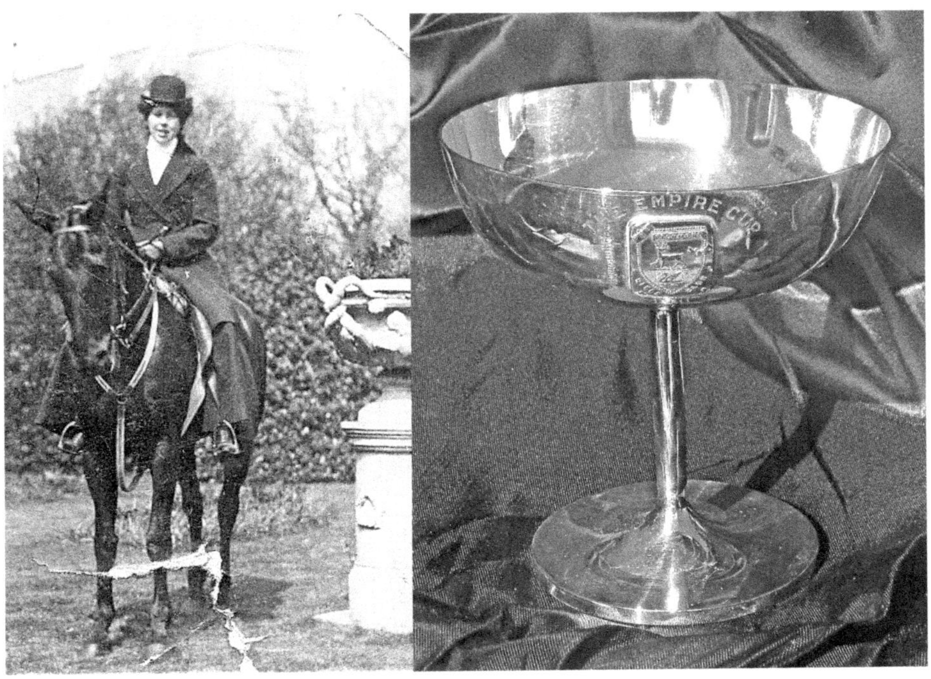

Grace on her horse Castor   *The Richmond Rifle Club Empire Cup*

1909 Girl who loved dancing

CHAPTER 2
Rebuilding The Corps

Grace determined to find out all she could about the Corps she had joined. The more she discovered, the more she accepted, perhaps subconsciously, that she had at last found her direction in life, and began to realise just how much she would have to do to mould the organization to her vision of it.

She threw all her energies into making this decision worthwhile. About her first meeting she wrote later: *"I turned up in my quaint uniform with fast beating heart to face the battalion of women"*. In fact, as she noted, the 'battalion' turned out to be six ladies at the riding drill, and three for stretcher training. She was disappointed, but not disheartened. She stayed on. *"Was it,"* she mused in her diary later, *"my Scottish reluctance to losing my guineas, or was it merely Destiny that made me remain?"* She added darkly: *"I left that parade in thoughtful mood!"*

The FANY Corps had been founded by an ex-Cavalry Sergeant who had been wounded in the Sudan Campaign some years before. After he left the army he brooded on the lack of immediate medical aid to those left lying wounded on the battlefield, and came up with what he saw as the solution. A troop of young women, able to ride well, and trained in First Aid, who would hover on the fringes of the field of battle, then gallop out to succour the wounded and get them back to a Medical Aid Post staffed by trained nurses. It was never made clear just how the wounded were to be transported, but it was assumed to be on the backs of the rescuers' horses.

Grace dug further into the Terms & Conditions. Uniforms and First Aid kits were to be provided by the young ladies themselves. They also had to pay a 10 shillings joining fee, six shillings a month subscription to HQ and a Riding School, plus the cost of horse hire! This was no bar to the well-heeled young ladies, and the idea caught on. Many middle and upper class women were bored and dissatisfied with the restrictions of their Edwardian lifestyles, and saw this as a way of escape to a more exciting world.

Recruits poured in, especially after the Corps' successful appearance at the Royal Naval & Military Tournament of 1908. Baker's daughter Katie, promoted to Sergeant Major, was given the task of overseeing recruitment, and the year 1909 started off extremely well. But it was then, Grace discovered, that it all began to fall apart.

A show held in June to raise funds produced a princely £170, mainly to obtain an Ambulance Wagon. Then the money vanished. Of the ensuing rows and investigations there is very little information, but there was a faction within the Corps which was very critical of, and dissatisfied with, the way Baker was running it. This faction, led by a very strong-minded and able woman, Mrs St.Clair Stobart, a practising suffragette, managed to tear the Corps apart when her group of followers signed a motion disassociating themselves from Captain Baker and his Corps.

Months later, it transpired that the missing £170 had been deposited by Mrs Stobart in an account opened in the name of The Women's Sick & Wounded Convoy Corps, set up and run by Mrs Stobart herself. Eventually, after a good deal of legal wrangling, the money was split 50-50 between the two Corps. Stobart was forbidden to use the FANY name in any context, and she left the FANY, later reappearing with her much depleted Women's Corps in Serbia.

This was well-nigh a fatal blow to the FANY. 'Captain' Baker, as a Sergeant of Cavalry, may have been able to put the fear of death into his troopers, but faced with a bunch of well-off, incorrigibly independent ladies, was out of his depth completely. His Corps, 100 strong the year before, could now barely muster a dozen. Interest waned and died.

The more Grace delved into the recent past of the Corps, the more she realised how Baker was burying his head in the sand. Things were far removed from the picture he had painted for her when she made enquiries before joining. Once she had grasped this, she determined she would change things.

From that time on, the Corps entered an entirely new phase, and would never look back. Over the next year or two, Grace took it by the scruff of the neck, and shook it back to life...

The small group of FANYs who gamely stayed on after the

fiascos of the past year were staunch and true supporters of the Corps and its aims. Baker and his daughter Katie were still nominally in charge, but they were shaken by the recent events, and their ideas for publicity and recruitment were uncoordinated and unsound.

One of the FANY in particular who remained loyal, was Lillian Franklin. She had joined the Corps in 1909, the year prior to Grace, and was to become the firm foundation on which Grace was able to build a strong and virile Corps, unfazed by the often wild and unexpected way in which Grace sought to expand its identity and sphere of operation. Already on the promotion ladder as a Sergeant, she and Grace became Co-Commandants of the Corps. Known affectionately as 'Boss', Lillian went on to be sole Commandant of the FANY in the immediate post-war years.

She and Grace were chalk and cheese. Lillian, quiet-spoken, totally unflappable, confident, steady, never given to histrionics, a woman who carefully thought things through before taking any action.

Grace, on the other hand, was emotional, impetuous, always ready to jump in where angels would fear to tread; plans and ideas tumbling headlong out of her, one after the other; on to the next project before the last was properly up and running, but confident it would be. And almost always right, probably because of the sort of girls she led – spirited, determined, and all guided strongly by their unofficial motto "I Cope"!

Between the two, Lillian and Grace made an incredibly effective combination, but inevitably on occasion were very much at odds with each other. There is no doubt at all, however, that without the seemingly tireless, forceful determination of Grace, and her constant enterprise both in the early pre-war days and during the dreadful war years, the Corps would never have survived. Not only did it survive, it grew, both in numbers, influence and activities.

But in 1910 Grace was a newcomer, and had to play the waiting game, something she did not excel at!

One of the first assignments Baker gave her was to act as an usher at a London East End factory dance, handing out not only programmes, but also recruitment leaflets for the FANY. This was highly unlikely ground for enrolling 'young ladies of independent means', a fact which Grace pointed out to Baker in no uncertain terms when she went to his Holborn HQ to speak to him and express her dissatisfaction with the whole set up. As a result, and no doubt recognizing in her future officer material, he asked for her help in future projects.

This was just the opening she had been working towards. Having been given an inch, she lost no time in seizing the proverbial mile. She redesigned the totally impractical uniform; out went the scarlet jacket, the voluminous dark blue skirt, riding side-saddle – as all respectable young ladies were taught.

In came riding astride, khaki tunics, divided skirts with riding breeches beneath, boots and puttees (a long narrow piece of cloth wound tightly and spirally round the leg from ankle to knee); and to begin with, that great symbol of the British Empire, the 'solar topi', or sun helmet. She followed this up by arranging the drills, and writing a First Aid Directive based on the Royal Army Medical Corps (RAMC) Training Manual.

The new breed of FANY had been born. It was just a start. There is no doubt that Grace was a genius at organizing things, and possessed a flair for spotting opportunities. Unfortunately, she tended to see only the big picture, leaving the detail of ground-level problem-sorting to others. This rather cavalier attitude was to arouse deep antagonism among some colleagues in the war years ahead.

CHAPTER 3

Publicity Stunts

The priority now, however, was to increase numbers through publicity, and raise their profile. This would also involve working to overcome the then current attitudes of the man – and woman – in the street. Their usual reaction to the sight of FANYs in uniform was ribald laughter and jeers. This had to be overcome. To aid this process, Grace was working on rebuilding the image of a FANY as a woman of daring and adventurous spirit, with cheerfulness, humour, and a touch of glamour, plus ability and efficiency.

It was a process which would have its problems, one of which was to make sure the girls knew the boundaries. Grace was already looking on the Corps as *her* Corps, and frowned on any behaviour seemingly frivolous, or bringing discredit to it. After one incident Grace sternly laid down that *'no member shall be allowed to sit on the box of an ambulance in the arms of a young man'!*

Over time, she took on the task of organising personnel. She hunted round for recruits, and pestered her friends to join. On the other hand, she was keen to weed out those who did not come up to scratch, or take things seriously. *"Amongst them,"* wrote Grace, *"a soulful young lady with peroxide hair, very fat and hearty, who insisted on wearing white frilly drawers under her khaki skirt. She also insisted on falling off her horse at every parade and displaying them. She had to go!"*

Grace, now a Sergeant-Major, involved herself in other publicity events, bringing the FANY and their uniforms and abilities to the general public's gaze and attention. In one such stunt, with no real experience, but confident in her own ability to cope with any situation, she drove a large 2-horse ambulance round London, via Knightsbridge, past Harrods – plenty of ladies of independent means there – navigating Hyde Park Corner, getting almost hopelessly mixed up in the heavy traffic along Piccadilly, past Green Park, through Piccadilly Circus, and thence safely back to the Holborn HQ.

Another of her escapades, which she later admitted she was *'happy to forget'* was to lead a Troop of six inexperienced FANY on horseback from Hyde Park, round Marble Arch, down Oxford Street and down to the Embankment, alongside the Thames. Stressful it may have been, but it was seen by a large number of Londoners, and got some press coverage the next day. Mission successful!

By this time, Grace had organised riding lessons with the Surrey Yeomanry, and the Hussars from Hounslow Barracks; membership was increasing, and confidence in the future of the Corps had recovered completely from the traumas of 1909. With this new confidence came a determination to show themselves off more often.

On the death of Edward VII in May 1910, Grace and Katie Baker went to Buckingham Palace with a red and white Maltese-Cross-shaped wreath on behalf of the FANY Corps. This gesture was later personally acknowledged by Queen Alexandra. It was a start.

As a follow up to that action, Grace approached the Metropolitan Police, offering the services of a fully equipped horse-ambulance and stretcher-bearers to help with the crowds who would be flocking to the funeral. The offer was declined. Undeterred, Grace arranged for members of the Corps to attend the Lying-in-State in uniform, where some were able to give First Aid to several who fainted in the heat and the crush.

A small detachment of FANYs, under the supervision of Nurse Isobel Wicks, a strong-minded, devoted and outstanding FANY, attended the Finchley Hospital Carnival, a magnificent, spectacular and crowded event, getting more coverage all the time.

The Corps also turned out in force for Derby Day at Epsom, helping out with minor ailments, such as 'ladies wilting under the sun'. It was on their way home, however, that they were able to flaunt their usefulness. A man had fallen off the back of a car, and, though not seriously injured, was taken to the Epsom Cottage Hospital, at his request by some of the FANYs. Later on, while the remainder were on their way home with the ambulance, they came across a more serious case of a motorcyclist who had been knocked off his machine by a motor car. The FANYs immediately administered First Aid. *"Blood was pouring from his head, and one eye was badly torn"*. Once patched up, they took him off to the South Wimbledon & Merton Hospital. Again, their actions and uniforms gained attention.

After that, attendance at the Derby became a regular event for the FANY. In fact, the following year they had to convey the body of a policeman struck by lightning to a mortuary.

Grace, though very active, had not yet got fully into her stride, and in 1911, with the two Bakers losing ever more control, she herself arranged for Headquarters to move from Holborn, where it had been since Baker set up his Corps, to a flat she had rented in Lexham Gardens, South Kensington, which was much more accessible to the Corps Members.

There they were able to carry out more training under RAMC Sergeants and Army signallers whom Grace had managed to co-opt, and who actually came to the flat to do the training. On top of this, never one to take 'no' for an answer, she cajoled the 19th Hussars at Hounslow Barracks to give them cavalry drill, and ride there also. Later on, when the flat became too small for the numbers being attracted, she arranged for the instruction to be done at the Surrey Yeomanry Barracks.

As a result of all this specialist training, the Corps set its sights higher still; at the great Festival of Empire at Crystal Palace, for instance, attended by people from all over the world in fact. That they were allowed to take part at all says a great deal for their negotiating expertise, as well as their connections. It was to be a demonstration of the original, but now obsolete, concept of a FANY's role, galloping onto the field of battle and attending to the wounded. A mock battle had been orchestrated between soldiers who had served in the Boer War, and scores of other veterans disguised as Zulu warriors, armed with the short stabbing 'Zulu' spears and *knobkerries* – long, thin but deadly clubs. Boss and Grace were to be the FANYs involved.

Grace wrote in her memoirs 'Five Years with the Allies': *"We had to come in at full gallop, leap from our saddles, and gallop off again* (with our wounded) *amid the shouts and spears of Zulus, and to the wild applause of thousands of spectators. One admiring and rather drunken gentleman forced his way to us at the end of the performance. He hiccupped at me 'I'm half Scotch myself', to which I tartly replied 'Yes – and the other half soda!' which had the desired effect of making him vanish."*

Wearing their original uniforms of scarlet jackets, dark blue skirts, white belts and First Aid kits, and scarlet caps with shiny black brims, they made a huge impression on the crowds who had flocked to watch. Good, stirring British Empire stuff, naively unaware of the shocking reality that they were to face three short years ahead.

CHAPTER 4

Corsets And Camps

By now, there was absolutely no doubt that Grace was firmly entrenched in building a future for the FANY. Funds were needed, as well as ideas and publicity, and she was to become equally adept at that side of her campaign. One of her money-raising schemes involved a well-known firm of corset makers, Sandows. Grace agreed to place an advertisement for their product in the FANY 'magazine' which Grace was publishing at her own expense, 'Women & War'.

The advertisement took the form of a four-page Supplement. On page 1 it introduces the *"NEW CORSET – Tested and Approved by the Editress of Women & War, and already worn by several members of the Corps"*. It continues in this vein, and explains that *"Mr Eugene Sandow, who is recognized as the greatest authority on the subject of the human form, has produced a unique garment, known as 'Sandow's Patent Health & Perfect Figure Corset'…"*

The inside pages continue the eulogy, and include a photograph of Grace in the full parade regalia of a FANY Corps Staff Sergeant, looking extremely smart and slim. She is quoted as saying, *"I have worn your corsets regularly while performing various duties of the Corps (First Aid work, Stretcher Drill and Riding) …they preserve the outline of the figure better than any other I have used!"*

Just how much money she raised through this is not known, but Grace would certainly have squeezed the last penny out of them for her FANY!

The other great way of increasing expertise were the weekend, or longer, summer camps. Despite, frequently, a lot of discomfort, the ladies loved them and thoroughly enjoyed themselves. Before Grace arrived on the scene, Baker had organised a couple in 1908 and 1909. Unfortunately, very little record of them survives. The first FANY camp was held at a place called Chiddingfold, in Surrey, on an estate owned by a Mr Waechter. He was a great supporter of the Territorials in particular, and the military in general. He took an immediate and keen interest in one of the earlier FANYs, Lieut D'Arcy, whom he subsequently married, and she was to become Lady Waechter in the course of time.

Grace, who had done a lot of camping herself with her brothers in the hills and mountains of Aberdeenshire, was quick to realise the value of these activities, not only for the benefits of training in the field, but for the bonding that would follow from shared discomfort and hardship. She could also see that it could be useful in sorting out those who were seriously dedicated to the new role from those who were inclined to be lukewarm about it all. In fact, she wrote in an early edition of The Gazette: *"It is not a Corps of shirkers, but of workers. Those who look upon the training of the Corps as a pleasant pastime are advised to think twice before offering themselves at Headquarters as recruits!"*

From 1910 onwards, the number and scope of the camps increased as Grace extended her grip on the Corps. After her meeting with Captain Baker asking for her help, she admitted, *"I spent the next few months fighting for my way in the office."* It looked as though she was winning.

Years later, in her fascinating history of the Corps, 'FANY Invicta', Dame Irene Ward said of Grace, "She was an energetic, forceful personality with a flair, which never deserted her, for seeing where there were openings for the FANY to operate." Grace spotted immediately the possibilities of media publicity, as well as getting closer to the regular Army contingents at these camps. She was beginning to achieve her goal of greater numbers of recruits and a higher public profile.

To give him his due, Captain Baker had endeavoured to do just that, when in June 1909 he had organised a ride from London to St Albans, 50 girls on horseback accompanying a horse-drawn ambulance. They had received a right royal welcome from the Council, with the Mayor turning out in all his finery, surrounded by his councillors, and treating the FANYs to a sumptuous tea, before they set off back to London.

However, when Baker and Katie decided that in November 1910 they would repeat the ride with an epic journey from London to Edinburgh, Grace was aghast. Never one to turn down the chance of publicity, in this case she was realist enough to see the enormous problems associated with this. She wrote to Katie, who had been put in charge of the project, and pointed out the huge administrative difficulties – the weather for a start, changes of the horses *en route,* accommodation, cost. She also pointed out that if the enterprise failed, the resultant adverse publicity would probably far outweigh any applause from success. She followed this up with another letter to Baker himself, and the whole idea was quietly laid to rest.

The power struggle between Baker and his appointed officers was heating up, and he was beginning to lose ground. A letter from the Duke of Argyll in February 1911 was addressed to 'Miss Franklin'; and another from Lord Valentine merely to 'Madam'. Baker was being sidelined, and it was around this time that Grace arranged the transfer of HQ to her flat at South Kensington. The writing was on the wall for the Bakers.

As the camps were all held close to London, Grace persuaded the Surrey Yeomanry and 19th Hussars to continue to train them in their camp venues. There were two camps in 1911, followed by two more in 1912, at Haslemere and Bourne End, both highly successful. At Haslemere in particular, only a weekend camp, Grace's hopes for publicity were amply fulfilled. She recalls: *"masses of people came to tea, including the Marquis of Sligo, then Lord Altomand and his family, and over 100 visitors on the Sunday afternoon."* Unfortunately, swamped with visitors as they were, not a great deal of training was fitted in.

A few months later, Grace organised a week-long camp at Bourne End. It was much quieter, but very successful in terms of training and *esprit de corps,* aided as ever by the Army instructors on loan. This camp was part financed by Grace herself, as were some of the others.

Though Grace went on record as saying she felt that 1912 was the real turning point in the path of the Corps, the 1913 camps were much more successful. The first, at Brookwood, was FANY Pat Beauchamp's introduction to the FANY. She became one of the better known of the early FANYs, and later lost a leg when her ambulance was hit by a train at an unguarded level crossing, just minutes after she had finished loading the last of her wounded into a hospital ship. In the first of her two books, 'Fanny Went to War', she wrote about her arrival at the camp to 'test the waters', at Grace's invitation, before joining: *"There was a large Mess Tent, some half dozen or more bell-tents, a smoky but serviceable-looking Field Kitchen, and at the end of the field were tethered the horses."* Having been shown into the Mess Tent and told to wait for the C.O., a thunderstorm erupted, and rain was *"pouring through the roof in small rivulets. Even in peacetime, comfort in the FANY was at a minimum"*. It was the sort of challenge the ladies met so well, as they demonstrated in such an outstanding and inspiring way in the years ahead. Pat wasted no time, and signed up immediately!

Later, another weekend camp held at Norbury was featured in The Tatler, with a glowing article about the FANYs. Deliberately underlining the similarities, it was printed immediately next to a photograph of a group of debutantes being presented at Court!

The camps became more disciplined and militarized – largely through Grace's influence, possibly a throwback to her adolescent years spent with her two brothers. She had been promoted to Lieutenant along with her senior, 'Boss' Franklin. At about this time she issued another set of Standing Orders: *"Officers' Orderlies will make the beds in the Officers' tents, clean their boots each morning, and polish the brass on their belts."*

The long summer camp at Pirbright in 1913 brought their greatest windfall so far – again through Grace's enthusiasm and expertise in networking among friends and acquaintances. The Guards regiments held their summer camps at Pirbright, and Grace, who admired them greatly, hoped to someday obtain their backing.

Always on the lookout for opportunities to advance the cause of the FANY, once again Grace had found a possible opportunity, and seized it. She recalled: *"Thanks to my sister and I shooting at Bisley I had discovered a farm at Pirbright"* (the venue for many of the Regular Army's camps and manoeuvres) *"which was ideal for camping out"*. She booked a suitable field there and then.

Her efforts to woo the Guards succeeded. There was a natural affinity between Guards Officers and the FANY, both groups from the same social backgrounds. They took the FANY under their wing and lent them most of the equipment they needed. In the past, the girls had had to hire what they required from the Army & Navy Stores at Victoria. Now those days were gone, though they still had to rent the field at 15 shillings a week!

It was not just the Guards, though, who helped out. Their old friends from the 19th Hussars provided cavalry instructors to improve their riding drill skills. They also cheerfully provided a supply of hefty troopers to act as 'casualties' for the FANY to bandage and remove to safety.

It was apparent, too, that there was some competition among these elite regiments, vying with each other to look after this band of attractive, vivacious and adventurous young ladies in uniform. The Royal Horse Guards, generally known as 'the Blues', were delighted to help, preparing equipment, setting up a Marquee, bell-tents and a kitchen. However, when a sergeant of 'the Blues' asked her if they would like a swimming pool, Grace thought he was joking. *"Oh yes, rather,"* she laughed. *"You fix it!"* And fixed it was. She recalled later the welcome – it was a very hot summer – appearance of a large canvas pool filled with cold water.

During that 1913 camp, the Rescue Races, as they were called, were becoming more competitive, and more popular with the FANY, and were getting a lot of Press coverage. Horsemanship was at a higher standard, more risks were taken, more falls recorded. The young ladies were remarkably tough and resilient. Dame Irene Ward records in 'FANY Invicta' that at one of these events Grace fell from her horse, which then rolled on her shoulder. *"Only a flesh wound,"* she laughed as she got up, and was in the saddle again next morning. This was typical of the way the FANY took everything in their stride.

The Irish Home Rule Bill had been published earlier in the year, and Grace, with her nose for seeking any expansion in the role of the FANY, writes: *"I offered the Corps to Sir Edward Carson as an ambulance unit for the Ulster Army. Sir Edward accepted provisionally."* As a result, Carson sent a Colonel Davis, Principal Medical Officer of the Ulster Army, over to inspect the FANY at training. This was very successful, and was followed by an invitation to Grace to go to Belfast and discuss the idea with Sir George Richardson of the Ulster Ambulance Service, and also meet Sir Edward Carson personally. Grace went, taking another FANY, Cicely Mordaunt, with her. There was mutual accord, and the FANYs were thrilled to bits at the opportunities opened up. The Press got wind of it – no doubt Grace had something to do with that – and The London Budget ran an article at some length under the headlines 'WILL ULSTER FIGHT?' describing the FANY as 'gentlewomen' prepared to take a brave part, declaring "these ladies, at least, are **Ready to Take the Field!**". The paper also mentioned the aristocratic and military connections – always a good selling point – and pictured Grace with four scions of the Irish aristocracy.

It all came to nothing. In a long and disjointed letter to Grace, the Secretary of the Medical Board at Unionist HQ in Belfast expressed the unfavourable military view of ladies exposing themselves (to danger) in a travelling ambulance. He went on, "I do not want to dishearten you but if we do have a row here the rowdy element, which is a very cowardly one, would necessitate guards being supplied to any woman in the field… the military people are looking rather askance at the idea…" He ended, perhaps as a sop to possible hurt feelings: "Your Corps is of such good material I would love to have you over."

Though that was the end of that little scheme, it resulted in a lot of media attention, especially at the 1913 Pirbright Camp. Grace wrote about the start of that: "*We rode down* (to the farm) *at Whitsun, and were absolutely mobbed by reporters. Unfortunately we had five ardent Sinn Feiners in the ranks, and still more unfortunately they were in the foreground of every Press photograph, and appeared all over the country as 'Off to Fight for Ulster'!*"

Although it hadn't worked out quite as she had wanted, the publicity the attempt received put the FANY Corps firmly on the map. Not only did the whole thing give the members of the Corps a lift in morale, but the jeers of the public that they had had to endure suddenly became very muted.

Maybe not quite yet accepted, but they were well on the way.

CHAPTER 5

Camps And Conspiracies

By 1914 the Corps was on a high. Membership was well up, as was morale and confidence. There had been two good years of working and training together, and all the murky past of 1909 was behind them and forgotten. There was a strong, effective leadership in Grace and Lillian. The halcyon days of peace were drawing to an end, but the camp at Pirbright in the summer of 1914 was truly memorable. Not only did the various Guards Regiments look after them more than in previous years, giving them greater support than ever before, but there was a marked feeling of respect for each other and what they represented, that perhaps had not been there before.

The FANYs worked hard at these camps. As Grace had laid down in the Gazette, 'it was not for shirkers'. They were up at 5 a.m., and before breakfast at 7 o'clock there was a Mounted Parade and Inspection, and the horses to be groomed, fed and watered. Immediately after breakfast there was a tent and equipment inspection, followed by a lot of First Aid training – bandaging, identification of various conditions and wounds, stretcher bearing. Grace had also arranged for groups of FANYs to help out at the Guards Camp Reception Hospital, getting 'hands on' experience as opposed to purely theoretical.

Lunch was at 1 o'clock, with various lectures through the afternoon, until tea at 4 o'clock. After that, from 5 o'clock to 7 o'clock they practised cavalry drills, with supper at 8. From 9 until 10 there was Morse Code or Semaphore instruction, by which time they were all ready to fall into bed. The camps were a great success. They loved it, so different from the pampered life most of them lived normally, and it was their choice. Most felt they were doing something really useful. Grace wrote: *"Everyone loved the camps, we had a heavenly time, lots of hard work and discomfort, but unfailing cheerfulness, fun and good fellowship."*

It was at this last pre-war camp, too, that Grace demonstrated yet again the capacity of her FANYs to exploit situations to their advantage, especially if it involved initiative and quick thinking. Some time before, she had attended a Hygiene and Army Sanitation course addressed by an RAMC (Royal Army Medical Corps) Officer, Major Smallman. Speaking to him after the lecture, she asked if he would visit them at their camps and see their work. He agreed, and came to more than one. He was impressed with their performance, and asked Surgeon-General Woodhouse if he would inspect them.

On the day, an RAMC, Sergeant Pepper, who had long been an instructor at FANY gatherings, arrived very early, removing any identifying items such as his cap and tunic.

When the General arrived with Major Smallman, he barked at Grace. *"What do you want to show me? I've seen hundreds of VAD shows."* He added that he could *"only spare half an hour"*.

Grace replied innocently, *"We're not VADs, so this will be a change for you. What would you like us to do?"*

He hummed and hawed a bit, then told Grace he wanted so-and-so done. It was, in fact, an unusual and intricate bandaging procedure, used as a trick question in RAMC tests. Grace had never heard of it. However, using her amateur stage experience, she kept a confident smile on her face, and suggested that as he was pushed for time, he might like to inspect the Cookhouse. Here they had stationed the most attractive young FANY at the camp. He was almost immediately captivated by her blue eyes and "face as sweet as God ever made", as someone wrote afterwards. She kept him talking for quite some time, before he returned to the bandaging squad.

Pepper had had ample time to show them how to bandage him, and brief them on the whys and wherefores. The General was at first unbelieving, then suspicious. *"Why d'you do that?"* he asked. The girls had all the answers.

"By Gad," he barked, *"it's the first time I've ever seen that done properly."*

"Yes," said Grace, *"it's the first time you've been to see our Corps."*

He still looked suspicious, and peered at Sergeant Pepper. *"Who's that feller there?"*

"Oh," replied Grace artlessly, gazing back at him, *"we get soldiers from the Guards camp to act as patients. They're very decent like that."*

The General's 'half-an-hour' stretched over both lunch and tea, being shown the whole gamut of FANY activities. As he prepared to leave finally, the General turned to Grace and said, *"Go up and see Arthur Sloggett at the War Office. Tell him I sent you. He should be able to fit you in somewhere."*

Grace would never let an opportunity like that slip through her fingers. Within a few minutes, FANY Walton was galloping down to the railway station with a telegram. It read:

> *Sir Arthur Sloggett War Office*
> *When can you see me recommended ask immediate interview by General Woodhouse breaking camp Monday.*
> *Grace Ashley-Smith, Lieutenant, FANY Corps.*

It was a Saturday night, but was in time to be handed in at Waterloo. On Monday a reply was received:

> *Lieutenant Ashley-Smith, FANY Camp Pirbright*
> *10 o'clock Tuesday – Sloggett.*

Grace was there at the War Office right on time. Sloggett told her they were having trouble getting the Red Cross and St John's Ambulance to work together. *"Where can we put you?"* he asked.

"Attach us to the RAMC," she replied confidently.

"Hmmm," he said. *"Well, I won't forget you. I'll do what I can. Come and see me again."*

After that triumph of ingenuity, there followed what to Grace was close to the pinnacle of her ambitions. The FANY were attached to the Skeleton Army, as Britain's small, but highly trained Regular Army was known. The bare bones of Britain's fighting Army, out in the fields around Pirbright on their final manoeuvres before war struck, had the FANY Corps alongside them, something no women's unit had yet achieved. The real zenith was reached that same fortnight, when they were invited to take part in the Guards' Church Parade, the first time women had ever been invited to do so.

Grace was over the moon. In her memoirs she remembered, *"One of the Grenadiers was our 'marker'. Franklin and I went up to salute Lord Bernard Gordon Lennox, who was senior officer that day. Bishop Taylor-*

Smith preached, and I was thrilled and bursting with pride to be there at last with the FANY, the Grenadiers on one side, the Coldstreams opposite, the Scots Guards on our right and the Irish Guards alongside. There are certain supreme moments in everyone's life. That was one of mine. It was worth all the labour and slogging, and self-denial and discouragement – all the ups and downs, all the jeers and sneers and laughter – to be there at last – part of the Army – yes, and with the best of it!"

It was an extraordinary experience, the end of an era, lifting the chins, straightening the backs and raising the spirit of every Member of the FANY, just weeks before they marched off to the War to end all Wars.

CHAPTER 6

Back Home To The War

On August 4th 1914 Grace was on her way to South Africa to visit her sister Caroline, who was married to a South African doctor, when she heard that war had been declared.

She had made the decision to visit, full of faith in *her* FANYs, as she always thought of them, confident they were in very good shape, ready for anything. She was still on a high and glowing with pride that she and the FANY Corps had been accepted by the Brigade of Guards at the Pirbright Camp, and invited to join with them at the Guards' Church Parade. She had absolute confidence in 'Boss' Franklin who was as dedicated to the FANY as she was.

Now, aboard the *Guildford Castle*, her reaction to the news of war was typical, earning a stern rebuke from the Captain. She wrote in her diary, *"We all stood there speechless. I was the first to speak. 'Thank God it's come now.'"* Her emotions ran too strongly for her to think of explaining, as she did in her diary later – *"while I'm still young enough to be in it"*.

The Captain swung about and faced her, anger sparking in his eyes and voice. *"God forgive you for that, my girl,"* he growled.

But it did little to diminish her naïve delight. Like so many of her background and generation, she believed in the jingoistic idea of war – heroism, gallantry, glory. The true face of war in all its horror and devastation, broken bodies and broken hearts, was to be revealed in the four ghastly years lying ahead of her. But for now, it was *her* war, *her* FANY, and she was proud to be in both. The spirit of youth and adventure was strong in her; she couldn't wait to get home, get her girls across to Belgium and into action.

For much of her girlhood she had grown up sandwiched between her two brothers, one older, one younger, both a bit wild and adventurous. Always with Charlie and Bill, Grace too became wild and adventurous, headstrong and confident.

She didn't hesitate for a moment. Within an hour of her slight brush with the Captain, she had cabled ahead to the Union Castle

Line office in Cape Town, with instructions to book her on the first available ship home to England. They took her at her word and booked her onto the *Edinburgh Castle*, due to sail for England within hours of its sister ship's arrival at Cape Town. On arrival, Grace spent four hours on the docks organizing the transfer of her luggage from ship to ship, and was off back to England and *her* war.

By good fortune, one of the passengers on board was the Belgian Minister for Colonies, M. Louis Franck. Never one to pass up a good opportunity, Grace asked him about the chances of helping out in Belgium. As a teenager around 17, she had spent a year at a Belgian Convent, and spoke a fluent, though slightly fractured, French. It was enough to cement a friendship that would shortly stand her in good stead. He was in receipt of daily signals from the Belgian Government keeping him up to date with what was happening, while Grace told him about the FANY, what they could do, and offered to send the first Convoy to Belgium. There was little Louis Franck could actually do, but at least a connection had been made.

The ship called in at Gibraltar to pick up a number of Civil Servants and Diplomats, and was provided with a Naval escort vessel for the remainder of the trip home. Shortly afterwards they came across an Austrian boat suspected of mine-laying. After firing a shot across its bow, and taking all its crew aboard as prisoners, the Navy set about sinking it, with conspicuous lack of success to begin with. Watched with breathless anticipation and patriotic pride by hundreds of passengers lining the rails, it took a long time. Grace recorded in her diary later, *"It (the Austrian boat) was so light they couldn't hit her below the water line at first. Then lo, the boat had gone. We who had tarried to the end and had our rewards, rushed in to dinner."*

This rather callous attitude to destruction was largely born of patriotic fervour that affected everyone, no doubt coupled with the fact they were well distanced from the actual scenes of carnage. It was in stark contrast, certainly in Grace's case, with the revulsion and despair she was to experience only weeks later, when faced with the vile reality of war. She wrote in her journal, after visiting a tiny Belgian village, Holstadt, ravaged suddenly by modern war: *"I looked, with an awful horror in my face. We all stood with our eyes fixed on the charred and blackened body that lay there. I had never known a human skeleton would look so small when the flesh was gone round it."* This small incident was her first close contact with the ruthless reality of total war. All this and more lay ahead of her.

The *Edinburgh Castle* and escort made all speed back to England. Arriving near Portsmouth, Grace was again to experience – and later express – the patriotic pride born of tradition at the sight of Britain's Naval might.

"Out from Portsmouth Harbour," she recorded, *"with blood-red sun behind them, came the long line of ships. Silently, majestically, they passed on either side – massive Dreadnoughts, torpedo-boat Destroyers, Battle Cruisers. We stood entranced, our throats too dry to speak. We could only watch in awed silence. The most wonderful sight I've ever seen – the British Fleet going out to war."*

That was September 5th 1914. Grace herself was soon to sail into battle herself – battle with the Establishment, the War Office, the Red Cross – all those who during the year before had assured her of how highly the FANY were regarded, and who now turned their backs and slammed doors in their faces.

CHAPTER 7

Ronald McDougall Joins The Fray

Ronald McDougall sat quietly at the bar on Johannesburg Railway Station, sipping a cold beer. Outside on the platform waited his 'Boy', his African servant, guarding the small trunk and suitcase Ronald was taking back to England with him. He smiled wryly to himself. Not much to show for – what was it? – sixteen, seventeen years in South Africa. Not quite the fortune he had hoped to make. Going home for the first time since that hurried and secretive departure.

He thought of his father, who had died two years before, patriarchal and overbearing, insisting that Rannie, as he was usually called, study and become a lawyer; and the useless, wasted arguments he put up against the idea. Perhaps it was his father's Scottish obstinacy that he wouldn't listen. Finally, given the money to settle him down at University in London, he made his decision to run away. Again he smiled to himself. 'Run away' was a bit Boys' Own Paper-ish!

Instead of ending his journey in London, he had gone on to Southampton, and booked a Cabin Class ticket to Cape Town. He'd show them, he thought, when he'd made his fortune in gold or diamonds. He landed at Cape Town, still with a bit of money in his pocket, but oh, so wet behind the ears. He was lucky at last, when directed to a Boer Voortrekker who was off to the Transvaal with his family, but wanted an extra hand who could ride and shoot. At least Ronald could do both, a bit of an expert with horses and rifles. He could still see that old Boer glaring at him, with those piercing dark eyes, and hear his thick accent *"Trouble with you bloody Englanders, you're too soft. You have to learn to kick these bloody Kaffirs around a bit more. The only way to get work out of them. And you bloody Englanders, too."*

Then he had to demonstrate he could ride and shoot, before the old man took him on for the trek. It was an experience, not a pleasant one, but at least he grew up fast. It was really living rough.

The family slept in the wagon, except the elder son – he and Ronald were in sleeping bags alongside. He had never experienced anything like it before, sometimes desperately short of food, often a scarcity of drinking water. But he learned to live off the land, how to hunt game, and grew fitter than he had ever been before. Except for the three weeks of malaria, when, to his surprise, he was looked after with great kindness by the Boer family and made a complete recovery.

At journey's end, he was genuinely sorry to say his farewells, finally joining another small group of professional outriders heading back to Cape Town. This involved him paying his own way, and by the time he reached the Cape, he was once again almost broke. This time he was not so lucky getting a job. The possibility of a civil war was looming, people were putting off treks into the interior, putting off plans to set up in farming, unsure of the future.

Then salvation came out of a clear blue sky. A crack Militia Regiment was being expanded, in view of the tense situation between the Boers and the English. The Cape Mounted Riflemen were looking for young recruits who could ride well, and were able to shoot. Ronald fitted the bill, and on the 8th August 1898 he became No.3365 Private Ronald McDougall. He was delighted. No worries about money, accommodation provided, and three square meals a day.

Gazing into his beer, he remembered the elation he had felt, dressed for the first time in his new uniform – high collar khaki tunic, riding breeches, black Rifle Corps buttons, knee-high leather boots, and bamboo swagger tan tucked under his arm. It was a wonderful feeling.

Nearly five years he served, right through the Boer War, then when it was over, Ronald bought his discharge for £3, on 15th May 1903. For the next three years he roamed the velt, through Transvaal again, up into Rhodesia, prospecting for precious metals or diamonds, never finding anything. Then into Natal in early 1906, just as the last Zulu rebellion broke, a result of a £1 a year Poll Tax, and the killing of two white Policemen near Durban. Once again low on funds, he saved his situation by joining up, this time with the Natal Naval Corps, part of the Natal Militia Force, and served with them for eight or nine months, as 'Seaman 1st Class' until the uprising was finally dealt with!

Ronald recalled his sense of futility when he was once again discharged; no job; nothing to get back to; wasted years. This time he gave up prospecting, travelled to Boksburg in the Transvaal, where he had acquaintances, and the local gold mines were booming. 'By God,' he remembered, 'if I thought soldiering was hard, it was luxury compared to down the mines' – the heat, the dust, the danger, even though the Africans did most of the hard digging work.

He buckled down to the job, worked hard for and obtained his Blasting Certificate, authorizing him to carry out blasting operations. This was one of the really important jobs down the mines: one miscalculation and hundreds, or even thousands of tons of earth and rock could come crashing down on the poor devils in those deep tunnels. It happened all too often. But it was well paid because of this responsibility, and at last Ronald could move into quarters of his own, and live reasonably well.

It all came to an end in August 1914. The first he knew of the war was arriving at the surface of the mine after a shift, to be met with the news from the overground teams, full of excitement.

It was later that evening, washed and refreshed, that Ronald made up his mind. For a long time he had dreamed about going home to England, but what for? There had been nothing there for him. But now there was. His country was at war. He was a trained soldier. If he could get home, and join up, it would perhaps make up for the disappointments of his long absence in this beautiful, but harsh country.

The next day he went to the office to tell his bosses of his decision. One, he remembered, slapped him on the back, said *"Good for you, Rannie."* Another growled, *"Don't be a fool, man. You're too old for fighting anything now."* But his mind was made up. By selling off his rifle and one or two other possessions, plus his final pay, and what little he had saved, he could afford the train fare to the Cape, and a cheap passage home on a minor line ship.

He took out his half-Hunter watch, a present from his father when he was sent to University, finished his beer, and made his way onto the platform. The hissing and shunting of the great black engines drowned out almost everything. He found his carriage, his

Boy trotting along behind him, trunk on his head, suitcase in one hand. Before settling onto his bunk in the two-berth compartment, he lowered the window, paid his Boy a farewell bonus, and gazed around the cavernous place in the semi-darkness. Great gouts of steam rising. Shouts magnified a hundred times under the huge cavernous roofing, noise echoing everywhere. Then the clamorous grunting and puffing and hissing of the massive engines overwhelmed all other sounds, as vast plumes of smoke coiled their way skywards.

Ronald grunted, dropped back into his seat, and prepared himself for the two-day journey to Cape Town… then Southampton… then… what? He wondered if he would ever be back. For all its faults and his failures, he loved this wild, rolling, treacherous country…

The thought of marriage never crossed his mind. Nor any idea that the girl he was to marry would shortly be heading home to England after the briefest of stays in Cape Town where he was now heading.

The Guard's piercing whistle cut through the bedlam of sound, and, amid great billows of steam and smoke, the train growled its way slowly into the African night.

CHAPTER 8

Fighting The Establishment

On the outbreak of war, Boss Franklin and her Sergeant Major, Edith Walton, immediately contacted Sir Arthur Sloggett, as Director General of Medical Services at the War Office, to offer the services of the FANY – the same Sloggett, who had been so complimentary and apparently impressed after Grace's discussion with him only weeks before.

Now, however, he became totally unhelpful, stonewalling all their efforts to get his help and support for the FANY. The Establishment line was, very firmly, that a battlefield was no place for a woman and that was the position that he was determined to hold at all costs.

Fortunately he was not quite as patronizingly disparaging as some. When a certain Vera Matthews applied to the Admiralty, prepared to accept any kind of job at all, she was brusquely informed by their spokesman that *"we don't want any petticoats here"*.

Vera, much later, became Director of the WRNS!

Again, a Dr Elsie Inglis, Head of the Scottish Women's Hospital Unit, applied to the War Office, volunteering to take a qualified team of medics with their own ambulance, across to Belgium, and was told even more rudely, *"My dear lady, go home and sit still!"* It was an attitude that prevailed almost everywhere in the male dominated establishments of the time. Later, Grace herself was on the receiving end of a similar rebuff on the quayside at Folkestone.

Fortunately, Lillian Franklin was a woman of great strength of mind, known for her calmness and unflappability. She accepted Sloggett's decision calmly, though inwardly seething with frustration, and returned to FANY HQ apparently unperturbed. There she organised sewing parties, collected any sort of equipment which could be useful, and got staunch, dependable FANY Margaret Cole-Hamilton to come to London to sort out, list and pack that equipment for a time when it might be needed.

Such was the situation when Grace returned to HQ and was briefed by Boss Franklin. Already, as a result of the Establishment's attitude, many of the FANY had resigned to take up other posts, some with the VAD, or the Red Cross, convinced that there was no chance of service overseas with the FANY. Only a small band of dedicated and steadfast members remained, and on these stalwarts – Cole-Hamilton, Mosely, Nora Cluff, Walton, and of course the rock-steady Lillian Franklin – the future of the FANY was built.

Disgusted with Sloggett's attitude, Grace swung into action at once, demanding an immediate interview with him, which he finally and reluctantly agreed to after some initial prevarication. Even she – tough, confident, using Scottish bluster and feminine wiles, reminding him that trained nurses with an ambulance were desperately needed – couldn't budge him from the Establishment line.

Ever resourceful, she changed tack, asked to go across the Channel alone, look at the situation, and report back to him. Perhaps this sudden change of tone, almost subservience, reassured him that he was still in charge. Little did he know. He agreed to her plan, *but only* if she herself could get the necessary passport and permit to take her across, *and* the prior agreement of the Red Cross, as they would be providing the transport. Sloggett was convinced she would get neither. How wrong he was!

Grace lost no time, went straight to the Red Cross HQ, completed the form they gave her, then badgered the Red Cross secretary unmercifully until she got it signed. All this happening in one visit was almost unheard of. From there she made a beeline for the Passport Office, arriving shortly before 3 o'clock, and it closed for the weekend at four. She was horrified at the number of people waiting to be processed, but she was in her khaki FANY Lieutenant's uniform, which gave her a psychological advantage over the majority who were mostly civilians.

Handing in her application form to the policeman on duty, she watched him slide it beneath the pile in the tray, then she sat quietly waiting for any opportunity that might arise. It came, when the policeman took a handful of forms from the top of the tray, called the names of the next small batch of applicants, and led them through to the processors in the main office.

Grace rose quietly to her feet, deliberately slow moving, though her heart was beating nineteen to the dozen, strode over to the in-tray, moved two or three of the last-in forms, including her own, to the top of the pile, and returned to her seat. It was England, and nobody said a word.

The policeman returned, standing watchfully, until the buzzer went for the next lot, when he picked up the forms, and read out the names. Grace's was first. The policeman frowned at her suspiciously, but noting her officer's uniform and Lieutenant's 'pips' trod carefully.

"Yours?" he queried.

Grace gazed at him, eyes wide and innocent. "Mine," she answered.

A moment's hesitation, then he led her and the others into the main office. Grace got her Passport and Channel Permit. But the battle wasn't over yet. She dashed back to Red Cross HQ, and was confronted by the same sour-faced secretary who couldn't – wouldn't – believe that Grace had got it sorted so quickly. But persuasion, persistence and perseverance won the day. Besides which, it was going-home time for the Red Cross staff, and they could see that with this particular customer, it would be a lot easier and quicker just to give way. They did. Grace got her Embarkation Permit signed and stamped and was off.

The episode was typical of Grace's attitude throughout the war to red tape or awkward situations. She would seldom, if ever, take no for an answer. She hurried back to FANY HQ, then to her flat, weary but triumphant. There she gathered a few things together, and next morning headed for Victoria Station and the train to Dover. Two days later she was in Belgium.

CHAPTER 9

Alone Into Belgium

On September 10th 1914 Grace arrived in Ostend.

This was something of an achievement considering that only 5 days before, she had been aboard the *Edinburgh Castle* docking at Portsmouth. This one-woman whirlwind was just getting under way, throwing herself into the sort of crowded, hectic itinerary that was to become her hallmark throughout the war. She had somehow found time to visit her mother in Edinburgh, a proud feisty woman whose comparatively humble early life had instilled a powerful sense of work ethic in her family. Admittedly, she had a struggle at the same time, trying to calm the wilder ideas of the three youngest family members, Charlie, Grace and Bill. Her advice to Grace when war broke out was to slow down, and "do something really useful, like working in munitions".

Through one of her many contacts, Grace heard of a temporary hospital in Antwerp. By-passing the usual channels, possibly through the auspices of her fellow passenger on the way home to England, Louis Franck, she was officially permitted to join it. It was a Field Hospital set up in a building in the Boulevard Leopold, tending both British and Belgian wounded. She arrived there, immaculate in her FANY officer's uniform, to be summarily confronted by the stark reality of wartime nursing. It was both chaotic and heartbreaking, She later recorded in her journal: *"The top floor has 60 beds and no lavatory, and only one little water tap and sink which serves all purposes – dishwashing, rinsing of urinals and bedpans, surgical basins and instruments."*

Matters were made worse by the growing volume of needs battling against the two great shortages – staff and time. Grace wrote: *"The next floor down is the same, though there is a little corner screened off round a commode."*

There is no doubt that the conditions were terrible, but once the initial shock had worn off, her personal enthusiasm, toughness, and innate organizing skills took over.

The Head of the hospital was a Dr Beavis, who must have been satisfied that she would be able to cope, even allowing for his desperate shortage of help. Or because of it! In any case, he put Grace in charge of the two wards on the third floor, and agreed whole-heartedly to her suggestion that she bring over a whole contingent of FANYs.

This was the opportunity she had been hoping and waiting for. Manna from Heaven! At the same time she was offered a 300 bed hospital to run on behalf of the Belgian Army, in Antwerp, showing how desperate the authorities were at that time. Grace immediately sat down to compose a telegram to 'Boss' Franklin with the good news. As soon as the telegram arrived, 'Boss' and her team sprang into action. In a matter of hours they were ready to leave. But, as it turned out it, they were already too late. The Germans, building up overwhelming strength, were poised outside the city. The FANY contingent were waiting at Fenchurch Street Station when the news arrived that Antwerp was about to be evacuated. Bitterly disappointed at this last minute hitch, they returned to HQ to wait and hope desperately for the next opportunity.

In the meantime, Grace was able to assert herself at least within the confines of her third floor 'empire', consisting of two wards with 16 and 12 beds respectively. But before she did so, she spoke to Dr Beavis, acknowledging that she was totally inexperienced in nursing apart from the First Aid training she had done with the FANY. She was concerned that she would now be expected to not only dress dreadful wounds herself but also direct other experienced nurses. Admittedly, since her arrival at the Field Hospital she had worked for some days alongside Dr Beavis, dealing with dreadfully mutilated men, but for once her confidence was waning slightly.

Dr Beavis fixed his gaze on Grace, and told her she was to carry on as best she could. It was all hands to the pump, and he was counting on her. That was enough. Her diary entry for that day simply says: *"At least I had a good idea of what not to do!"* And with her usual energy and authority, she set about improving cleanliness and sanitation in her two wards.

She watched, horrified, as an overworked nurse wiped out a cup for a patient to drink from, using the same cloth she had used minutes earlier to clean a bedpan. From working downstairs in the main wards Grace had suspected that this practice went on, but now the full realization of the awful truth hit her, and she was in charge.

Grabbing every cloth and rag she could lay her hands on, she washed them in boiling water laced heavily with disinfectant and washing soda. Then she stained some with patches of blue ink, others with red, and some she left unstained, hanging them all up in a line. Above this she placed a notice, written in French, with greasy crayons – 'RED FOR BEDPANS – BLUE FOR FACES AND HANDS – PLAIN FOR CUPS AND PLATES'. It certainly had an effect, not quite the one Grace expected, but perhaps inevitable given the circumstances the nurses were working under. It created a wave of disharmony and acrimony among the existing staff. They were doing their best to cope in dreadful conditions, and took it as direct criticism of their professionalism. And well they might. Here was this upstart *foreigner*, not even a qualified nurse, only been there a few days, put in charge of *their* wards, and giving *them* directions.

Diplomacy had never been Grace's strong point, but now she showed that she was able to adopt a calm and measured approach on occasion. Compared to the independent minded ladies of the FANY, these overworked, tired nurses were won over with ease. Grace sat them all down, and faced them. She admitted that her skills at nursing were non-existent compared to theirs, agreed that she had only been there a few days, but perhaps that was an advantage. She could take a fresh view of things, whereas they had been working under terrible conditions for weeks, short of everything, from medicines and equipment to sleep. They had done a marvellous job.

But they must try to think of their patients. They were men who were willing to give their all for their country, defending these very nurses from *les Boches* at the gates of their city. They deserved the best. Choosing the right cloth was a small price to pay. How would they feel drinking from a cup wiped clean with a bedpan rag?

She had made her point, with no ranting or bluster, no 'I'm in charge' attitude. It worked. The nursing staff accepted it, and her.

As a result, shortly after, she was given still more responsibility: a larger ward with men who were much more severely wounded. Again she told Dr Beavis of her doubts, lack of qualifications and experience. *"I know you can cope, Miss Ashley-Smith,"* was all he said. *"Now, just get on with it."*

She did. It wasn't easy, but she didn't expect it would be. She learnt as she went along. She learnt not to touch a wound, but gently apply a mix of iodine, or flush it with salt and water. She learnt the difference between clean wounds and septic wounds, the different kinds of dressings to be used for each. It was an enforced learning curve which turned out to be a godsend later on, as more and more FANY convoys found their way over to the battlegrounds.

Grace certainly worried about her capabilities, her lack of training and experience. It was evident within a short time that this was an opinion not shared by the doctors and senior medical staff there. They were impressed by her work and her attitude.

CHAPTER 10

War At The Sharp End

Although Grace had quickly proved her worth at the Field Hospital in Boulevard Leopold, willing to undertake any task asked of her, she longed for more direct action. She changed dressings, assisted doctors during operations, and carried out the many varied and often unpleasant tasks which so many of the wounded were unable to do themselves. But her upbringing and adventurous nature conspired to channel her thoughts and ambitions to more active participation in the war.

She got her chance. One afternoon, officially off-duty, she was asked if she would go with an ambulance to help collect the wounded from just behind the front lines. This was exactly the chance she had been waiting for, determined to prove herself away from the confines of a Military Hospital. She needed no further urging and leapt aboard the ambulance. This first foray for her was in the direction of Lierre. As they were approaching the front line zone, they met up with a cyclist, who waved them down. He explained he needed help removing the wounded further along the road. Away they went, the cyclist in front leading the way. Grace, who had never done this before, was full of excitement, smiling wryly at the thought of the Corps' original aim of ladies galloping onto the field of battle to succour the wounded in colourful uniforms of red, blue and white. And here she was, a few hectic years later, doing much the same, but in a motor ambulance and in a drab khaki uniform.

They stopped at a small brick house by the roadside, but before Grace could get out, both the driver and the cyclist had taken to their heels and were running wildly down the road away from the house. The countryside was flat; a ditch ran alongside the road. In the distance, Grace caught a glimpse of some cottages. On the road itself, she was aware of small puffs of smoke in the sky above her, wild explosions, then ahead of her, *"great clouds of smoke bursting from the ground"*. She wrote later, *"Suddenly I felt a great exaltation, and I ran – ran my hardest – and stood on the edge of the trench and looked in.*

There were three or four figures there, very still.”

This was her 'blooding' – her baptism of enemy fire. There was more to come. Two men began lifting another out of the trench, and a third man *"with a ragged, untidy moustache, and a white face was trying to climb out. One of his legs was all torn – clothing, and blood and bandage"*.

Grace leapt down beside him, wrapped his arm around her shoulders, and struggled out onto the road. She was deafened by a massive explosion close by. Half dazed by the sheer volume of sound and the breathtaking impact, she lost all sense of thought. She stood quite still, unable to move. A thick cloud of dark smoke rose not far away, and a frightening unfamiliar smell spread with it. She was alone. All the men had gone. But where? Forcing herself to swivel round, a feeling of dread within her, eyes blinking in the dust and smoke, she found them, all crouched again in the ditch.

At last she realised what had happened as her mind started to clear. A shell had burst just a few yards away. The soldiers, experienced, and recognizing the sound of one approaching, had instinctively flung themselves back into the ditch. Grace, of course, had had no such experience to draw on. Recording the incident in her diary, she notes, *"The men were looking at me with stolid unconcern. They were rising, going back [to the ambulance]. I went too."*

Then one of those many instances of black humour that occasionally occur when men are locked in combat imprinted itself in Grace's memory. As Grace hurried behind the other men, she heard a loud, wailing scream. Another shell? she wondered. The soldiers all stopped, grouped behind a very small, young tree. She records: *"I stopped, too, facing them, looking into their faces to question them. To me it was all new. I did not understand. All I saw was these white, scared faces – in them a sort of dumb appeal. A demon of mischief awoke in me of what we must look like – four hefty people hanging on like this to a little thin tree. I laughed, and their white faces and troubled eyes glared at me!"*

Leaving the 'shelter' of the tree, they ran to the ambulance, where Grace found two other men lying beside it. One was conscious and moaning. Grace gave him a shot of brandy that she carried with her. Then the two badly wounded men were loaded onto the stretcher racks, leaving the others sitting on folding chairs inside. Grace waited in the road with one last casualty for whom there was no room. The car's owner, sitting in front with the driver, glanced at her and raised his eyebrows. Grace shook her head to indicate she would stay behind. The owner immediately jumped out of his seat in the front, settled the last wounded man into his space, and told the driver to go on back to base.

The house, larger than it appeared from the road, contained a bar. A number of Belgian soldiers stood around. *"Ragged, unwashed heroes"* Grace called them, just out of the firing line for a few hours. They were a revelation to her, took her inside to see the holes in the roof and walls, broken glass and china scattered everywhere. In the back yard, Grace recorded, *"lay a dead pig, raising a stench of protest to the sky!"* A young lad brought her a jagged piece of shrapnel, still warm. He asked her if she had been afraid. *"Yes,"* Grace answered him, *"very afraid, terribly frightened for a time."* The soldier just shook his head slowly from side to side, and shrugged his shoulders.

Eventually the ambulance returned, more wounded were loaded in, and this time Grace sat in front alongside the owner and the driver. The patients were unloaded at the Boulevard Leopold hospital. They then drove to the English Medical HQ in Antwerp, where they were then directed to yet another Forward Aid Post. There they found crowds of soldiers, many wounded, but most already treated and bandaged. By this time Grace was becoming almost blasé. She recorded in her diary: *"We filled the car and sent them in. I was left alone and waiting for their return. The men I was left with were all very curious. They all wanted to talk, asking if I was an officer; why had I left England to come and help the Belgians; had I helped many?"*

Outside in the roadway, reinforcements headed for the trenches – marching men, lorries, cavalry, artillery and ammunition carts, and staff cars. Most expressed amazement at seeing an Englishwoman in khaki standing there; as well as rousing cheers, some, to Grace's amusement, saluted her as they passed. She recorded in her diary: *"The sun was setting, and far away the loud roar of guns cut through the evening stillness. This was war!"*

This was indeed war, any romanticism torn out of it. Here she came upon a British soldier, trudging slowly, very slowly, towards her. Her surge of pride in seeing a British uniform waned, as he stopped every few steps, *"looking fearfully behind him"*. The Belgian soldiers fell silent, watching him and Grace. Seasoned troops could read the signs and body language new to Grace. He claimed to have just delivered a message to some trenches about a kilometre away. On his way back he had seen a Priest driving an officer in an open car; a shell had exploded nearby, and the officer's head had rolled into the road. He was shaking and looking for sympathy. Grace wrote of the incident in Nursing Adventures:

"I returned his look coldly, for I was too new at the game to realise what a nerve-strain these gallant fellows had to undergo. Many a time since I have regretted my hardness, my stupid lack of understanding, for the poor lad had been through hell!"

It was a lesson that remained with her forever afterwards.

The overall experiences at Lierre were to be repeated again and again during the days she was based in Antwerp. She got to know well the villages and towns in the area – Malines, Bucherout, Vieux Dieu, all near the wavering front lines of the time. Only the Belgians were prepared to allow women to do the dangerous work of driving their ambulances out to treat and pick up wounded from forward zones. Neither the French nor the British would even consider it, but Belgium was desperate for help. Their small and badly equipped army had no Medical Service, as such. But even in their desperation they drew only on the services offered by foreigners, seldom involving their own Belgian ladies.

But Grace, and later the FANY Corps as a whole, were infinitely grateful. Without the active support and encouragement of l'Armee Belge in those early days, it is almost certain that the Corps would not have survived. It was through the example of dedication set by Grace, originally on her own, and followed by those FANYs who came later into France, that so impressed the sceptical and suspicious in the military hierarchy that led to their being invited to work with both the other Allied Armies.

One of Grace's more memorable trips was to an old and quite beautiful church at Bucherout, badly shattered by shell fire, with walls partly collapsed and windows blown out. It was being used as a

Forward Aid Post with an English doctor in charge. Those casualties ready to travel were loaded into her ambulance, and despatched to Antwerp hospitals. Grace remained to give what help she could. By now she was becoming quite adept at dressing and bandaging a variety of wounds, some quite serious ones.

The Sacristy of the church was littered with packets of cotton wool, bandages, bottles of iodine and a bottle of chloroform – almost beyond worth in that place at that time! Two severely wounded men had just been brought in: the first, shot through the buttocks; the second with an arm hanging loose – "by a thread of flesh" – as well as having been shot in the stomach. Grace assisted the exhausted doctor as best she could, but in spite of their combined efforts the soldier *"shouted and writhed, and at last his head fell back: then, with a mighty effort, he raised himself and opened his mouth to speak: but only a stream of blood gushed forth, and a brave soul had gone to his God"*.

Much of Grace's writing about the early part of the war is in this vein. It is difficult now to understand whether it was one way of getting these dreadful experiences and memories out of her mind; or, as the book was written and published at the height of the war, it was, perhaps, to draw attention to the real and so often unseen, horrors undergone by the men in the trenches. Experiences the men themselves were loth to talk about at home.

By the time Nursing Adventures was published, of course, FANYs were serving with all three Armies. It was written anonymously, as a tribute to all those FANYs who crossed the Channel. Not just an account of *what* they had to put up with, but *how well* these "elegant, high-spirited, well-bred young ladies" coped with the dreadful and often revolting tasks they experienced in hospitals and Aid Posts, having voluntarily abandoned their lives of well-heeled ease at home. They frequently found themselves living under dreadful conditions, willing but ill-prepared to face and overcome the stresses they were subjected to. But with humour and selflessness, they were able to subordinate everything to the well-being of the sick and wounded in their care.

Meanwhile, back at the church, the ambulance, full once again, was sent back to Antwerp to drop the men off at whatever hospital would accept them, while Grace remained behind. On this occasion, with treated wounded piling up awaiting transport, Grace once again demonstrated her imagination, decisiveness, and disregard for red tape.

A large Army Service Corps bread wagon appeared, and on the spur of the moment Grace pulled rank on the sergeant in charge, and commandeered it. The fact that she had absolutely no jurisdiction over anyone other than FANYs was a point she was not prepared to argue, even if she gave it a thought. However, despite his initial objections, the sergeant entered into the spirit of it. Between them, they spread some blankets under a covered gateway and unloaded all the bread. Then, dragging the sergeant into nearby shattered and derelict houses, they collected mattresses, blankets and cushions, turning the flat bread wagon into a haven of comfort and warmth. When the doctor in charge saw it, he was delighted. A big wagon, it cleared almost all the wounded awaiting transport, and so with a broad smile on his face and an exaggerated salute, the Sergeant set off back to the city.

While all this was in progress, those soldiers and officers in the vicinity were keeping eyes and ears open for the direction of the ever-present artillery barrage. If it was directed onto a certain road outside the town, that was the signal for all to leave as quickly as possible. Troops were passing in all directions, mostly between Vieux Dieu and the front line trenches not very far away. One of the most frequent visitors was Winston Churchill, First Lord of the Admiralty, who passed by several times in his Staff Car, encouraging and speaking to some of the 3000 men of the Naval Brigade he had sent in to help the Belgians defend Antwerp.

As Grace's car returned, a call came in to pick up three wounded from an outpost about four kilometres up the road, which was unfortunately under shellfire all the way. Grace noted, *"Luckily my little ambulance was ready, and off we went."* Arriving at the lonely outpost, she met an Englishman wearing a Belgian soldier's cap; he had been attached to the Belgian Service, and Grace was to come across him again and again in the days ahead, always cheerful,,and in the thick of it. As they pulled alongside, there was *"an earsplitting skirl"* as Grace described it, and all bolted for their lives round the side of the small building, as a shell ploughed its way across the road, knocking down a tree on the far side.

Grace and her driver had a long wait, listening to the occasional shell targeting the road from time to time, while a Priest and the Englishman brought the wounded to the ambulance. When they got back to the Dressing Station at Bucherout, there was a rousing cheer from the St John's Ambulance men who had arrived in their absence. It was this sort of camaraderie that helped everyone to maintain morale in the difficult and dangerous conditions they were working in.

As evening approached, the workload grew lighter, and Grace rode back to Antwerp on the footboard of the last ambulance to leave. Apart from collecting the wounded, she had been interpreting for the English doctors, none of whom spoke French. Back at the British Medical HQ, she was asked to try to get a complete list, if possible, of all British wounded in Antwerp. This looked like a formidable task, but the Belgian owner of the ambulance she had been using assured her he had 'connections and would get the information for her. He was as good as his word, and during the next day had them ready for her.

That morning they left early for Bucherout, by way of Vieux Dieu. To Grace's surprise, the latter village was completely deserted, the English HQ empty, and the odd shell bursting in the streets. They left hurriedly and headed direct for Bucherout.

A Staff Car with two British officers aboard drove towards them, and Grace waved them down to ask if Bucherout was still the collecting station for the local wounded. The officer Grace first spoke to had no idea, nor did his companion. *"Go back at once,"* she was told, *"this is no place for an ambulance. The firing line is 200 yards from here."* And they drove off!

Some Belgian soldiers appeared in the distance, and they drove on to meet them. The soldiers were not much help. They said there must be wounded about, but they didn't know where. They added that the road wasn't too dangerous if the Mademoiselle stayed behind! This, 'Mademoiselle' declined to do, and they drove on and into Bucherout itself. So busy yesterday, but today it was quite deserted. Driving on a little further, they came upon a group of English Marines with a wounded Belgian in a wheelbarrow.

One of the Marines was trying to re-bandage the soldier's leg, which was swamped in blood. The Marine in charge said gruffly, "Let Sister do it", which she proceeded to do. The small party was completely lost, with no idea of the way to Antwerp, and spoke no French. Grace gave them directions, then loaded the Belgian into the ambulance. She wished with all her heart that she could load these wonderful countrymen of hers into the ambulance and take them on their way, but it was just not possible. She waved good luck to them, and set off once again into war-torn, bleak desolation.

CHAPTER 11

More From The War Zones

For much of this period, the war was chaotic and disorganised. It was still largely a war of movement; the era of set lines of trenches had not yet begun, and communications were erratic and unreliable. Much of the medical services were provided by men and women like Grace, a FANY, with no official attachment to a particular Army. Other volunteer services, St John's Ambulance, or the Scottish Ambulance Service. for instance, were doing what they could. Even privately owned ambulances driven or operated by the owner, like the one Grace had been attached to for some days, played their part.

This was just another instance of the confusion and lack of cohesion in those early days. Some of the group of Belgians they met had retained their rifles and equipment, while others in the group had thrown them away. Troops were split up, totally disoriented. Grace was slowly coming to terms with this, and beginning to understand just what these men had been through. Time and again she was hearing the same story from different allies, Belgian and British. *"The guns. We had no guns. What could we do?"* The men were referring to the big guns, the artillery with which the German Army was plentifully provided – but in those early days the Allies had nothing comparable.

This little party of disorganised Belgians had the same tale, the same lament. In the midst of it all, four wounded men staggered in to join them. Grace got them loaded into the ambulance, and, now full, it headed back to base Aid Posts and Hospitals.

On yet another occasion, and underlining the general disorder of things, on a road to the Chateau de Tragenham, they came across an English Doctor in a 'shell proof' dugout, fully equipped and ready to deal with any casualties, and very confident, but with no patients. He was also very surprised to see possible back-up from motor ambulances. The following day, when Grace passed that way again, the doctor was gone, along with all his supplies and equipment, his dugout empty. Just another unsolved mystery.

Back in Vieux Dieu, deserted a couple of days before, British soldiers and Marines were busy digging trenches and preparing defences, aimed at blocking the road to Bucherout, the expected route of any attack. The ambulance driver asked Grace if she was afraid to go any further. She told him there was no question of fear, only wounded. They drove on, leaving behind the safety of the khaki figures. Crouched in the car, Grace prayed, then scribbled her mother's name and address on a piece of paper, which she thrust into a pocket. She felt better.

At Bucherout all was destruction and desolation. Churches and houses reduced to so much rubble. Dead horses lay around, polluting the air with the sickening stench of decaying flesh.

Then came the whiz, whiz, whiz of shrapnel nearby, the shriek of shells and explosions, and close by the crash of falling masonry. Having raced to take cover before the explosion, the tension broke, and there was a concerted rush back to the ambulance. Grace was becoming quite used to this by now, learning quickly in those conditions. She recorded in her memoirs, *"the chauffeur broke all speed records on that return trip!"* They all were happy to get back inside the barriers erected by the English soldiers and Marines on the edge of Vieux Dieu, with only inches to spare as they sped through the sandbagged entranceway.

Once safely inside, Grace reported to the Medical Officer there, and he took her to see his 'hospital' in the fort, with stone cellars and earth piled all around outside walls to lessen the impact of shells. He had no dressings – they had been forgotten in all the panic and confusion – so Grace sent her ambulance back into Antwerp with a 'chit' for the Belgian Red Cross. She also entrusted her driver with what money she had, with instructions to buy white bread, butter and cheese.

With little else to do, she was offered a sandbag to sit on and watch the 'fortifications' going up. Never a fan of red tape, Grace had always imagined it to be found only in Ministry Buildings, or the Civil Service sanctums. She certainly didn't expect to find it here, almost on the front line. She was to learn differently! Sitting there, she noticed two tall, stone, tower-like structures reared up over the main barriers. She mentioned them to one of the English officers supervising the operation. Naively stating the obvious, Grace told him, *"If they were to be hit by a shell, surely they would crash down on the barrier trenches killing anyone in them? Couldn't they be knocked down?"*

Quite naturally under the circumstances, the officer exploded in frustrated wrath: *"We have been asking all day to have these houses taken down, and we can't. Why not? It's all red tape; a fussy old staff officer came along and said they were not to be touched!"* She felt so sorry for him.

Shortly after that, she was to experience another example of red tape at work, putting men's lives at risk. One strategically important section of the trenches being dug on the outskirts of Vieux Dieu got special treatment. The men slaved over covering the section with heavy wooden beams, covered over with a thick layer of earth, making them safe from anything other than a direct hit. It had taken them a long time and much effort.

Then to everyone's dismay, the same 'fussy little Staff Officer', who had to be obeyed, came along and ordered the officer in charge to have all the covering removed immediately. The reason? The Instruction Manual decreed that all supports were to be iron, not wood, in case of fire. He listened to no arguments or pleas. All the protective roofing must be removed. At once. And he strutted off self-importantly to his Staff Car and drove off. Of course, there was no suitable iron available; the coverings had to come off, leaving the men, and the defences dangerously exposed. Just one more burden heaped on the shoulders of the front-line fighting men, already battling against great odds under dreadful conditions. Grace wrote in Nursing Adventures: *"My heart ached for them. The men were disheartened and furious, and many a curse fell on that Staff Officer's head, and personally I think he deserved them!"*

CHAPTER 12

Escape From Antwerp

Eventually, Grace returned to Antwerp, and after helping out in the hospital for a few hours, settled down for the night in a cellar she had been offered in a nearby house. It was a night she remembered. She wrote, *"I washed in the kitchen sink, got into bed and wrote up my diary. That took some time, and as midnight was striking I closed it, and was snuggling down in my pillows, when…whiz-zz-zz – boom, came the opening salvoes of the German final attack on the city."*

It was the beginning of the end. Her days in Antwerp were numbered. The Germans at the gates were determined to seize it with all possible speed. Bringing their massive superiority in guns to bear, they began an unceasing 12 day bombardment of the city. Defended to the death by the tiny Belgian Army, and aided by the British marines sent in by Churchill, it was a forlorn hope, because the German Army was just too powerful. Antwerp could not hold out.

Preparations for evacuating the wounded commenced, a task which made a deep impression on Grace, and one she never, ever forgot. It tore her apart emotionally, being part of it first in Antwerp, then, not long after, in Ghent. She wrote in her diary, *"That was a terrible night. For two and a half hours we worked carrying men downstairs – top floor first with its 69 beds to clear (for by that night there were extra set up in the corridor), then the 2nd floor, and lastly the fracture wards on the first floor, though to me that seemed a mistake. It was down slowly with a heavy stretcher, and up rapidly with an empty one. My wrists and legs ached after the first ten men."* But it was just a start.

She was to feel a lot worse, helping one 'Dresser' to carry down no fewer than 30 cases. In Nursing Adventures, she described the chaos: *"Down below, the scene was horrible, a mass of helpless men, some on rugs, some on mattresses – all exhausted with suffering and want of rest, racked by the pain of their wounds, but brave as the gods of old."*

The long night wore on. Transport for the wounded had been organised – four motor coaches – but there had been the inevitable delays. Doctors and nurses worked as best they could in the flickering light to relieve the suffering. In the background, the roar and crash of German shells. With all patients now downstairs, it became a waiting game. Staff huddled together on the front steps, watching and listening – and responding to the occasional cries for help, or water, or just comfort.

Upstairs, someone had somehow managed to organise coffee and bread and treacle, a feast for the gods indeed. The thundering bombardment continued, random shelling spreading death and destruction. On and on it went, whizzz-boooom, the whistle of shrapnel. Some fell very close – one hit the upper floor of the darkened building. Still they waited, still no coaches. By this time Grace, and others, had been on duty continuously for more than 24 hours. Outside, the air was clean, the moon bright. She found a wooden bench, dragged it away from the wall of the building, and lay down to snatch some rest. A doctor kindly brought her a blanket from one of the wards, but she refused it with a shudder at the blood and filth on it. Someone covered her with a coat. There was to be no sleep.

She lay counting the explosions. She wrote, *"One shrapnel… two… three… eight… nine… ten. I began to feel proud of myself when number eleven arrived. Its hissing seemed to go through my brain. In wild unreasoning terror I bolted to the wall and crouched there, holding my breath, praying madly. The great BOOM was followed by an appalling crash – part of the house next door had gone."*

Grace and two or three doctors and Sisters headed for the top floor of the building, climbing a ladder to see out across the city as the first flush of dawn lightened the sky. Everywhere the orange glow of fires burned among heaps of masonry visible through gaps in the skyline. More shells flew overhead on their deadly errands. With a degree of understatement, Grace recorded: *"I wasn't sorry to climb down and return to my bench in the yard!"*

As dawn broke, men, women and children passed along the road, clutching whatever possessions they could carry, desperate to get away before the hated Boche marched in.

The Belgian Red Cross had promised Grace that she would be picked up by ambulance–car at the hospital. By now it was long overdue, as were the coaches for the wounded. She decided to walk through the almost deserted streets to their HQ in Place du Meir. *"Once I passed some weeping women beside their house, of which two storeys had fallen in, and I had to whistle to myself and hum snatches of song as I walked, to keep my spirits up."*

It was a wasted journey – none of those still at the HQ knew anything about any transport, and were busy packing up before leaving. *"Two passing English doctors caught sight of my uniform,"* wrote Grace, and they gave her a lift to the English Medical HQ, where she was told three buses were definitely going to collect the wounded from the Field Hospital and evacuate them. She walked back to the hospital, and passed on the good news to the patiently waiting staff. Then she took it on herself to go back into the building, as she obviously wasn't going to be picked up by the Red Cross, and collect bandages, dressings, scissors, and anything else that was easily portable and might be useful on the journey.

The dawn gloom gave way to daylight before the first detachment of wounded were loaded onto buses and ready to leave, under the command of an American doctor from Red Cross HQ, Dr Hoyle. To him, Grace entrusted her small personal suitcase, as she was staying behind with the remaining casualties and helping to nurse the new wounded arriving all the time. It was lost in all the confusion and she never saw it again. They were to be evacuated as soon as transport was available. *Les Boches* were expected hourly, and when they came it was generally thought that *sauve qui peut* (run for your life!) would be the watchword.

As the morning wore on, more buses arrived to take the remaining wounded to safety, and again Grace experienced the long, painful, heart-wrenching process of packing wounded men, some in awful agony, and desperately ill, into every available space.

Then it was down to the quay and into the ghastly confusion of terrified humanity, women and children weeping, crying out, many lost and hopeless. In the evening sun, some of the buses rolled across the pontoon bridge, bound for Ghent, and yet another motley collection of temporary and makeshift hospitals.

CHAPTER 13

The Nightmare That Was Ghent

By now it was into October. As the small convoy headed for Ghent, Grace realised to her amazement that so hectic and busy had she been, she had lost count of time and dates. Winter struck early and hard that year. Temperatures dropped and night came more quickly. Grace sat perched on a small, narrow seat in one of the buses, wrapped in a thin blanket – precious little protection against the creeping chill.

From time to time, one or other of the buses would get stuck in the almost freezing mud. All who were able would force themselves out into the cold to push it free. Then seemingly endlessly onwards, jolting and bumping over rutted roads, every jerk a stab of agony to the shattered and broken bodies hunched in the darkness.

In Nursing Adventures, Grace makes clear, on a note almost of despair, of how wrong she had been about war. *"To me, in the past, war had meant romance and heroic deeds, not the awful hell of agony it is."* This was to be a recurring theme in the bleak years ahead.

The heavily laden buses with their grim cargoes rolled into Ghent in the chill of another October dawn, rattling *"along the endless streets of tall, narrow houses,"* she recalled. At the Hotel Flandria, commandeered as an auxiliary hospital, the first of the wounded were unloaded. While this was going on, Grace and a nurse from a London hospital found the hotel kitchens. Here they heated a huge pan of milk, the only thing available, carrying trays of hot cupfuls to cold, tired and suffering men waiting in the remaining coaches.

The last of the coaches bore the worst cases, again making an indelible impression on Grace's memory, still taking in the ghastliness of total war. She recorded these impressions later. *"Every man was livid, with a drawn face, and lines of agony stamped on every mouth."* She remembers one of the first to be offered the hot milk, a young 18 year old English lad, who *"twisted his lips into a smile, and said 'give it to that chap there, Sister, he needs it more.'*

"That boy's smile," she wrote, *"broke through my calm, and I was*

crying bitterly while we finished our round. It was the saddest moment of my life so far."

Then the convoy moved on to a big convent, the Maison Saint Pierre, run by nuns from l'Ordre des Dames Christiennes. Grace writes with great feeling about the 'gentle, kindly nuns'. They were waiting at the entrance with hot coffee and English tea, a great comfort to the wounded and the medical staff alike. Here 32 wounded were unloaded and taken in, six or eight of them English.

The Mother Superior approached the doctor in charge, asking if it would be possible to leave an English nurse at the Convent, as the nuns spoke little English, and had no nursing experience. Looking back to her happy year spent before the war in a Belgian Convent, Grace was eager, almost desperate to accept, but it was not her decision. She waited with bated breath. It appeared that none of the English nurses were happy at the idea, and Grace waited no longer. She rushed to the Mother Superior and begged to be the one allowed to stay. Her offer was welcomed delightedly and *"with great joy in my heart"* she wrote later.

The buses moved on once again, with more wounded to distribute, finally stopping at the Hospitale Civile, where all the remaining men were unloaded. Grace, like the others, already worn out through lack of sleep, found this additional task both saddening and wearying. She remembered the hospital as a grim, forbidding place, and her heart went out to the badly wounded men who were to be left there.

At last the transfers were complete, and the buses moved on to rendezvous at a local café. Here there was a disorganised rush by tired and hungry nurses, orderlies and helpers. There was no way Grace could get any information about what was going on.

Instead, she took a taxicab to the home of a Belgian doctor whose address she had been given before leaving Antwerp. To her relief she found that Dr Hoyle was expected that morning. The Belgian doctor's wife made Grace most welcome, giving her breakfast and allowing her to wash and freshen up.

Dr Hoyle arrived as planned for a brief visit. He tried hard to get Grace to go with him and his group of medics back to England, but Grace wouldn't consider it. After he had departed, the Belgian doctor's wife and daughter offered to take her back to the Convent. They called at the British Consul's office on the way, to inform him of where she was, and that there were English wounded at the Convent. The Consul's daughter was interested to hear this, and promised to follow up to see what she could do to help in any way.

Grace was weary beyond words, and almost half asleep by the time they reached the Convent. It had been a long walk, on top of two days and nights of frenetic activity, excitement, and fear for her life. She wrote in her diary, *"I felt very much near the end of my tether. Above all things I longed for a hot bath, but though this was impossible, it was a luxury to get my clothes off and tumble into bed."*

Alas, there was to be little rest for her after all. Only an hour later she was awakened by one of the nuns, to tell her that another bus was at the door to evacuate the English wounded.

Slowed down by weariness, Grace dressed and stumbled down the stairs, to find that the bus had taken away all but three of the English patients. At that moment the Belgian doctor arrived, and at once called upon Grace to get the dressings-trolley out and do the rounds with him. Apart from the three Englishmen, there were now about 50 Belgian soldiers being looked after, most of whom were severely wounded, their suffering made worse by the sleepless night of the bombardment in Antwerp, and followed by another night crammed into buses.

Fortunately there were other helpers, the nuns and a few young women, who did what they could to ease the men's discomfort. The rounds took a long time, as Grace was the only one the doctor allowed to undo the old dressings, syringe the wounds, and apply new dressings. Much later, the nuns provided them with lunch, which Grace ate with a young Belgian girl, whose relatives had all been killed at Louvain earlier in the war. Although still only a couple of months old, the war was already beginning to feel like forever.

There was to be no respite for Grace. During lunch the doctor had asked her to do the rounds of all the patients, taking their temperatures, and making what extra notes she could about their condition. He would return at three o'clock. In the event it was five o'clock before he got back, and time for most of the dressings to be done again. It was a measure of her stamina and dedication that she accepted this without demur.

At last her day was done; she had supper at around 7.30, then fell gratefully into bed after writing up her diary. She remembered: *"the tiny cubicle amongst a dozen others, was a haven of peace..."*

Two hours later she was awakened by the sound of loud yells and cries. Springing out of bed and slipping on a coat, she groped her way towards the commotion, her *"brain a mass of chaotic thoughts!"*. A big figure in white suddenly erupted from a nearby cubicle, stamping and shouting. Half awake, completely disorientated, all kinds of things crossed her mind. A demented patient, perhaps – not for the first time? Or a thief? Or a German? She wrote later, *"I seized the figure and pushed it back onto the bed, and wondered vaguely if I could overcome it, or if I would be killed; and suddenly the mists of sleep cleared away, and I realised it was a woman with cramp in her leg!"*

Grace knelt down and rubbed the leg until the woman's companion turned up. Then, thankfully, Grace headed back to her bed again. A nun came to her with a message delivered for her from the Chief Medical Officer of the English Division in the town. He asked Grace to call in the next day, and let them know how the English wounded were getting on.

At a quarter to six next morning Grace was called by a nun, and another long day began. All dressings had to be inspected and changed. An English sailor from the Marine Division kept calling for her to 'come and look at him, now that he'd lost an eye'. *"Poor soul,"* wrote Grace. *"I remembered him from that last night of bombardment on the steps outside the hospital in Antwerp, suffering pain and thirst."*

That afternoon, after a hurried lunch, Grace was able to get to the English Division HQ and report. In spite of her great respect and regard for the Belgian troops, Grace always reserved her highest praise for British soldiers. After this visit to the Divisional HQ she recorded in her diary some of her feelings. *"There I saw lots of our own men – big and strong and confident; it is wonderful the moral (sic) effect conveyed by a big Englishman in khaki."*

She felt like this about our own troops throughout her service. A Highland Scot herself, and rightly proud of it, the word 'English' was largely a generic term universally used in those days for the British soldier. The sight of the khaki uniform always made her proud to be wearing one herself.

When she got back to the Convent, she was told that their only erysipelas patient was to be moved out at eight o'clock that evening. As the doctor had previously issued strict instructions that only Grace was allowed to touch him, she now had to get him ready, and then settled down to wait. By 10.30 nobody had come for him, and Grace got a First Aid helper to go into the town HQ and make enquiries. As a result, a one-horse ambulance-van eventually arrived to pick the poor man up. The driver flatly refused to go near the stretcher, or help in any way for fear of infection, so Grace and the First Aider had to manhandle it aboard by themselves. It was a bitterly cold night, the wretched chap had a temperature of 105 degrees, but orders had to be obeyed. The driver cracked his whip and the contraption moved away.

Once gone, Grace was left to clear the bed, soak the sheets in a powerful disinfectant, scrub and swab the bed itself, and all the floor space around it too. Nobody else would help her, in case of infection. After scrubbing and disinfecting herself, it was after one o'clock when she finally fell into bed.

Next day was Sunday, and Grace, with her strongly religious background, rose at 5.30 to attend the Service. *"It was a moving sight,"* she recalled, *"I knelt in the background, with the nuns, and the wounded who were able to get up and make their way to the Chapel."*

The doctor had also attended Mass, and immediately commandeered Grace for the rounds again, ignoring the fact that she had not yet had any breakfast. In fact, he was quite annoyed that the temperatures had not been taken! While doing the rounds, Grace, to her great surprise and dismay, came upon the erysipelas patient tucked away out of sight. He had been sent back to the Convent in the small hours of the morning, as the fever hospital refused to admit him, for reasons known only to themselves. Just another hapless victim caught up in the chaos of a retreating army.

Later that day, the Consul's daughter arrived to speak to Grace, offering to come back for night duty so that Grace could at last have an unbroken sleep. Her offer was gratefully accepted, as was an offer to give her a lift into town that afternoon to check on the patients at the Hotel Flandria, especially the seriously ill young Marine officer from Antwerp.

While there she met a very attractive woman, May Sinclair, a well-known novelist of the day, who knew nothing about nursing but was working for a detachment of the St John's Ambulance Association as a voluntary helper. The young Marine, Lieutenant Foote, was slightly worse. May and Grace got on well, and May agreed to visit the Convent later, in order to see the English wounded and help in any way she could.

As so often happens in war, the best laid plans fall apart. The Consul's daughter took Grace home with her to let her parents know what was happening. While there, a phone call from Ostend ordered the Consul and his family to leave Ghent immediately. So much for Grace's early night!

She hurried back to the Convent to tell the Mother Superior what had happened. All sorts of rumours had been flying about all day, and at last there was something official. There was news for her, too, which had come through from the Belgian HQ. All their wounded were to be evacuated at 8 o'clock the next morning.

In the middle of the preparations, May Sinclair arrived on foot, very late, having walked alone through the darkened streets. She had come to warn Grace that her small party were leaving Ghent before dawn, and she had arranged for Grace and the two remaining English wounded to go with them. This was a kind and thoughtful gesture, under very difficult circumstances. Grace walked with May part of the way back, then returned to the Convent to bring the Rev. Mother up to date with her plans.

The idea of a peaceful night was just a distant dream by now, and much of that night was spent with the nuns, making up small parcels of clothing to go with both the Belgian and English patients, in the hope that they might be of some use in the hours or days ahead.

While all this was going on, Grace heard the tramp of marching feet in the road outside. Running through to an outer window and peering down, she could see rank after rank of British soldiers marching out of Ghent. Yet another city was to be taken by the Germans. Grace could hardly hold back her tears, as the last of the marching men faded into the freezing night. Her diary of that night records: *"I still stood there; but of a sudden I felt desolate and very much alone."* Quietly and sorrowfully closing the window on the now empty street, she went back to help the nuns.

She never did get any sleep. Two hours after the marching men had gone, May Sinclair arrived with her car and three ambulances. The two English wounded were loaded aboard, and one, a Marine, moved them all to laughter. Dressed in white flannel trousers, khaki tunic and cap, he put on an aggrieved expression. *"I come 'ere a sailor,"* he remarked gruffly, *"an' I'm goin' away a soldier. Funny, aint it?"*

Grace was terribly saddened at having to say goodbye so soon, as were the nuns. *"I, too, felt my heart heavy,"* she recorded in her diary, *"for they had been the kindest of friends, and I loved them."*

The small party settled into the cars and ambulances, and set off into the dark, frosty night, with little idea of what lay ahead, or where they would end up.

Worn out, Grace managed to fall asleep, her head on May's shoulder. She would awake to find herself on the threshold of perhaps the most bizarre, dangerous and exciting experience of her life.

CHAPTER 14

Behind The German Lines

The cold was bitter and sharp; frost glittered on the road. The small convoy had stopped outside a large house in the village of Ecloo. It was 5.30 in the morning. Grace climbed unsteadily out into the freezing dark to join the others entering the house, where a big fire burned in a large comfortable room.

Beds were offered to the ladies, but refused, and they all – drivers, doctors, nurses, and a clergyman – sat round the fire together, relaxing in its warmth. May Sinclair, however, appeared to be arguing fiercely with a tall elegant woman Grace had not seen before.

Listening closely, it appeared that the young English marine, Lieutenant Foote, had been left behind at the temporary hospital in Ghent, too ill to be moved. May had been keeping an eye on him for a day or two prior to the evacuation, and although he was not her patient in any way, she felt responsible. She wanted to go back to help him, but had no nursing experience at all. The Parson also spoke of returning, but he would be even less use than May.

In her typically impetuous fashion, Grace rose and, putting on her coat, left the house. May and the clergyman hurried after her, out into the icy road, and asked what they should do.

"Stay with the group, and help the wounded you have with you," said Grace. *"I'm going back to Ghent."* They tried to dissuade her, but once Grace had made up her mind she could be very stubborn. May and the Parson walked with her to the railway station, where, by one of those strange quirks of war, there was a train due shortly for Ghent, only now just occupied by the Germans. Poor May was terribly upset and in tears because she was not a trained nurse and couldn't go.

Grace walked up and down the unheated train, trying to keep warm in the bitter cold. The Guard arrived and laughed cheerfully when Grace admitted she had no ticket. He told her that Ghent was full of Germans, telling her to *"go back, Mademoiselle. The Boches are brutes. It is no place for an English lady there now"*. But when she explained that she had no choice because of the English officer left on his own, she recalls *"tears came to his eyes; he pressed my hand, praising the doctors of the Red Cross"*.

At Ghent Station there was much confusion; men and women desperate to get away were loaded with trunks and cases. At sight of her uniform, many rushed up to her, to ask if the English were coming back!

She managed to find a taxi driver prepared to take her to the makeshift hospital at the Hotel Flandria. She wrote in a letter a little later, while still holed up in Ghent, *"The relief of the young Englishman when I entered, repaid me tenfold for the terrors I had undergone."* He couldn't understand why he had been left alone, why nobody had come to wash him, dress his wounds or give him anything to eat for so long.

There was disorder and chaos everywhere. Grace had difficulty finding clean water, basins, jugs, cups, almost anything. Eventually she was able to boil water on a small gas ring, wash him, and change his dressings. Then she went to check the adjacent rooms, all of which were dirty and untidy, with beds unmade and sheets and blankets tossed about. A young Belgian girl in a kind of nursing uniform came into the room. She stopped abruptly when she saw Grace with the young Englishman.

"Oh," she gasped, "you will stay with him? I am going. My father and mother are ready." Pulling off her cap and overall, she threw them to Grace, and disappeared out through the door.

Going in search of some help, and desperate to get word to the Convent that she was here, and to ask if they would take this poor, suffering boy, Grace ran into a big, bearded man who looked as though he might be in charge. She asked how she might get a message delivered. "I am not a porter," he growled, and stumped off.

After an unsuccessful hunt for anybody who could help, a short time later Grace was back in Lieutenant Foote's room. The same big, bearded man clumped in, and stared at the two of them. "Are you a doctor?" asked Grace. "I can find no charts or treatment book. What does he get?"

The man's expression didn't change. "I am not the doctor," he said, and walked out. Grace was getting desperate, when some time later an elderly Belgian lady arrived. She turned out to be very deaf, but kind and helpful. After several attempts to speak to her, the lady produced an ear trumpet, and Grace was able to explain the situation. The old lady was a Godsend; she knew of a Nursing Home not too far away, and rushed off to make arrangements. She returned with two rather surly porters who had agreed to carry the patient to the home. It was not a happy journey; the men knew nothing about lifting gently, and seemed to care even less. Grace finally took the front handles herself, leaving the porters to take the rear ones.

Grace was exhausted when at last they arrived at the Home. In a letter she wrote to her mother while still nursing the wounded man there, she recalled, *"To my great surprise I found a lovely clean Nursing Home with English nurses – one is an Edinburgh girl trained at Guy's, a Miss Fletcher – and everything beautifully clean and comfortable"*. The relief was too much for her, she remembered, *"after the long night, suspense and misery of it all, and realizing I was no longer a forlorn Scotchwoman waiting the arrival of wicked enemies; I had found friends, and my wounded officer was in good hands."*

She was given a clean room, something she hadn't experienced for days, weeks even, and a comfortable bed. She slept for four solid hours, stretched out just as she was, still in tunic, belt and boots. Once again, though, war was to intervene. She woke to a vast explosion, said to be the Belgians blowing up a bridge not far away.

"Then a German Regiment marched by," she wrote. *"Little men, all of them, and I watched in a fury of despair from the window."* Worryingly, no fewer than seven German soldiers were billeted on the Home that night, but to her surprise they were apparently quite civil, although Grace kept well out of sight, hidden in the attic with the Lieutenant. In fact, Maude Fletcher told her, the men went about on tiptoe when they knew there were *malades* in the Home. For obvious reasons they were not told about the wounded officer.

That first day passed. A Belgian doctor was quietly brought in to examine the lieutenant. He just pursed his lips, shook his head and said he wouldn't live till sunrise. She wrote to her mother, *"I sat up with him all night, and thank God, he is still alive. That awful night in the motor bus from Antwerp about finished him – poor boy, he is so patient and suffers so."*

Grace was obviously a very worried woman, fearful and under

great stress, not just for herself, but for her wounded and suffering charge. She mentions the seven Germans billeted downstairs, and says she sat by him *"in terror at every sound – there are such awful tales of their barbarity"*. But in a sudden change of tack, she refers to the demeanour of those Germans at the Home as being 'civil' and 'walking about on tiptoe' – an indication, perhaps, of her inner turmoil at the ongoing and constant fluctuation of her fate and fortunes, with no idea of what the outcome would be.

She continued the long letter to her mother, more to settle her nerves and find solace, and to fill in the long hours alone with Lt. Foote. *"It is heartrending to see German Regiments marching about, where English Tommies had been cheered and cheered only nights before…It seems very hard to see what England is doing. She sent men – too late – to Antwerp – and sent them defenceless to be shot down."* She may not have understood, but she felt deeply for the soldiers. *"Now the 7th Division and French troops were here* (in Ghent), *badly equipped – bad horses – torn tents, and what has happened? The English and French retire the night before the Germans enter, and poor little Belgium loses one town after another."* The distress had obviously got to her.

At the same time there is a strong sense of anger or shame, as she writes of English Ambulances and hospitals leaving hurriedly in a seeming panic, while English nurses outwith the military stay on looking after the last two English wounded left behind. Lt. Foote is one, and she mentions for the first time a Marine Brant that she nursed at the Convent, who had been brought to this same nursing home for an operation just before the evacuation. Of him she writes, *"He is Royal Marine Light Infantry too, not an officer, but so plucky. He is shot in both legs and an arm."*

During the day she washed all her clothes in her bath, mentioning that she had only brought one uniform with her, and the blouse was filthy, and she apologises to her mother for writing a very selfish letter all about her. She looks ahead a bit, and comments on how lucky she has been. *"I have had the greatest chances in landing on my feet, so far. …I may, of course, be taken prisoner by the Germans. I hope they leave the prisoners alone, they have suffered enough."*

Even in the dire circumstances she found herself in, she made a point of including nurse Maude Fletcher's home address and asking her mother to write to Maude's parents, saying that their daughter was alive and well; adding *"she is an awfully nice girl"*.

Grace also had moments of madness. Towards the end of the letter she mentions a vague plan she has to try to blow up a German aerodrome on the outskirts of Ghent with dynamite. It was, of course, a quite impossible plan under all the circumstances, but another indication of the way she felt about the Germans, and her own adventurous, and slightly belligerent, leanings!

With an added touch of the dramatic, she ends that part of the letter with a far from reassuring comment. *"I suppose, if this falls into their (the Germans') hands I shall be shot. Much love to you all. Gracie."*

It was not the end of the letter, however. She went on: *"Poor Mr Foote. It will be all over in an hour or so. I have been with him all night. He is quite conscious, and I wrote his mother, but he doesn't know he is dying."* Peritonitis had set in, and there was no hope left. Grace considered briefly getting away that night, but determined to stay on and see that he got a proper burial.

She finally finished her letter, which she hoped to get out through one of the Consulates. *"Goodbye, mother – I feel very miserable – it is easy to be brave when there are horrid wounds to do up… but to sit helpless hour after hour and just watch and be able to do nothing…*

"He is dead! I shall try and leave here tomorrow after the funeral."

Her long ordeal with the wounded and dying Lt. Foote had ended. It is obvious that the emotional drain on Grace had been considerable. She had seen it through to the end, following the hurried and impetuous decision made on the freezing road in Ecloo. But now she faced another series of equally important and fateful decisions, any and all of which bore down heavily on her immediate future.

She spoke with Maude Fletcher, discussing whether to go direct to the German HQ in the town, to ask – or even demand – a military funeral for Lt. Foote. Maude strongly advised her against such a step; it might well jeopardise the future of the Home itself, and its elderly and vulnerable patients too.

For once, Grace accepted advice. Putting aside her uniform, she borrowed some civilian clothes, and set off to see the American Consul, to ask if he would attend the quiet funeral she and Maude were arranging with a local undertaker, and also if he could lay his hands on a Union Jack? Horrified, he told her there was no way he would meet either of her requests, and not to approach him again.

Disappointed, she returned to the Home, where she and Maude prepared for the funeral the next day. In a special despatch for the British Press in the event of her getting home, or being able to send it through one of the Consulates, Grace wrote…

"So next day a gallant officer was buried by three Nurses – a Scotch nurse in Guy's Hospital uniform, a Belgian nurse, and I, in my khaki FANY uniform. We followed his hearse – we passed through lines of German soldiers who eyed my khaki uniform with amazement, but did not molest us – and there, in a Foreign country, we came to the bit of ground set aside for soldiers. There were ten graves already, and into one we lowered our countryman's body, and I, a woman in my khaki British uniform, supported by two nurses, read the burial service over him. It was a sad, strange scene, on a dismal Autumn day, a group of poor Flemish people standing near in reverent silence, and German soldiers in their drab uniforms all around. So we left him at rest, no Union Jack, no 'Last Post' to mark his passing."

CHAPTER 15
Escape From Belgium

That afternoon, she told Maude of her plan and gained her agreement, then made herself as immaculate as she could under the circumstances, and drove in a horse-drawn carriage to the centre of Ghent, where the Germans had set up their Headquarters. Striding between two astonished sentries, Grace approached the Corporal of the Guard, and demanded to be conducted immediately to the General Commanding. It was pure theatre. There is no doubt that her success as an amateur thespian, her love of dressing up and her highly developed sense of the dramatic was the driving force behind this display of audacity, and enabled her to carry off the entire charade so successfully.

The Corporal, utterly out of his depth, just threw open the massive entrance doors to the spacious ante-room within. The usual hubbub ceased; a dead silence descended on the Officers and men congregated there. All heads swung round to stare at her. One or two, possibly mistaking her for a man, saluted without thinking. *"I saluted gravely back,"* she wrote later, *"and looked round for a likely interpreter."*

She goes on to record: *"A very dapper ADC asked my business. I stated it quietly. 'I am English. The officer I have been nursing is dead. I want to return to England'."*

A small group of officers gathered round her. All spoke perfect English, and made plain that they would not permit her to return to England.

She would have to go to Brussels and from there she would be sent to Germany.

This was just the sort of Establishment confrontation that Grace revelled in, and excelled at. She continued to press her point. She was a nurse; she would go to England to nurse English, not to Germany to nurse Germans. This sort of logic obviously puzzled them; they couldn't understand it. The discussion was brought to an end by a senior Colonel ordering her to present herself at the HQ at

9 o'clock next morning, when her papers to Brussels would be ready for her.

Always one to go for the last word, Grace replied that if they wished her to go to Brussels they would have to send her, but it was her intention to go to England.

Savouring the drama of the situation to the end, Grace records, *"So, with many salutes we parted, and I swanked out through the courtyard filled with Germans, as if khaki had never before been so fittingly worn."*

The whole episode had an air of fantasy about it, and it was some little time before the sheer folly and danger in it began to sink in. Going back into enemy territory in British uniform; hiding a British Officer from the Germans; disguising herself in civilian clothes, in the streets of an enemy occupied town – all this was almost an invitation to be shot as a spy!

Grace acknowledged later that the Germans were not the devil incarnate that wartime propaganda had made them out to be. Prior to her impulsive decision to make the journey back to Ghent, when she still believed them to be heartless killers of men, women and children, her personal fear must have been strong. It was an indication of her strength of character and courage that she faced up to the Germans and all the possible consequences.

Having met them face-to-face and talked with them, she wrote in her final despatch from Ghent, *"The Germans are friendly on the whole. Up to now* (they are) *very civil, and not arrogant or brutal. I hold no brief for the Germans. I have seen such sorrow and suffering as I never dreamt of, for which I hold them responsible, but one must give the Devil his due."*

There is little doubt that at some point the adventure became almost surreal; she was acting a part, floating across a vast open stage, calmly, coolly, her lively actor's mind making up the script as she went. It was this, along with inner determination and confidence, that finally carried her through to the Last Act.

Instead of 'presenting herself' at German HQ next morning, as ordered, in a characteristic act of defiance Grace recorded: *"At 9 o'clock next morning I breakfasted in bed!"* It was a sort of throwback gesture from her early days of tomboy-ism, growing up with her two fearless brothers. A 'put that in your pipe and smoke it' message to the Germans.

The rest of that day was spent in a buzz of activity. Play-acting she may have been on one level, but she was no fool, and knew that, busy as they were with more important matters, the Germans would come looking for her sooner or later. The final stage in her odyssey was to ensure her escape back to England – no easy matter given the circumstances.

Grace was fortunate in her past contacts. While in Belgium before the war, at various horse trials and Gymkhanas, she had become good friends with a rich and influential Belgian lady, Baroness de Crumbrugge, and she went to see her now, to see if she would be willing to help in any way. The Baroness was delighted. A Town Councillor she knew well, a M. de Weert, was involved in smuggling much needed supplies of food across the border from Holland, to help the more vulnerable folk in the already occupied areas. She would contact him immediately.

Grace had other plans while the contacts were being made. Still dressed as a Belgian woman, she visited the town's major cemetery and with the help of the Graves Superintendent, recorded the details of any British military personnel who were buried there. Then, with time still to spare, she headed for the military hospital, and managed to get the names of most of the British wounded. On her return to England, this was a very effective tool indeed in getting the attention of the War Office.

After some persuasion de Weert agreed to take Grace with him, but warned her of the possible consequences if they were caught. As far as he knew, he was not yet under suspicion, but there would always be a risk.

Grace never hesitated. Getting home again was what she desperately wanted, so she could bring her FANY people across to run one of the hospitals she had been offered by the Belgians. So far she had sailed through everything safely, and was determined to continue. As a Town Councillor de Weert had access to a car and various papers. For this trip, he drove, while Grace sat behind as if a person of some importance.

They passed through the checkpoints set up by the Germans with varying degrees of ease. De Weert had provided them both with some old Flemish parchment documents from the Town Hall, with large and impressive seals attached. It was only at the final checkpoint that the major hold up occurred. Grace sat with her heart in her mouth trying to look relaxed and disinterested, once again playing a role, lounging back in her seat with an imperious look on her face, as discussions went on.

At this point in the proceedings a Dutch police officer strolled across to ask the Germans what the hold-up was. Peering into the car, he gave a start of surprise at seeing Grace's khaki uniform stepped back and saluted smartly. Whether the salute was a result of pure surprise, or planned by the Police Officer to impress the German sentries is not known, but it had the desired effect. The Germans handed the documents to de Weert and waved the car on across the border into Holland.

Grace wrote: *"What a blessed relief it was to leave the last German sentry behind, and be greeted by the friendly Dutch sentries with smiles of welcome, and to unfurl the Belgian flag on our car!"*

She found herself in the small port of Ternhuisen, crammed with refugees from far and wide. A welcoming but curious Dutch Army officer was most intrigued with her uniform, told her she was the first woman in uniform he had ever seen, and asked to take her photograph. *"He told me, that while the people supported the British, the Royal Family were for the Germans."* He had a look of disgust on his face when he spoke of the Royals.

Grace made her way to the steamer offices, where she was given a ticket for a refugee boat leaving the following morning for Folkestone, and also a berth. Boarding the ship, she went in search of her cabin, and was dismayed to find she would she be sharing it with a mother and her fairly mature son. So she began to explore, and found a small single cabin, apparently unoccupied. Noting the number, she went back to the shipping office, and persuaded them to transfer her. Going back on board, she waylaid the steward when he came on duty in early evening, and got clean sheets from him. She wrote in her diary, *"Indeed, the sheets in use looked as if many a strange being had inhabited them!"*

Despite all the danger, stress and strain she had been under since her defiant breakfast of the previous day, Grace was still prepared to tackle any problems – minor though they were by comparison – that circumstances put in her way.

Grace had supper at a small local hotel. Maybe it was her Aberdeen origins that caused her to record in Nursing Adventures, after all her extraordinary adventures, and the dangers she had encountered and surmounted: *"A poor meal for an exorbitant charge!"* Then it was back to the boat through the ever-present *'crowds of homeless wanderers'*. She felt such sorrow for them, but being almost a refugee herself, there was little she could do apart from listen to some of their tragic stories.

Early next morning, the ship pulled away from the quay and headed across the North Sea to England. As so often happens at the closing of a dreadful experience, time almost stands still on the last bit of a journey home. It was the same for Grace. She wrote: *"Never shall I forget the interminable weariness of that crossing. I suppose it was the reaction after the constant work, but as the hours went by, I felt almost sick with the endless monotony of it all."* Halfway across there was a long, exasperating delay *"whilst someone on a little minesweeper harangued the bridge through a megaphone"*.

At last the boat arrived at Folkestone, followed by the train journey to Victoria *'in a fever of impatience'*. She recalls: *"None of my people were in England, only friends, to whose flat I hastened; and as I ran out of Earls Court station, I wondered wildly if I would find them out, but that blow was spared me."*

She was greeted as one returned from the dead. Neither friends nor family knew what had happened to her, where she had been, or whether she was dead or alive. For Grace, there was an enormous feeling of relief. She was home! She was safe! Soon she *would* be with her family again. Her first great wartime adventure was at an end. In so many ways she was a changed woman. No longer the girl who, only a few weeks before, her head full of romantic notions of war – glory, honour, heroism – had sailed so excitedly across the sea to France. Now she had experienced reality, seen for herself the random and senseless death and destruction; shared the horror and fear and feelings of loss; witnessed the carnage, the personal hell of innocent people caught up in the maelstrom of conflict.

Suddenly she had matured, learned so much from her

experiences, which were so far removed from the comfortable, self-indulgent life-style she had enjoyed before the war. She ended the account of her short stay with a subdued, flat statement:

"And that was the first chapter of the War for me; and the second is, perhaps, stranger still, for Providence led my comrades and myself into as strange places as ever women went before. This at least the Great War has done – it has proved to men that women can share men's dangers and privations and hardships and yet remain women."

CHAPTER 16

Trail Blazers

Grace's homecoming was a huge load off her shoulders. During those few weeks in Belgium she had gone through a host of new experiences and emotions, totally alien to her life so far. She had seen death, destruction, appalling human suffering. She had been gripped at times by overwhelming terror. She had found the courage to face periods of dread and fear. She had been filled, too, with a fierce pride whenever she saw her own countrymen at war.

Back again in England, she allowed herself the luxury of reuniting with family and friends. There had been times in the past weeks when she thought she would never see them again. But, for all her joy at seeing her loved ones again, she was dominated by one ambition, reinforced more strongly than ever now, and that was to get back to Belgium, this time with her FANY comrades. Back to the War. No time for reflection. She knew instinctively that this was her destiny. There was no stopping her. She *would* do it.

She was no fool. Reflecting on her recent adventures, she realised that her best, possibly her *only,* chance of getting the necessary permits for her group reasonably soon, was to get hold of a Motor Ambulance.

On a flying visit to Aberdeen, with the help of her younger brother Billy, she persuaded her guardian, to advance the money to her, while she sold some shares to cover it. Then it was back to London, where Billy knew of a firm of coachbuilders in Earls Court – Brown, Hughes and Strachan. The latter partner was an Aberdonian, and there was an instant empathy between the three, Grace, Billy and Strachan. Through him, Grace purchased a Unic chassis, on which the firm would build an ambulance body as a priority.

In the last few weeks Grace had learned a lot about ambulances at first hand, and put a few of her own ideas forward. She asked Strachan how long it would take, and he jokingly answered "about a week".

"That's absolutely topping," said Grace. *"Bill and I will be popping in*

to see how it's going."

Protests were unavailing. Strachan had said 'a week' and he soon recognized a fellow-Aberdonian's mind-set.

Luckily for Grace, her prime aim of getting the first FANY contingent across the Channel was enthusiastically shared by 'Boss' Franklin, who was much better suited to the detailed preparation of kit and supplies, so essential to the success of the mission. This left Grace free to oversee the operation as a whole, and spend a lot of time at the coachbuilders' urging them on to greater efforts.

In this she was much helped by Billy, impatiently awaiting his call to the Colours. By the time he had got home from Rhodesia, tens of thousands of volunteers had rushed to join up, and there was a huge man-power log jam while the Army struggled to cope with the sudden influx. Frustrating though the delay was to Billy, it did leave him time to watch over the work going on on the new ambulance.

True to his word, although part spoken in jest at the time, Strachan had the ambulance built, checked and ready to go within the promised week, quite an achievement. Grace was, of course, absolutely delighted. This really was a trump card to have in her hand. She wasted no time. Unperturbed by the earlier rejection of 'Boss' Franklin's offer of the FANY to Sir Arthur Sloggett, she badgered the authorities until she got an interview with Sir Alfred Keogh, Director General of the Army Medical Services. She was able to inform him triumphantly that not only did she have a trained team ready and waiting to go, but a brand new, fully equipped motor ambulance into the bargain. Keogh was extremely sceptical at the idea that Grace had been able to obtain an ambulance sooner than the Army was able to get them.

However, when he realised that she actually had an ambulance, he relented slightly, and arranged for her to see Sir Arthur Stanley, Head of the Red Cross, who turned out to be on their side, and issued the necessary permits for the Ambulance and its FANY contingent to cross to France on the official Red Cross yacht in service at the time.

This was a fantastic break-through for Grace – just what she had been striving for. She raced back to the HQ at 192 Earl's Court Road, and broke the news to 'Boss' Franklin and the others, who were equally excited. Within a matter of hours, they were ready to go.

This first 'convoy' was 12 strong – among them FANY names that recur again and again in the annals of the Corps' history – Grace Ashley-Smith, 'Boss' Franklin, Molly Marshall (later to win the Military Medal), the indomitable Sister Isobel Wicks, Edith Walton, and Violet O'Neil Power. Grace's brother Bill, still waiting his papers, drove the Ambulance – the only male ever to be enrolled as a FANY! Also in that first contingent were three trained nurses, paid for by the Corps, and two male dressers, a Mr Bretton, and Eric Hickson, a young medical student.

The group made its way to Folkestone, and spent the night in the Waiting Room on the dockside. The next day, there was the inevitable delay. Wounded were flowing in from the battlefields of France and Belgium, and, never one to miss an opportunity, Grace approached the RAMC Colonel responsible for the transfer of the patients from waiting areas to ambulances, and offered the help of her girls,

Here she herself came up against the infuriating condescension that other women offering their help had come up against from members of the Establishment. *"Dear ladies,"* waffled the Colonel, insufferably patronizing. *"Do they think their soft white hands can carry a stretcher?"* A colleague is quoted as remembering that Grace turned 'white with anger', and retorted that her girls had been fully trained by RAMC Sergeants, and were completely capable of doing the job properly. In the face of this female fury, the Colonel backed down, and subsequently had the grace to apologise, thanking them for their hard work.

Later that day, the 27th October 1914, Grace took the first FANY Convoy across the Channel and into a war zone. The date, a memorable one in the annals of the Corps, is remembered and celebrated every year with a reunion lunch, at which both ex-FANYs and those still serving, meet and remember old times and places and friends. It marked the start of the first 100 years of dedicated service in both war and peace.

Perhaps the proudest, most satisfying moment for Grace in all her service with the Corps during World War 1, was leading her tiny group of high-spirited, well bred young ladies to war, who, in typical self-deprecating manner, referred to themselves as 'The Band of Hope'. Grace wrote later of her feelings at this time. *"Away I went, light-hearted, taking with me willingly the responsibility of eleven other beings. Wise counsels of parents, the cautious teachings of friends, were listened to and lightly disregarded."*

It summed up her mood perfectly. The fact that her 'eleven other beings' had not undergone her traumatic experiences of the last few weeks and had no inkling of the scenes of horror they would soon be involved in was never considered. She had absolute faith in their strength of character, and their decication – a faith well-founded as it turned out. They met every situation head-on, with courage and humour. They coped. So much so, as hundreds more crossed to "that troubled land", their willingness to tackle any task combined with their high spirits became a byword with all who worked with them in the three armies.

On their arrival in Calais there was no time to relax, or become acclimatized to conditions there. Less than 50 miles away the First Battle of Ypres was in full swing, and casualties were already pouring into the town in thousands, to be evacuated as quickly as possible, either further down the coast, or across the Channel to England in a motley collection of converted hospital ships.

In no time at all, the FANYs were engaged in ferrying wounded men from temporary Aid Posts on the dockside to either buses or ships. There was no let up; the work went on day and night. It was late October, the day after their arrival, remembered and vividly documented by Grace.

She writes, with great feeling: *"Storms of rain and wind, cold and wet and cheerless, swept the town. Calais the cruel, the pitiless, along whose quays one never-to-be-forgotten night, rows of wounded lay in the darkness and the cold, and the rain."* It paints an appalling picture of the dreadful conditions the wounded had to endure through lack of foresight and preparation, and the sheer volume of wounded pouring in.

CHAPTER 17

Dear, Dirty Old Lamarck!

While Boss Franklin, the indomitable Sister Sergeant Wicks, and the others of their small group worked ceaselessly fetching and carrying sick and wounded off the Hospital Trains that arrived hour after hour, Grace made time to contact the Belgian authorities in the port, urging them to fulfil their offer of a hospital for the FANY to run for them.

The Belgians needed little persuasion, but the usual red tape and national jealousies involved seemingly endless discussions with French officialdom, as well as British military and civil authorities. It wasn't easy, but so great was the need as casualties poured in from the Ypres front – 8000 in five days – that even the French gave up on their usual blank, stonewalling tactics without too much of a struggle.

Actually getting possession of the premises, however, was not easy even then. Years later, another author, writing about that time in Calais, recorded that "the FANY were immediately seized upon with enthusiasm, and given an empty school". Grace scribbled crossly in the margin of her copy, *"ROT! We had to ask and ask."*

They were allocated a school, an old, empty Convent School. A huge amount of credulity was required to consider the place as suitable as a hospital, but the saying *'needs must when the Devil drives'* was as true then as it is today, and the Devil was surely in the driving seat in the Calais of October 1914.

Forty eight hours of discussion, cajoling, asking, almost begging, and the Belgian Army was finally able to hand over the shambles that was Lamarck Hospital. Grace and Boss were delighted, as were the FANYs with them. It was theirs; the future was now in their hands.

But, when Grace and Boss Franklin first set eyes upon the Convent, entering the main gateway, it took their breath away. Literally! Immediately in front of them was a long row of latrines. The stench was quite appalling. Cecily Maudant, who had accompanied Grace to Belfast for the meeting with Ulster's Medical Director before the war, noted in her diary that the only way she could describe the smell of the latrines was 'indescribable'!

In her book, Grace remembers that memorable day, *"when I marched the squad up to the yard to take over. An imposing gateway led into a dirty courtyard, where two long, ungainly buildings lay parallel with each other. Opposite the doorways were rows of latrines, and the odour from these made one shrink back in disgust"*. Venturing further into the totally unprofessional 'hospital', the enormity of the task ahead of them became only too evident.

The building was already partly operational, run by two Belgian doctors, a Quartermaster, and a few Belgian auxiliary nurses. Grace and Franklin went on a tour of inspection, which did nothing to allay their worries. The 'wards' – schoolrooms – were dirty and untidy. The few patients at that time lay on straw mattresses, or *palliasses*, on filthy, unswept, littered floors. There were a very few makeshift beds – wooden planks supported on short iron legs, known as *chalets*, even more uncomfortable than the *palliasses* and, as they later discovered, a breeding ground for bed-sores.

In a small room by the front door opposite one of the 'wards', they found the two doctors, and half a dozen nurses boiling water on a small old-fashioned stove which resembled a drainpipe. The only other furniture, a wooden table and bench.

Continuing their inspection with some trepidation, they found a small wooden staircase which led to another 'ward'. Here there were 16 patients, some of whom appeared to be very ill. Next to this was another smallish room, equipped with a couple of wooden benches, leading into a third ward. There was another floor above, but they were told not to go there, as the rooms were owned by the ex-Headmistress of the school, who also had private rooms downstairs.

To get to the second building, which they were told was empty, the only route was outside and around the courtyard. When they finally got there, they found the same ingrained dirt and general air of neglect and desolation that hung over the whole scene at Lamarck. Grace and Franklin looked at one another, realizing immediately the extent of what lay ahead of them and their small team.

The first priority was to clean the whole place up, from top to bottom. In spite of their frenetic activity of the past 48 hours, there was no hesitation. The 'Band of Hope' straightaway buckled down to transforming the place from a refuse tip into a hospital worthy of the name. They didn't realise it at the time, but this 'up Guards and at 'em' attitude to the task ahead was to become an integral part of the FANY character in the years and generations to come.

It is worth bearing in mind the backgrounds of these young women, Grace, Franklin and the rest, all raised in wealthy or certainly well-off families, all with maids and servants who carried out the accepted domestic chores – cooking, cleaning, washing, fetching, carrying. The work that lay in front of them was totally alien to their previous lifestyles. But all had that vital spark within each of them, the strength to cope with whatever their chosen life threw at them. The RAMC Colonel, who less than a week before had been proved so wrong when he queried the ability of their 'soft white hands' to cope with stretcher-bearing, would not be surprised to see them at work now.

Scrubbing brushes, brooms and disinfectant were obtained one way or another, even though it meant digging into the precious £12 'kitty' they had brought with them, which was all the money they had to see them through those early days. Everyone got involved – Grace, Franklin, their girls, men dressers, and Grace's brother Bill – scrubbing walls, floors, tables, seats, stairs. Everyone had a job to do. When the packing cases arrived with the supplies their colleagues in England had got ready, the men carried them inside and emptied them, scrubbed them, adapted them where necessary, and set them up as cupboards in the side room.

The nurses, led by Sister Wicks, at once attended to the patients, many of whom were badly wounded, two suffering from sceptic pneumonia. These last two had not had their dressings changed for two days, because the Belgian doctors and nurses had decided there was not much hope for them!

Grace and four FANYs scrubbed the upstairs room, and the 'kitchen'. She noted in her diary: *"The Belgian orderlies watched us, at first resentfully, then curiously, and at length one came and took my bucket and scrubbing cloth from me, and himself continued washing the floor and stairs"*. Shortly after, others followed his example, finally convinced that the 'Eenglish Mees' as they called the girls, could work, and so they would, too!

Between them all they cleaned out the school desks to use as storage places for bandages and dressings. They even carried some of the desks to an empty, upstairs room, which the FANYs laughingly dubbed 'The Theatre'. Each desk was allocated a particular use – bandages, dressings, iodine, chloroform – whatever supplies they could get.

They kept at it all that day, and when, at around 6 o'clock, the two Belgian doctors finally arrived for their evening 'rounds', they were totally amazed and unbelieving at the difference in their hospital.

There was still a huge amount of work and organizing to be done before the place could really be thought of as a Hospital. But, in Grace's own words: *"We were exceedingly fortunate, too, in our Belgian Quartermaster."* He was kind and helpful, and had spent all that first afternoon directing what staff he had in filling mattresses with fresh straw, and also setting up dozens of *chalets,* this time with mattresses to protect the suffering patients. To him, the transformation of the place was a wake-up call, and from that time on he was a tower of strength. Grace wrote later: *"To him I went in despair over the question of cooking."* He looked her in the eye, a half-smile on his face. *"Mademoiselle,"* he said, *"tout est possible."*

He was as good as his word. Within a couple of days the almost bare, depressing 'kitchen' was equipped with a cooker, tables, chairs, plates, cups, cutlery, and – perhaps most useful of all – a great cauldron for boiling water, so essential for maintaining hygiene and cleanliness.

Again, making use of old packing cases and boxes, makeshift cupboards were constructed, and such bed linen and 'bed' shirts for the patients that were available, were neatly stacked and labelled.

By this time, under the watchful eyes of both Grace and Boss, the whole atmosphere of the place had changed. All were working together, with infectious enthusiasm – FANYs, the team they had brought with them, the Belgian auxiliaries and orderlies. They all had a common purpose: to get the hospital up and running properly as soon as possible, and provide the best service for the sick and wounded. Grace expressed her feelings at the time – and frequently the same sentiment in the years ahead – *"All we could spare went to our blesses, and overtime was never thought of. Somebody was ill, and that meant a night on duty to follow a hard day's work, but that was nothing. To us all, War spelled work, and work spelled war; and we never looked beyond."*

This was the sort of dedication Grace fostered in *her* FANY, and it was the kind of dedication the FANY gave freely and cheerfully under all conditions. It was this attitude of single-minded commitment to their patients that endeared them to all units of any of the Allied armies that they came in contact with, and drew their respect throughout those years. To the Band of Hope and the many others who followed on, and toiled in Lamarck Hospital, it was always referred to with nostalgic affection and a touch of dry humour, as 'dear, dirty old Lamarck'!

CHAPTER 18

Calais The Miserable

Getting their hospital into shape, clean, tidy and fit for their patients, was just one of Grace's worries. Finding accommodation for her team proved to be an even greater headache. Leaving the running of the hospital in the safe hands of Franklin, day after day she spent hours badgering the Council Offices for billets for her girls, then trudging through the streets in bitter cold to find them and make arrangements with the owners. Only too often she was met with blank refusals from the householders, or found the house unoccupied and locked up. Then it was back to the Council Offices to try again to fix something up.

Many Calaisians had developed an unbelievable approach to the English in their midst. Perhaps it was a throwback to some old folk memory of the past when the English occupied much of that part of the French Coast, but the feeling was that if the English gained a footing in the town, they would never leave. This extraordinary attitude was even supported by Councillors and some Civil Authorities. In Calais it fell to Grace to do all the negotiating, as she was the only FANY officer who spoke French.

In 'Nursing Adventures', Grace expresses her feelings at the time with some intensity: *"It meant going to the Mairie (Council) to get new billets, then going round the billets to inspect them, and very often returning to the Mairie to report empty houses, or inhabitants who flatly refused a room. Taciturn and almost insolent clerks had to be propitiated, and personal feelings had to go to the wall when one was confronted with the possibility of seventeen or eighteen English girls being left homeless and without beds for the night!"*

Grace hated this part of her duties. She would far rather have been working on the wards, or driving her ambulance collecting patients and delivering them to the hospital ships going to England: so many of the jobs they were all involved in.

Time and again Grace came up against rudeness and insulting remarks from officials as well as proprietors of the places allocated as billets. She had great difficulty in keeping her temper. Grudging permission was given for the team, in ones and twos, to stay over with registered guesthouses, but only for two, or at most, three nights at a time. The excuse used by many authorities at the time was 'the fear of spies getting in'!

After doing these seemingly interminable rounds day after day, week after week, Grace wrote, with feeling and passion, never one to mince her words. *"The French civilians hated the English people and resented our presence; they hated the Belgians, and were furious with the English for coming to nurse them."* To write like this about a people she had liked and admired, Grace must have been near the end of her tether.

Whatever reasons the French may have had, perhaps a deeply ingrained distrust of anyone foreign to France, it was an unfortunate fact that they constantly put difficulties in the way of British and Belgian military and civil organizations.

Once the hospital really came under FANY control, the Belgians made sure it was well supplied with patients. The wards began to fill up, and more FANYs came over from England to staff it. The patients were not all wounded soldiers. A particularly virulent form of typhoid fever had hit the Belgian Army. Lamarck's two blocks of wards were divided into 'wounded' – *blesses* – and typhoid patients – *'les typhiques* – and the latter was soon filled to capacity, with over 100 patients. None of the other hospitals in the town, French or British, would take them. But, as usual, the FANY coped. The redoubtable Sister Wicks made them her special charges. With her small but committed staff she grappled day and night with disease and death. With a frighteningly low survival rate of patients it was a terrible time for them all, but they battled on.

Attached to the hospital was a horse-drawn hearse, known as the Coffin Cart, and daily – frequently hourly in those early days – it rolled in, collected the dead, and rattled out again. The long, hard struggle went on. None of the FANYs – apart from Sister-Sergeant Wicks – was a trained nurse, but it seemed there was nobody else prepared to come to look after *'les typhiques'.* The girls gave it everything they had, pulling these emaciated men back from death. Gradually the Coffin Cart came less often, and the battle was almost won.

Throughout this time the girls worked tirelessly during the day, and every two or three nights they would find themselves taken to a different 'home', more often than not with suspicious, unwelcoming landladies offering them little in the way of comfort or cheer.

At last, Grace's luck changed. Constantly on the lookout for somewhere permanent they could call their own, and after countless stormy scenes, she was sent to see the owner of an abandoned corner shop. This was indeed an oasis of hope as far as she was concerned. Previously offered to the Authorities by its owner as an overflow hospital, and refused, it was called Le Bon Genie. And such it turned out to be. Grace noted it had *"bare rooms, dirty walls, one table, five chairs and 20 beds, but it was rent free and available at once. A little flattery and coaxing soon brought good-humoured assent from the owner"*. Once again, her single-minded commitment had won through. Her FANYs had somewhere to call their own. They lost no time moving in.

Ever resourceful and never afraid of hard work, the girls got down to creating a home from home. Impressive shop windows, full size, extended round the side as well as the front. The girls covered these with brown paper to ensure some privacy, leaving the top parts to let in light. The shop floor was cleared of almost everything, and beds reorganised. A small room leading off the main shop was allocated to Sister-Sergeant Wicks. Of course, much cleaning and scrubbing was needed, but this was now almost second nature to the FANYs. It was to be their home, and they would make it something to be proud of. The best thing for Grace was no more endless worry about billets for her girls.

As more and more reinforcements arrived from England, there were not enough beds to go round. The girls accepted the situation with their usual aplomb and good humour. Night staff arriving back from the Hospital, usually exhausted, tumbled into the beds the day staff had just vacated. There was no bathroom at that time, only a washstand, jug and basin, but at least running water was laid on. To the great delight of all, a bath was installed later, something sorely missed and longed-for by everyone.

They repainted the walls, brought in chairs and cushions for an upstairs 'common room', put up pictures, and made the very best of it. Of course, many of the girls couldn't resist writing home to their horrified families, telling them with great glee, that they were 'sleeping in a shop window'! It was a splendid release for them all, getting away from the tasks most of them were having to carry out at the hospital. They could relax, be themselves, and somehow keep cheerful.

As the weeks rolled by, they became more organised, more established and accepted. Grace was able to acquire another home from home in the shape of a flat above a sort of rather *risqué* night club called Le Bijou. Every night there was music and singing from downstairs. The FANYs would gather in the rooms above, listening to the catchy tunes and the choruses as the audiences joined in. They loved it, at one point considering disguising themselves as civilians and going down to join in the fun. However, discretion won the day, as it really wasn't 'done' for well-bred young ladies to visit that sort of establishment, certainly not without a male escort. Despite the huge changes to their lifestyles as FANYs, especially where their work was concerned, the Corps imposed a strong unwritten set of rules governing their behaviour off duty. These were seldom broken.

CHAPTER 19
Tribulation And Triumph At Lamarck

Work at Lamarck continued to be a hard, seemingly endless, slog against time, awful wounds, and the dreaded typhoid. There was an ongoing shortage of dressings, medicaments, bandages and bed linen. Grace recalls that on one occasion they spent ten days cutting bed sheets in half, to provide enough to go around all the beds. Shirts and socks had to be washed every night, or there would not be enough to meet the needs of the next day.

The typhoid wards were the most unpleasant to work in. By the nature of the disease there was a frightening amount of uncontrollable violence by the patients while they still had the strength. Prior to the arrival of the FANY, the relatively few typhoid patients had been looked after by nuns, who courageously did their best, gave great spiritual help and guidance, but were never successful, or trained, as nurses.

Grace and Franklin had their quarters at the top of the main building in Lamarck Hospital, on hand day and night. One end of their room was curtained off, for whichever two FANY Ambulance drivers were on duty, as they had to be immediately available on the premises overnight to cope with any emergency. It was hard, backbreaking work for all of them. Water was always contaminated, and had to be boiled before use. Food was in short supply, particularly milk, eggs and brandy, the latter a great tonic and morale builder among the patients, not to mention the FANYs! But their Belgian Quartermaster *"showed a wonderful energy in getting larger supplies than other hospitals could obtain"*.

Proper beds, too, were still desperately needed, and once again Lady Luck stepped in. The FANY's English Chaplain visited, and, wrote Grace: *"a few of us dined with him at a hotel on the Quay"*. They were joined by the Senior Medical Officer in Calais, a Colonel Alexander, *"a gallant and kind-hearted officer, who never threw us a crumb of praise when inspecting our hospital, but who made ample amends for that in his official reports"*. Through him, the Director

General of the RAMC also paid them a visit, resulting in *"the arrival of a splendid supply of spring beds, bedding, blankets, sheets etc"*.

Little triumphs like these helped Grace and the others to overcome the ongoing gruelling routines that they had to endure, and did much to lift their morale. It frequently needed lifting. In spite of the strict supervision of water hygiene, many of the FANYs were struck down with bad attacks of dysentery, and had to double up for each other on duty, covering for those who became ill. It got to them all at one time or another. For some it was desperately serious, for the more fortunate, a dreadful inconvenience. Grace herself wrote about her *"constant dysentery"*, and how difficult it was *'finding places'* to run to, as each emergency struck! It was not only debilitating and embarrassing, but involved everybody in extra duties and tasks.

In addition, many had infected fingers, painful and persistent, sores so easily picked up in the unsatisfactory hygiene conditions in which they were forced to work, in spite of everything. Bacterial infections were rife everywhere, affecting the smallest cut, or even through chilblains.

But above all, they were young and enthusiastic, and according to Grace's 'Five Years With the Allies', tackled all the dirt and discomfort with cheerfulness and good humour. They were all volunteers, and in their own way each had a bit of the rebel in them, driven by a hidden desire to defy those oppressive social conventions imposed on girls of their upbringing to follow a set social path.

However, being only human, inwardly they must have had doubts and fears. Grace herself probably voiced those doubts and fears they all had, when she confessed *"how awful, heartbreaking and tiring this endless work was, and at times I could barely hold back my tears"*.

Edith Walton, one of the original 'Band of Hope', the youngest FANY at the time, and later a lifelong friend of Grace, was almost certainly right when she confessed: *"We were too young really, or too inexperienced, to realise, perhaps, the seriousness of it."*

Nursing the sick and wounded and coping with all the problems of poor hygiene conditions, alongside food and equipment shortages, were only part of the life of a FANY at Lamarck. Now that the hospital was a secure base, more were arriving from England, all of them keen and eager to get into the action. Driving Motor

Ambulances had superseded riding onto battlefields on horses as their *raison d'etre*. Of course, when they first arrived in Calais they were called upon time and again to collect and deliver wounded to the trains, boats and various Aid Posts in the port. This was largely because of a crying need and desperate shortage of cars and drivers. Neither the French nor British Armies permitted women to drive for them in any capacity. The 'Top Brass' of both viewed the idea with horror. It took both time and commitment, but this attitude was finally overcome.

Unfortunately, when this invasion of male space actually took place, the male drivers and mechanics *in situ* of both armies took strong exception to it, and were singularly uncooperative, even going so far, in some cases, to sabotage the motors in petty ways, standing back and leaving it to the girls to put things right. To the credit of the women drivers, they generally managed to do so!

As these early weeks at Lamarck slogged by, their one ambulance, Grace's Unic, was joined by others – two Fords and a Mors car, converted by its owner into a vehicle for 'walking wounded' rather than stretcher cases.

The history of that Mors is typical of the disorganization and *laissez faire* of the time. Owned by a Mr Hargreaves, too old for military service himself, he answered an advertisement in a national newspaper for drivers and ambulances to join the First Aid Nursing Yeomanry. It was only when he arrived at FANY HQ for interview that he became aware that the FANY was a women's Corps. He was highly amused, and offered himself and his Mors to be attached to the FANY entirely at his own expense. He also paid the salaries of two hospital nurses, and for all the petrol used. Becoming known universally and affectionately among the FANYs as 'Uncle', he was a pillar of help and support for them all.

Originally, much of the driving of their one ambulance in Calais was done by Grace's brother Bill, still awaiting his call to the Colours, which came in January 1915. The arrival of the Fords and the Mors involved them in constant repetition of the original task – collecting wounded from the hospital trains and distributing them to their allocated destinations.

Here the wounded all had labels attached to them by the Train

Doctors. FANY drivers would check these, and drive the men to whatever destination was indicated. Once 'booked in' it was their job to strip off tunics and any other filthy clothing, then slip on clean nightshirts, at which point hospital staff would take over, whether on land or hospital ship.

That was the comparatively easy part. Battling against the elements was the worst. Out with their ambulances in all kinds of weather, and with the insistence of Grace and Franklin on building a reputation for dependability, along with their own pride in the service they gave, the girls frequently worked through the night repairing and servicing their vehicles. As a direct consequence of their efforts, even the French were sufficiently impressed to overcome their scruples about using women drivers – so long as they weren't French!

On one occasion, for instance, desperate for more assistance at a particular area of their Front Line, they asked the FANY for help. Four of the girls drove more than 120 miles to a place called Cayenne, far removed from their normal operating area, spent a whole night ferrying French wounded from the trenches to hospital, and drove back to Calais the following day.

No other military controlled unit or organization could have responded so quickly to a request between two allied armies, but the uniquely independent position of the Corps made that sort of response possible.

They didn't just cope – they coped well.

CHAPTER 20

Aid Post At Oostkerke

Grace was entitled to be content with the amazing progress and changes she and the FANY had brought about to the shocking state of the so-called hospital they had been allocated at Lamarck. There is no doubt she was, but resting on her laurels was not her way.

The daily chore of finding billets for her girls may have been over, but she was still saddled with almost daily trips to the Quay to organise the unloading, checking, paperwork, and dispatch of FANY supplies arriving from England. As the only French-speaking FANY Officer available, this, too, was her responsibility.

But in the midst of all this, she never lost sight of one of her main aims: the expansion of new outlets for the Corps. During October she had managed to find time to renew her contacts with the Belgian Medical Services, and at their request agreed to take over the running of an advanced dressing station, a Regimental Aid Post (RAP) at a town called Oostkerke, not far from Calais.

Now, in addition to the hectic daily – and nightly – round of work at Lamarck Hospital, the FANY provided two girls to staff a RAP less than a mile behind the Front Line. This was part of the Medical Team of the 3rd Chasseurs, a crack Cavalry Regiment belonging to the 5th Belgian Infantry Division holding that part of the line. The FANYs would forge close links with them during the three months they were there. Grace happily referred to the RAP as the *'Poste de Secours'*.

Life there was dank, dirty and dangerous – and Grace loved it! For her, it epitomised her reasons for joining the 'Yeomanry': a life of adventure, risks and a chance to push back the parameters of her own life, at the same time as helping others. She revelled in the freedom she experienced from the constrictions of life at home. Serving alongside an elite fighting regiment was an added bonus.

Describing the routine of life at the RAP in Nursing Adventures, Grace writes: *"Every morning between 8 and 9 a large number of men came in from the trenches half a mile away to report sick, or get slight wounds dressed. Dr Hannsens examined them, and we stood by ready to put a fresh dressing on, or administer a dose of medicine"*. Through these, and following passages in her book, we can sense her excitement at being part of this, to her, great adventure.

A better description of her *Postes de Secours* might have been Post of Discomfort, of which Grace was only too aware, making it her business to experience things in person. Here the FANYs slept on straw mattresses on the floor, often short of rations, especially basics such as bread and butter. Frequently, if they had the one, they didn't have the other. Their staple diet was potatoes and black coffee – milk was seldom available.

Grace remembers – probably with a shudder – their main 'meat' course – *plaitre* – a sort of Bully Beef in tins, that *"we stewed, fried and boiled, and mashed up with potatoes, And once, from the troop kitchen, we got five packets of 'Little Mary Custard Powder', and as milk was an unheard of luxury, we made custard with water, and it tasted better than the best custard ever made at home!"* Such were the conditions they cheerfully endured.

Because of the cramped situation of the RAP, normal conventions were set aside and ignored in this world of men. The building only had two rooms; the FANYs slept in one, while up to 40 Belgian soldiers were crowded into the other. According to Grace in her memoirs, *"Chivalry was the outstanding characteristic of the men, and up there alone in the midst of the Belgian Army, we were as safe as in a London drawing room"*.

Close to the Front Line as it was, the rolling thunder of war was ever present, shellfire daily churning up the earth around, which the heavy November rain quickly turned to mud. Indeed, mud was the dominating feature of the RAP. It was a grim, exciting, and often dangerous round of dressing wounds of men straight from the trenches.

Grace recalls one dreadful night she experienced in November, when a heavy, localised attack on the Belgian line resulted in a sudden surge of casualties pouring into the RAP. The conditions were appalling: a massive storm brewing, an ice cold, bitter wind sweeping across the desolate landscape of war.

Inside the crowded dressing station, doctors worked frantically treating the men. Many were dying, too badly injured to even try to save, when so many who could be saved were waiting. Preceding the attack, the heavy artillery bombardment had taken its toll, doctors probing and searching desperately for fragments of shrapnel in the shattered bodies.

The room was turning into a temporary hospital, unable to keep up with the influx of pain-wracked patients pouring in. Making matters worse, the RAP ran out of anaesthetics, leaving men screaming in agony.

"Each time the door opened I groaned inwardly," wrote Grace. *"Would this procession of suffering never stop? The cold wind would bite through us all; the candles would flicker and splutter; big muddy men would tramp in with thick muddy boots, dump down their burdens on the cold stone floor, and go out, banging the door loudly to make it shut…and it would all happen again."*

This stark account of that one dreadful night was typical of so many others stretching on and on, week after week, month after month. Throughout it all, the morale of the FANY remained high. They never faltered in giving aid and hope and cheer to these terribly injured men. Their cheerfulness – though perhaps forced at times – remained constant.

There were certain compensations, however. Almost all the FANYs had an adventurous streak in them, and longed to get up to the Front Line. From this forward RAP, once morning sick parade was over, they got the chance, being so close, and forming friendships with the officers of the units holding that part of the Line. Grace was one of the first to seize the opportunity. She tells of her first trip, escorted by the CO of one of the Belgian battalions.

It was a rather better day than so far this cold and wet November, the sun actually shining. They were quite close to the Lines when a hare suddenly leaped up and raced across the ploughed field they were skirting. Two soldiers jumped after it with sticks, pursuing it across the field to shouts of laughter and encouragement from the troops watching. She wrote later: *"How well I remember it all, even now… .the fields with the trenches thrown up, and the happy faces looking over – for the Belgian soldier is as gay as he is brave, and here and there in the earth just above the trenches, and very close to the edge, little wooden crosses caught the eye."*

This idyllic scene was brought abruptly to an end by the German guns, the high-pitched whining scream of the shrapnel shell – whizzzzz-booommm – drowning out the cheerful Belgian voices, the men chased back to their trenches by the officers.

Just a brief, happy, fun-filled episode lighting up a moment in the darkness of war for Grace. This extraordinary Scotswoman experienced so much, soaked up into her consciousness, images that stayed with her always, about which she thought and felt deeply. Passing through a small devastated village she remembered: *"One or two scattered and shattered buildings to complete the picture – church towers that pointed to the Heaven we all profess to worship – the Heaven that heard the prayers of Allies and enemies, and ordered all things as it thought best."*

What went through the mind of this young woman whose early childhood had been so governed by a strictly religious father, whom she loved dearly, and whose goodness and generosity to those in need only came to light after his death?

She paints a very different picture of an occasion not long afterwards. She and Sayer, one of the girls on duty at the RAP at the time, set off for the trenches with a Medical Officer. From previous experience they were loaded down with bundles of clean new shirts, gloves, mittens, cigarettes, and, in particular, woollen socks. All items greatly valued by the troops. These came as a result of hard work of the FANYs back in England's fund-raising contributions.

"It was raining – hard, steady rain; the railway lines were broken up by shellfire and the fields were swampy. We scrambled along zigzag communication trenches. My field boots buried themselves in the mud and my skirt was tucked up to my knees, and my buckskin breeches were soaked through at the knees with slimy, greasy mud."

Looking about, little could be seen in this dreary landscape, until a drenched and sodden officer suddenly appeared apparently from nowhere, and greeted them with broad smiles. He clapped his hands, and all around camouflaged grass-sod roofs and doorways were cautiously raised, and unexpectedly dozens of smiling faces appeared, *"like rats in a hole"* wrote Grace.

She draws a picture of the extraordinary lives those Belgian soldiers were forced to live, and also the extraordinary experience the FANYs shared with them in those early days, through the bitter winter of 1914/15. Getting the gifts to the men was a wearisome and sometimes exhausting ordeal, gladly undertaken by the girls of the FANY, not just through a sense of adventure, but for them to see the looks of joy and delight in the faces of the men.

That made it all worthwhile. Handed a clean shirt the man's face would light up, his happy, heartfelt *"Merci beaucoup, Mam'selle"* would ring out, a dirty shirt would be tossed to the floor, a clean, new one hastily pulled on. The girls were always amazed at the cheerfulness of the troops, and their apparent utter unconcern for the squalor and danger they lived with daily.

Trudging back through the mud to the RAP with empty packs and bags, they came across some French cavalry troops in stables, and a Senegalese soldier acting as cook. Hunting through their packs and pockets, Grace and Sayer found a packet of cigarettes between them, and gave them to the Senegalese. It was obvious he was deeply touched, almost overcome with emotion. He fumbled in the neck of his tunic, and after a lot of fiddling and pulling, eventually produced a German ear from a necklace.

This he handed to Grace with much solemnity, and a low bow. It was their tradition to cut the ears off all they killed and string them round their necks as souvenirs and symbols of their prowess!

Grace accepted it with quiet glee, but at the same time assuring him it was an honour to receive such a gift from him. This was indeed something to show to her brothers.

CHAPTER 21

Battle Of The Big Guns

On another memorable occasion, returning from the trenches, Grace, Walton and Sayer were invited to an afternoon coffee celebration by the doctors of a different regiment, not far away. One of them had just been awarded The Cross of the Legion of Honour for great gallantry.

When they arrived he was wearing, with much embarrassment, a laurel wreath the others had made for him. An orderly had cycled 10 miles to fetch a bottle of champagne, and it was one of those cheerful, happy occasions which suddenly spring to life in the midst of war's desolation – six doctors, a Colonel, and an English officer who had blown in from nowhere.

"Champagne, biscuits and coffee," wrote Grace, *"were passed gaily around. Speeches were made, and the cheery scenes were strange indeed."* Outside, in the icy chill of winter, the guns rumbled sullenly on. The long stove in the room, red hot, spread its warmth. Grace was vastly amused that the English officer just couldn't get over seeing three English girls in uniform in this lonely outpost.

Suddenly, in the midst of the festivities, a frantic banging on the door brought things to an abrupt halt. It burst open and a rain-drenched, blue-uniformed Belgian soldier lurched in, one arm clutching his rifle, the other swathed in ragged, bloodstained bandages. Two stretcher-bearers with a wounded man followed him.

The party ended abruptly.

Medics leapt into action.

Grace describes the scene: *"Back went our chairs and coffee cups. In a moment the hero of the feast was ripping the trouser leg off the moaning figure on the stretcher, and we were bandaging the shoulder and hand of the other man. The leg was an ugly sight, and before it was dressed another stretcher was carried in, and a lad with half his head shot off lay at our feet. Outside a lull came in the storm, and as the rain ceased the clouds cleared and a dull red sunset flamed across the sky."*

When the ambulance had finally driven away, Sayer and Grace

stood for some time watching the sky. At this moment, a few hundred yards away, an armoured gun-train rolled up over the rails they had walked along that morning. Grace described it as *"cumbersome, quaint and wicked-looking"*. The two of them stood watching it, fascinated.

For Grace it was one of the most memorable days so far. A combination of merriment, tragedy and the sudden change in the sky to a majestic orange glow. Then the battle ensued between the great guns on the armoured train, and the prodigious German canonry away out of sight at Dixmude, recently taken by the Hun.

She revelled in the unexpected excitement, describing the scene as she saw it, and her feelings: *"Then BOOM BOOM, and a cloud of smoke melted into the twilight, BRO…OOM – BROO…OOM, growled the angry guns at Dixmude, where the Boches had received the shot.*

"BOOM-BOOM spat the train, and BOOM-BOOM came the answer. It was an unforgettable thing. Up here alone, far from civilization, very far from the homes where, perhaps, our people thought of us, but certainly did not imagine our surroundings!"

She was carried away by this sort of personal euphoria, finding it amazing and exhilarating, experiencing: *"in this atmosphere of storm and war, living what surely few women ever dreamt in their wildest fancies, until this war began"*.

She went on, catching this moment in stark relief, her real self surging to the surface: *"My ears tingled; I breathed in long, deep breaths. Had I spoken, a sort of wild war song would have come from my lips. The Highland blood in me bubbled and frothed; I wanted to run for miles – to race, to climb – action at all costs. And then? … Well, along the road came weary, stumbling figures."*

From the heights of exaltation, Grace was suddenly brought face to face with harsh reality – dirty, muddy, footsore men shuffling along the road, some carrying stretchers, others on them, maimed, broken, moaning. The battle between the armoured train and the German guns in the glowing light of sunset lost its glamour. Once again, the reality of war hit her; no romantic ideas of heroic deeds here, only, she records, *"gaping wounds and quivering flesh"*.

They were a long time dressing the wounds, and it was quite dark when Grace and her two FANYs made their way back to the RAP, and a meal of hot coffee and bread and syrup. Her brother Billy had arrived back with the Unic ambulance; she found him in the roadway, covered in mud, changing a tyre.

Bone weary after the long day, the girls drew their straw from the piles tossed into the room by the orderlies, collected their blankets and a cushion each, and bedded down on the floor. The doctors did the same in the next room, while in the kitchen 12 soldiers grunted and snored the night away.

This was so often the lot of those 'high-spirited, well-bred young ladies' in war-torn Flanders – but they coped.

Another day of meeting challenges, overcoming appalling problems, witnessing distressing sights of suffering, along with inspiring displays of courage. A few short hours, minutes, of camaraderie, cheerfulness, laughter.

Grace remembered the unpleasant details in her book: *"The guns boomed; the smells from the backyard were overpowering; the cold was horrid; our damp stockings did not keep the straw from pricking our feet; my poisoned finger was throbbing. This was War!"* She ended: *"And this was sleep…"*

FANYs out in uniform

Painting by unknown artist

WOMEN AND WAR. [Supplement]

STAFF.-SERGT. G. A. SMITH, 1st Aid N.Y.C. and Editress of "WOMEN & WAR," who wears SANDOW'S Patent Health and Perfect Figure CORSETS, writes :—

"I have worn your Corsets regularly while performing the various duties of this Corps (First Aid Work, Stretcher Drill, and Riding), which involves much bending and constant change of position, and am pleased to say that your Corsets preserve their shape and the outline of the figure better than any other kind I have used."

The Special Form for obtaining advice on Corsetting is on the next page.

Grace proudly posing in her uniform

Mrs Mac's Quaich

The Binson Medal

Co Commandant of FANY

Grace with two shell cases

The FANY on parade

Band of Hope with Belgian Staff

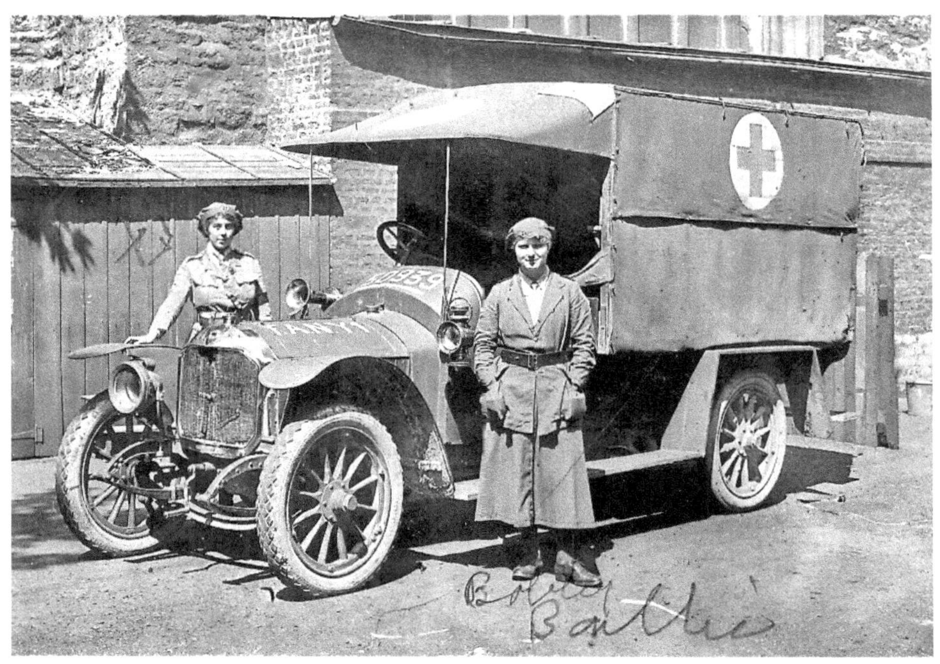

Grace and Bobs Baillie

Moses with Grace

Belgian Convoy Unit 5 Headquaters

Lieutenant Grace McDougall

Original cap badge

English Convoy Unit 3

Street in Pervyse

Shattered Chateau

Shell smashed church in Lampernisse

Water outpost on the Yser

Well dug in Belgian troops

Coastal defence line near Calais

Belgian trenches crossroads

Camouflaged Belgian artillery

Secret meeting King George V

Section of the Front at Dixmude

CHAPTER 22

Christmas In Calais

At the end of December 1914, the 3rd Chasseurs along with 5th Infantry Division moved to another section of the line, and the Oostkerke RAP was no more.

But already Grace, in her indefatigable way, had forged further links with the Belgian Medical authorities, and committed the Corps to opening and running a Convalescent Home for *Les Typhiques* from Lamarck when they had got over the disease itself.

Typical of Grace, given as she was to the foolhardy habit of jumping in where angels would think twice about the consequences, she gave little or no thought to details such as staffing, equipment, finance, or even telling her HQ what she was up to. This was the first of a number of increasingly bitter clashes with the FANY Corps HQ in London as the war went on. And, in this case, with the British Military Authority in Calais as we shall see.

It was getting close to Christmas; the Belgian Surgeon General had just completed another tour of inspection at Lamarck and was relaxing with some of his team. Grace could tell he wasn't his normal, cheerful self.

"What is the matter, Mon General?" she asked. *"Why the long face?"*

He frowned, and glanced at his deputy, a senior Colonel.

"Mademoiselle," he replied, *"we can find no place for the typhoid patients who are past the worst, and we must make room for others who will arrive."*

"Ah, Mon General," said Grace, half in jest, *"I will find you a place!"*

He and the Colonel laughed. *"Thank you, Mademoiselle. Then you can succeed where we fail?"*

"You shall have your Convalescent Home as a gift to the Belgians from the FANY!" Grace retorted.

And there it was, a commitment, spoken half in jest, just as Mr Strachan at the Earls Court garage had promised an ambulance in one week. Grace felt just as duty bound to make good; and was full of confidence. She described her feelings in her wartime memoirs, in her own sometimes slightly garbled way: *"When the need is great, there is always a way if you can find it."*

She got together with Billy, her brother, and Bond, one of the early FANY drivers and a close friend, and discussed the situation. Next morning they drove out along the coast looking for likely places. At Sangatte they stopped at a small hotel which was up for offer, but the owner was away in Paris, and there was little they could do in the meantime.

Then Billy remembered a Chateau, a bit off the main road to Boulogne, where some Belgian troops were billeted, and the three jumped back into the Unic and sped off. Time was of the essence.

Leaving the car at the gates of the Chateau, and resorting to direct bluffing, Grace swept into the impressive main hall, which the Belgians were using as an orderly room, with a rather startled Major in charge. Grace beckoned him to her with an imperious gesture, no doubt something she had learned in her days of amateur dramatics.

She informed him brusquely that they were nurses – *"English nurses"* – in the service of the Belgian Army, and needed the Chateau for Belgian soldiers convalescing after hospitalization in Calais. Giving him no time to digest this, she went on to ask him just how soon he could arrange alternative accommodation for his men.

All he could do was to gasp out that HE needed the Chateau for his men, that only three rooms were allocated to them by the owner, and added that the place was cold and damp, and totally unsuitable for sick men.

He then took Grace and the others on a tour of inspection, and it wasn't at all what Grace had hoped for. The Major accompanied them down the drive, where they parted amicably, Grace making the point before she drove off, that: *"If we find nothing better we shall return. Monsieur would not let the sick suffer for want of the chateau, I am sure"*.

As they stood chatting at the gates Grace spotted an elderly priest nearby. On a sudden impulse she approached him, asking if he was, by any chance, the *cure* of the village.

Not only was he the *cure,* but he replied in perfect English. It turned out that his mother was Irish, his father French. From the start they got on like a house on fire. It turned out that in his village of St.

Inglevert, they had a Church Hall he thought might be suitable for up to 25 convalescents.

Climbing into the Unic, they all drove off to the Church Hall where they talked drainage, accommodation in detail, took a good look round the whole premises, then gratefully accepted the Priest's offer. They drove back to Calais in a much happier mood. The major obstacle had been cleared, finding a home for *les invalides*. Obviously there were more hurdles ahead, which might prove even more difficult, but as usual, Grace was fired by irresistible enthusiasm, convinced that was enough to carry her through. It always had, and she saw no reason to doubt that it would now. Problems were there to be overcome.

However, as she wrote up her diary that night, she faced up to the fact that equipping the Home with beds, blankets and bed-linen was going to be a very different kettle of fish. She had virtually promised 'mon General' that all would be ready by the New Year. Not just the FANY honour was at stake, as she saw it, but that of England, too. She could never allow that to be jeopardised. Her mind in turmoil, she finally slept.

The next few days she spent organising and leading a team cleaning out the new Convalescent Home, with the help of a couple of FANYs, along with local volunteers dragooned by the *Cure*.

Satisfied that that part of her project was in the capable hands of the *Cure,* Grace headed for England just days before Christmas to raise funds and contributions towards the equipping and furnishing of the Home. It was probably the most hectic Christmas shopping spree Grace would ever undertake, and also the most successful and satisfying. Not only did she manage a flying visit to Aberdeen, where she raised considerable contributions for the Home, she was also able to spend some time with her mother. On her return to London she proceeded to shamelessly exploit any and all connections she had forged in the past with high ranking officials of the Establishment.

Her first targets were Sir Arthur Slogget, Chief Commissioner of the British Red Cross – *"the kindest and cheeriest of Directors-General"* she called him – and Mr – later Sir – Arthur Stanley – *"the most broadminded and generous of men"* – both of whom responded magnificently. Twenty five sprung bedsteads, along with mattresses and bedding, were immediately despatched to Calais for the typhoid sufferers in the wards of Lamarck.

Another major problem was solved. FANY HQ, though not at all happy with the way Grace had conducted the whole operation – out of the blue committing them to finding money to support this new venture, asking nobody's permission or opinion – rallied round as ever for the good of the Corps, and provided what funds they could spare, and a lot of donated 'comforts' for the Convalescent Home.

After three days of furious activity, Grace headed back to Calais, well satisfied with what she had achieved. One of the FANY Corps' great strengths was its independence from other organizations. When they felt it was necessary they could strike hard and fast, not waiting for permits, decisions, or agreements from above. It was just this independence of movement that so exasperated the Establishment, and led to bitter confrontations from time to time; and later on, between Grace and the Treasurer and the Secretary of FANY HQ as well!

Also, it may be said that this very same Establishment exploited this freedom from time to time, when they found themselves in difficult situations. As will be seen, the employment of FANY drivers by a British Base Hospital in Calais to get them out of a hole, without reference to higher authority, played a large part in the eventual – and grudging – employment of the Corps by the British Army in 1916.

Back in Calais, things were in full swing to make Christmas and New Year a very special time for their patients. Grace loved this time of the year, and all the FANYs, from Boss Franklin, down to the latest arrival from England, were infused with the festive spirit. Lamarck hospital was transformed. Despite her recent whirlwind trip to England, Grace was in the midst of all the activities.

Christmas trees were obtained with some difficulty, enough for most wards. Christmas Eve was a hive of activity. Candles and ornaments were used to decorate the trees, and, as Grace wrote: *"At midnight we went softly round each ward and placed a complete outfit of new clothes (i.e. shirt, vest, pants, socks, scarf, mittens and handkerchief) by each man's bed. Every bed was full, and we had two extra"*.

The Surgeon-General was invited for Christmas Day, and was

presented with a small lucky piggy off the tree. *"Tears came to the dear old man's eyes."* It wasn't only the General, though – everybody received a gift of some sort, as well as the bundles of new clothes.

These young, cheerful girls of the FANY were a magnet for many units around. On Christmas night the hospital filled up with visitors. There were officers from many surrounding units, doctors also, and an English naval officer from somewhere.

"What a spread we had, too," Grace remembered. *"Cakes and shortbread and sweets! We dragged the piano to the top of the stairs; and how the men loved the songs and the choruses."*

It was a truly Allied event, English, French and Belgian officers and doctors all made welcome. After tea was finished at about 7 o'clock, an English Tommy came along to sing to the patients, to settle them down, going round all the different wards.

This was followed by dinner in the kitchen for the doctors, orderlies and nurses, including, of course, all the FANYs who had worked so hard. *"For this very special event,"* wrote Grace, *"we had plum pudding and turkey!"* Then, as most had been up at 6 in the morning for early service in the hospital Chapel, they were happy to go off to their beds about 11 o'clock. So passed their first wartime Christmas in France.

CHAPTER 23

Celebration And Backlash

There was no time to relax. The new convalescent Home at St. Inglevert was still very much on the agenda. On Christmas Eve Grace, choosing her moment carefully, and *"with triumph in my heart"* had broken the news in as casual a manner as possible to the Surgeon General that she had found a place for the Home, and that it would be ready very soon. His spontaneous reaction – disbelief, amazement, delight – was, to Grace, worth all the worry and effort she had gone through.

True to their word, Sir Arthur Slogget and Mr Stanley had despatched the beds and accessories. They were now at the docks ready for collection, and Grace once more swept into action. She arranged for the new beds to be delivered immediately to Lamarck typhoid wards, where they were exchanged for the old wooden ones, and, under her supervision, scrubbed with boiling water and disinfectant, before being ferried by ambulance to the Church Hall at St. Inglevert.

Once they were in place, and satisfactorily lined up in true military fashion, the plentiful supply of mattresses, sheets and blankets followed direct from the Quay. Cecily Maudant and Evelyn Laidlaw, the first two FANYs selected to run the new Home, went with them, watching over their precious cargo like hawks.

There, along with the two or three temporary back-up staff attached to the Home for the first few weeks of the project to get it up and running smoothly, they buckled down to making up the beds, hanging decorations, and brightening the place up any way they could.

It would be a few more days before the convalescents occupied the place, but the girls would make sure that those poor, wretched men, who had been through the hell of that frightful disease and survived, would enjoy the best possible conditions it was in their power to provide. Especially at this time of the year.

About this Grace was adamant. She loved Christmas, birthdays,

Hogmanay, the traditional celebrations that went with them, and infused her FANYs with the same sense of fun and enthusiasm. Not that much urging was needed. Infectious gaiety was part of their lives at home, and in spite of the unpleasant, and sometimes shocking, conditions they lived under, the girls never lost that touch of good cheer. As time went on they became renowned for it.

The work and efforts of the FANYs still in England and staff at HQ in London were largely instrumental in providing these Christmas 'goodies'. They raised the funds for much of the decorations and trees, and most of the new clothing given to every patient on Christmas morning; while a great many of the FANY both at home and at Lamarck happily dipped into their own pockets to fund a lot of the festivities that went on over Christmas and the New Year. They made special efforts to give the new Home a cheerful, colourful look.

By Boxing Day the Home was ready! A rash promise was fulfilled, thanks entirely to the initiative, energy and hard work of the FANYs.

During the following week, the bulk of the patients from *les typhiques* who had recovered sufficiently to convalesce, were transferred to the Home at St. Inglevert, their places in the Typhoid Ward quickly taken.

The Christmas festivities were barely over, things slowly getting back to normal, when it was the turn of the Belgians to show how they celebrated New Year. They were much more emotional in their approach. At midnight on New Year's Eve the FANYs were invited into the kitchen. There they found the entire Belgian staff assembled. Most of these made long emotional speeches, according to Grace, praising the *"Eengleesh Misses and their devotion, and how we had left our homes to care for their homeless wounded"*.

The Belgians all wept, so touched were they by their speakers. And Grace had to try to make a suitable reply to match the feelings. She said at some length how *"honoured the FANY were to help these heroes who had saved Europe from the Hun"*. It went down well.

Then everyone kissed everyone else. This led to the Belgians singing a *"Flemish ditty which the English didn't understand, followed by Auld Lang Syne which the Belgians didn't understand"*.

Finally Grace and the other FANYs bade their hosts goodnight and went 'first footing' in the Unic. They were singularly unsuccessful. Their first 'target' was the Senior British Medical Officer, an Irishman who apparently did not understand Scottish customs, and was absolutely furious at being wakened!

They drove on to a hospital some way off, where they knew there were four Scottish doctors in residence. This, too, was a complete disaster, as *all four* were teetotal, and were *"sleepy and bored"* as Grace remembers, *"so we returned to our quarters to snatch a few hours' sleep before morning!"*.

Christmas and New Year 1914 had passed over in a euphoria of gaiety and goodwill. Grace wrote: *"Had anyone told us that we should spend our next Christmas in France, we would have treated them with scorn!"*

It was at this point that the season of goodwill among the various Allied organizations ended abruptly!

Between them, Allied Military and Civil administrators had built a complex system of jurisdiction within the Area. Obviously, Calais belonged to France, but in view of the military and logistical strength of the British Army in that part, in support of their section of the Lines north of Calais, it was nominally in the charge of the British. However, sizeable areas had been allocated to the Belgian Army too, for much the same reasons.

Bureaucracy being what it is, the ongoing petty jealousies between – and within – the various factions rose to the surface. Most units played by the rules, obtaining written permission from a Higher Authority to so much as blow their noses. The wheels moved ponderously and slowly, if at all.

Not so the FANY! Mavericks all, they revelled in their independence. They didn't just talk about doing things – they just went ahead and did them! It never occurred to Grace, for one minute, that she had to get somebody's permission for the Convalescent Home.

So it wasn't until the Belgian typhoid convalescents were actually in the new Home, that the British Authorities woke up to the fact that all this was going on under their very noses. And nobody had applied for permission for any of it.

Reaction was immediate and truculent. To start with, letters of protest were sent to FANY HQ complaining bitterly. Nothing had been authorized. The main road out of Calais and through St. Inglevert was under the control of the British. They even went so far as to threaten to withdraw Passes for all FANY ambulances and other vehicles to St. Inglevert and the Convalescent Home. The BRCS (British Red Cross Society), who had long resented the independence of the FANY, seized upon the episode with glee, supporting the British Administration wholeheartedly, saying, in effect, see – that's how they behave if left to themselves!

Grace was upbeat about the whole thing from start to finish, even though summoned to British Admin HQ to explain her actions. She commented cheerfully: *"Possession generally ensures victory."*

And it did!

One of the reasons Grace was on such a high at this time was the well-kept secret that she had become engaged. When or under what circumstances this happened is unknown. Where they met is not recorded. What is certain is that at the end of October 1914 she had not met her husband-to-be, Captain Ronald McDougall of the King's Own Yorkshire Light Infantry. But they were married at All Saints' Church, Bourne End, in Maidenhead on January 23rd 1915! It must have been something of a whirlwind romance. But then Grace was something of a whirlwind herself. Apart from a Marriage Certificate, all records or photographs of the event have been lost. What is known is that in her early days in Southern Rhodesia after the war, a lot of her papers were eaten by the voracious white ants, before she came to realise what a scourge they were. It may be that those records were among them.

Grace makes a brief, passing reference to the event in her memoirs, Five Years with the Allies: *"I spent three days in Scotland with my mother, and on my return* (to London) *found my brother and the man I was engaged to at the station with a Special Licence. It seemed absurd not to use it, so we dashed off to buy a ring and caught a train to Maidenhead in the morning. As it was the first wedding where the bride wore khaki, the parson was consumed with curiosity and rallied through the service to gasp out, "Who are you, do tell me what your uniform is?".*

"We had three wedding cakes, and everyone promised us presents when the war was over. (The war has been over for some time now!)"

Quite what that final sentence infers is uncertain. Perhaps that the promised presents hadn't been forthcoming after all?

What sort of honeymoon they enjoyed is also a mystery. Certainly it wasn't long before Grace was back in Calais, and Ronald's regiment, the KOYLI were headed for France. It is thought that the 'brother' referred to in that extract, must have been Billy, he who drove the first FANY 'Band of Hope' ambulance to France at the end of October. He had just received his long-awaited induction papers, and was commissioned into the KOYLI, Ronald McDougall's regiment.

Grace's marriage made little difference to her dedicated service to her Corps. With her new husband securely ensconced in the army, and shortly to be in the trenches, there was little in the way of wifely duties for her to perform. Whereas there was still much to be done for the FANY.

The main change to her service was that from then on she became known as either 'Mrs Mac' to the majority of the Corps, or plain 'Mac' to her closer friends.

Back in France, there was more work to be done. The ill-tempered Establishment stramash over the Convalescent Home patients soon blew over, and on her return to St. Inglevert after her wedding, she made sure all was going smoothly.

The two FANYs put in charge soon got it up and running, though it was hard work. It was an absolutely unique enterprise, new territory for them all. Grace was to admit much later that she should have used at least four girls to cope with the workload. *"They worked nobly,"* she wrote, and: *"the patients grew fat and rosy!"*.

It is unlikely the FANYs running the place did the same. They had a very long, full day. Reveille was a 6 a.m.. They held roll-calls, and prepared and served breakfast. The patients then made their beds and tidied up under the supervision of one of the girls, while the other got dinner ready; then, after a good meal, they went *en masse,* in crocodile formation, for a walk, escorted by the two FANYs. It must have been a strange sight! They all then settled down to coffee and biscuits on getting back, played games, read, and smoked till supper prepared by the girls. Then, after washing up, they went to bed, none more glad to do so than the girls themselves.

They slept in a farmhouse adjacent to the Home. The *Cure* would have been delighted to accommodate them in his spacious manse, but the laws of the Church were very strictly enforced – no females under the age of forty were allowed to sleep in the manse, even with an elderly housekeeper in residence to act as chaperone! Grace's amused comment was that the combined ages of the two barely exceeded forty.

Unhappily, there was no comparison in the quality of the rooms offered. The manse: large, comfortable, immaculate; the room at the farmhouse, shared by the two, described by Cecily Mordaunt as no bigger than 'a good sized cupboard'. It contained only a bed, covered with a large hay-filled mattress, and two thick quilts. No sheets or blankets, but numbers of small and active resident fleas and bugs. However, they were FANYs.

They put up with it, with their usual good humour.

CHAPTER 24

New Horizons

After the hectic Christmas and New Year festivities in Calais, Grace and the others faced the future with confidence. The grumblings and rumblings of the British Administration in Calais didn't really disturb Grace at all. Locking horns with the Establishment was something she enjoyed; apart from that there was the thrill and excitement of her recent engagement to Ronald McDougall Above all was her intense satisfaction at the way her FANYs had faced all their many problems in their first major test of efficiency, dedication and courage, and come out admired – if not fully approved in some quarters – by all, especially those sick and wounded to whom they gave all the care and attention they could.

Now Grace was back in France, generally overseeing the operation in Calais, but never losing sight of her principal aim – raising the profile of the Corps by getting them more work, and in the end, working for the British Army. It was not going to be easy. The Belgians were doing all they could to involve the FANY. From the early days, when Grace was the lone representative of the Corps in Antwerp and Ghent, to the setting up and running of Lamarck Hospital and other services, they had recognized and appreciated the huge contribution the FANY was making to their Army. Had it not been for the support of the Belgians it is more than likely the Corps would have ceased to exist.

The British and French authorities were fiercely opposed to employing women in any capacity other than traditional nursing. The British objections went much deeper than that; they could not bring themselves to acknowledge such an independent group, who made their own rules and went their own way, especially as they were women. It went against every tenet of male domination those at the top clung to.

As we know, Grace was not one to give up. She made constant and frequent approaches to both the British War Office and the French, offering them various services, changing tack from time to time to keep open the lines of communication.

But, as we also know, Grace was a woman who sought adventure, loved risk-taking, and always liked to be where the action was. She made time to go out with one or other of the Ambulances that daily roamed the areas behind the Front Lines seeking wounded wherever they could be found, at Forward Aid Posts (FAPs), RAPs, or even the trenches. Army units holding the lines got to know them very quickly, and were delighted at the service they gave.

These forays by the FANY Ambulances were, of course, primarily aimed at bringing in wounded soldiers, but all too often became involved with pitiful civilians from the very young to the very old, who had got caught up and left behind in the maelstrom of war. And here the FANY could step in and help, where the more hidebound – or regulation bound – military services could not.

And sometimes, if fortune smiled on them, they would find themselves unexpected, but honoured guests in officers' Messes tucked away in a hidden bunker near the Front; or perhaps a small, abandoned cottage, as yet untouched by bomb or shell, further back. For a short while there would be laughter and joking and some sort of food, perhaps a glass of wine. Then back again to the Ambulance, with smiles and handshakes from these young men in uniforms of Belgium, they might never see again. How Grace longed for the time those uniforms would be British khaki. 'One day,' she thought, 'one day.'

She often wrote about these trips. Of one, north of Calais, she set out with her driver and great friend, Chris Nicholson. Recounting the trip in her book: *"It was a perfect day, a cold wind blowing, but a blue sky overheard. The road between Calais and Dunkirk flew past; the walls of Gravelines and its narrow streets were left behind. Dunkirk itself was gay with Zuaves [French Colonial Troops] in their baggy red trousers. Along the canal we raced past ponderous convoys toiling up with their loads."*

They motored through Fismes – no longer a busy town, but now desolate and almost empty, its main square pitted with shell holes. Then on to Pervyse where they heard again the old familiar booming of the guns nearer the Front.

Revisiting the old '*Poste de Secours*' of the 3rd Chasseurs they knew so well, they were welcomed with delight by the strangers from a new regiment now in occupation. For the sake of old times they left them packets of cigarettes, scarves and socks to pass on to the patients there. As they were about to leave, a shell hurtled down out of the sky and exploded nearby, 'hastening their departure' with this reminder that war could catch up with them at any time, any place.

Passing through Lampernisse, their next stop, which they knew well, they saw just how badly the old church had been smashed. Grace remembered with sadness: *"its friendly tower, the throng of soldiers that had surrounded it, the gay faces of the little blue Belgians that had met us cheerily on every side"*.

It was here they were approached by the local *Cure* asking if they could take one of his last remaining parishioners to safety. He led them to a small, battered cottage, where inside they found a little, frail old woman on a mattress. Laying her gently on a stretcher, they carried her to the Ambulance, and drove her to a Convent which, the *Cure* told them, would take her in.

Unfortunately the Mother Superior adamantly refused: she was full up; no more, no more. At times like these Grace, and indeed all the girls, felt almost a sense of despair, They drove on many miles, to a place run by an Englishwoman for refugees like the old lady. They got there to find no trace of the Englishwoman, but left their patient in the care of some of the refugees. So many suffering in this way, so little to be done for them.

On this particular day they had been invited for lunch at the Belgian Divisional HQ, but were much too late after rescuing the old lady. However, they got there in time for tea, were greeted warmly, and looked after by the Belgian officers, happy to be entertaining two attractive young ladies. Feeling not only physically but mentally refreshed, and in a happier frame of mind, Grace and Chris made their farewells and departed.

On another occasion, in the war zone north of Calais, they encountered yet another small scene of misery and fear so often suffered by the innocents caught up in this disaster. Driving through a small, shattered village they were waved down by an officer commanding the troops stationed there. He asked if they could evacuate a young family still managing to exist there among the ruins. He was afraid for their safety – four little boys and a young mother expecting her fifth child, and absolutely terrified.

Grace and Chris agreed immediately. Wrapping the woman and her children in scarves and balaclavas to keep them warm, they drove them to the same refugee centre to which they had taken the old lady from Lampernisse a few days before, and settled them in. As they drove off, they were happy to see the four little boys waving from the doorway of the centre.

It was getting late by now, and, with no more wounded to collect, they headed to Ramskapelle for a previously arranged informal dinner at a Belgian artillery Mess.

Arriving at the cottage where the Officers' Mess was located, Grace recalled that: *"the whizzing and whistling overhead denoted 'activity at the front'."* She went on: *"In fact we ran at top speed up that garden path and hammered on the doors. Friendly faces greeted us and we were soon inside."* There they were again given a warm welcome, and enjoyed good food specially prepared to impress *'les petits FANYs'*, pleasant cheerful company, good wine, as well as some lively music. In the safety of this warm and cheerful Mess, windows heavily shuttered, they were able to relax, be themselves, be entertained. That would have been ample for them, but more was in store. *"Afterwards,"* Grace recorded, *"[we] …went up to the trenches. The rockets and flares were fascinating. Viewed from afar they are strangely remote, but very friendly here, when crouched down among all these gallant men."*

It was time to go. Before they went, they made sure from the Medical Officers that there were no wounded awaiting transport. It had been a long and strangely satisfying day helping lost and helpless civilian women and children on the one hand, and then finding themselves crouched in dark, front line trenches, illuminated from time to time by flares and rockets and the occasional bursting shells. It was an amazing and exciting experience, one that would live with them forever, but right now they were glad to be heading back to Calais, and a night in bed.

CHAPTER 25

Charlie And Grace Reunited

For Grace, April 17th was a day to remember, a day of intense excitement for her, as she strolled along the Quayside at Boulogne. Her much loved elder brother, Charlie, whom she had not seen for months, was due to arrive by boat. She had driven down from Calais the night before, with her great friend Betty Hutchinson as driver, in her own ambulance, the Unic.

She smiled to herself as she went, having just witnessed an amusing scene. Parked between a French and a British vehicle, Betty had decided to change a tyre which had been playing up. It was the differing attitudes of the French and English drivers on either side that had caused her so much amusement. Touched, to a certain extent, by national pride, it must be said.

Grace wrote about it later: *"The French driver protested it was a hard job for a woman – the English were courageous – an Englishwoman to change a heavy tyre like that! And he continued to sit and smoke his cigarette."*

Grace continued: *"The English driver strolled languidly round the car – sauntered slowly back to his own 'bus, strolled back to ours, levers in hand, and still in unbroken silence took tyre and nuts and operations generally, out of Betty's capable hands. Only when the new tyre was on, did he speak. 'That'll do, I'm thinking,' he remarked wisely, and strolled off again!"*

Grace herself wandered off, still smiling, but keeping a watchful eye on the harbour traffic.

As soon as she saw the leave boat approaching, she headed back to the Quay, and anxiously searched the crowds of khaki-clad figures on the deck, but it was only as he shuffled down the companionway that they spotted each other. She ran to embrace him as he hurried across to her. Their affection and comradeship, shared for so long as children, almost tangible, bridging those gaps over the years which had separated them – and Billy – from time to time.

Charlie had with him an old friend, Montague Johnstone, serving in another cavalry regiment, the Scots Greys. Introductions were soon over; they piled their kit into the Unic, and set off for St. Omer, GHQ of the British Expeditionary Force (BEF). Both men had orders to report there first and get instructions for joining their units. Off they went, Betty and Montague in the front, Charlie and Grace perched at the back dangling their legs over the tailboard. The years melted away. For these two it was like reliving one of their mad adventures of the past, though this time there were just the two, not the usual trio.

There was so much to talk about. In Grace's words: *"In wartime one does not see much of one's relations."* This final adventure stayed deep within Grace's memory. About it she remembers: *"The long hills, the wide stretches of country, the fascination of the vast views, held us too; and then the darkness came, slowly at first with a mellow golden sunset, and then – rain. Oh that rain! – but we did not heed it much."*

They drove on through the rain and the darkness, over roads that neither Grace nor Betty were familiar with – unsurprising, as it was well into the British sector, and women drivers were not normally allowed there. At last they reached St. Omer, where GHQ was situated, and with sighs of relief pulled up in the Town Square, in front of the large requisitioned hotel.

Here there was much activity: Staff Cars parked everywhere, men in khaki constantly moving around. Entering the hotel they immediately became the centre of attention. The buzz of conversation in the lounge died down, heads swung in their direction. Women at GHQ were a great rarity, especially women in British Army uniforms, and one of them an officer.

Charlie was delighted with all this, proud to be with his younger sister getting all this attention, proud of her in her officer's uniform. Montague, on the other hand, was obviously slightly embarrassed by all eyes being turned upon them. The two girls noticed his discomfort, but pretended to be unaware of it. Both knew that ladies, even in military uniform, were not supposed to penetrate the hallowed precincts of GHQ!

The two men duly signed in, got their travel instructions, and the four of them sat down to a much needed dinner. It had been a long drive in dreadful conditions. Refreshed and cheerful, they gathered themselves together, and once more set out into the dark and the rain.

It was difficult finding the way. The roads were thronged with military convoys, past sentries astonished at seeing women in uniform, through sleeping villages. At last they got to Hazebrouck, where Montague Johnstone of the Scots Greys was to be dropped off. Charlie wanted to send the girls back from there, taking his chances of getting further along to his own unit. Neither Grace nor Betty would hear of it. They were determined, in FANY fashion, to finish the job. Goodbyes were said, Montague promising to come and visit them in Calais the first chance he got. Charlie, Grace and Betty all sat in the front now, and headed for Boesinghe, where the 3rd Dragoon Guards were stationed.

In the tradition of the FANY, young though it was as yet, both Grace and Betty were enjoying this little adventure, driving around in the British sector where few women had been before, and where the Authorities considered women to be utterly useless unless they were nurses and nothing else.

They came upon an Army Service Corps (ASC) depot, and stopped to take some petrol on board. Two of the sentries at the depot were Scots, and according to Grace, were: *"Vastly overcome at hearing their own tongue being spoken by a woman in the heart of that little French village"*.

On they went until finally Charlie reached his destination, a small cottage, in the sitting room of which were laid out three sleeping bags. A small room off it was reserved for the Adjutant.

Charlie's batman made them some cocoa and produced some 'home made' cake to their delight. Then they strolled out to have a look at Charlie's horses, comfortably stabled in the back yard. The groom on guard duty was given a few packets of Gold Flake cigarettes from the stores they had brought with them, which cheered him up immensely.

Then it was time to go. Charlie was very worried about them going back in those conditions in territory unfamiliar to them, and suggested they stay until morning. Grace was wouldn't hear of it; she was catching the 10.30 boat in the morning, and that was that.

But first, Charlie wanted them to meet an old friend of his, originally from South America, whose billet was about quarter of a mile down the road. It was all in darkness when they stopped outside, and the three of them crept quietly up to a shuttered window. Tapping on it, Charlie called out, "Hello, Harry. Are you asleep?"

Grace remembers: *"And I, filled with the demon of mischief, laughed, and called out 'Hello, Harry. Are you asleep?'."*

Her woman's voice brought a shout of astonishment, and Harry appeared, with a 'British Warm' over his pyjamas, delighted to see Charlie again, and thrilled to see two ladies in khaki. Harry Dadson, a fellow officer of the regiment, was happy as a sandboy. He offered to sleep with Charlie if the girls would stay till morning. But both were firm: Betty had to get Grace to Boulogne for the 10.30 boat.

They all went out to where the Unic was parked in the road, alongside a small canal. It was about 1 a.m. and still raining hard. All four stood around the ambulance for a few minutes, "chatting gaily" according to Grace. She was trying to light and adjust the headlight – the other had been knocked off the night the 'Band of Hope' arrived in Calais at the end of October – when Billy had driven into a handcart in the dark!

Suddenly Charlie shouted, grabbed a flashlight, and ran to the rear of the ambulance waving it madly. Then he leapt backwards, and fell into the canal.

At the same time Harry yelled out *"jump for your lives!"*.

Betty burst out of the Unic and ran across the road.

Then, a sudden crash, and the Unic lurched towards Grace, who hurled herself away from it. The episode was etched into her memory: *"I leapt backwards – down, down into cold, slimy, horrible water. I fumbled wildly in the air; one thought alone dominated me – I had new boots on!"*

She was convinced momentarily that she would drown, until Harry reached down and pulled her out back onto the road. She recalls: "And all the gratitude I offered was *'my new boots will be ruined!'*."

Abruptly she remembered Charlie's first warning shout, and screamed out: *"Where's Charlie?"* and suddenly he was beside her, the moment of panic was past.

The cause of this unexpected fracas turned out to be a French Staff Car, with three officers in it, interpreters all, who had been driving far too fast for the prevailing conditions, and smashed into the back of the parked Unic.

In a letter to her mother a couple of days later, Grace summed it up graphically: *"Charlie fled for his life and fell into a small canal. Betty ran; Dadson leapt back. I, being on the other side, didn't see what was coming and only saw the Unic barge at me, leapt back clean over a milestone and into the small canal also."*

Her next remarks underscore the kind of stress that built up in those who were under constant pressure in adverse conditions. She went on: *"It was frightfully funny, and we laughed ourselves sore!"*

To the three French officers shakily climbing out of their damaged car, it must have been a bizarre sight: two British Officers and two women in British Army uniforms, shrieking with laughter, possibly having just escaped death by inches. It would have done much to reinforce the popular view of Continentals that the English were completely mad.

However, realizing and accepting their responsibility, they sought to make amends. As they approached Grace and the rest, one, slightly ahead of the others, called out in his practised English, *"Much damage, you fellows?"*

Grace answered, saying there appeared to be quite a lot. The Frenchman, taken aback at hearing a woman's voice, walked closer. Grace continues: *"His eyes peered into my face as he saluted."*

"I beg your pardon," he stuttered, *"I did not expect to find a lady!"* Then, poor chap, still apparently suffering from shock, took a step back, tripped over the same milestone that Grace had a short time before, and disappeared into the canal.

This incident produced further roars of laughter, but whether the officer concerned joined in is not recorded. However, he is on record as protesting that he was alright.

The French officers and their driver offered to repair the damage as best they could. As it was now about 2 a.m. Grace and Betty decided they would stay the night after all, rather than return through unfamiliar country in a damaged vehicle, in rain and darkness.

The gallant Frenchmen removed their jackets, and set to in their shirtsleeves as the rain continued to pour down. They persuaded the ladies to go inside and shelter from the elements, which they did, taking with them two stretchers for the men to sleep on, while they commandeered Harry's bed.

Meantime, Charlie set off on foot to recall his horses from the previously arranged *rendezvous*. This was to be a night to remember.

Back in Harry's billet the landlady appeared, having been an interested spectator, from an upstairs window, of all that had gone on. She produced coffee and rolls and butter, which was more than welcome after their experience. It was now about 2.30 a.m. and the old dear refused to go to bed until the meal was finished and Charlie had returned. Grace was convinced she felt it was her duty to act as a chaperone!

They were all in bed by 3 o'clock, slept until 6 a.m.. To their delight, the landlady was already up, with breakfast of eggs, rolls and butter, and coffee ready for them all. Shortly after breakfast the French returned having completed the repairs sometime during the night. They insisted that they must be there to see that the Unic started alright. While all this was going on, Charlie's batman cleaned the girls' boots and equipment, and dried them by the stove.

As a final gesture, the French officers had gathered bunches of early spring flowers to present to '*les mademoiselles*'.

The sun was now shining, and the road was already busy with military convoys rumbling past. The group were gathered around the ambulance. There were companies of British troops on the march, too, and as they passed the two girls in khaki, holding the bunches of flowers, all their usual march discipline went by the board. They broke lines to catch a glimpse of them, call out greetings and cheered them loudly.

The time came to go. Grace and Betty climbed aboard the Unic. Harry wished both of them *au revoir* telling them they must return next week. (They did, but sadly, both billets were empty and the area deserted. The regiment had gone to the Battle of Ypres.)

Grace had reached one of the most poignant moments in her life. Her account of the parting with Charlie in Nursing Adventures reflects this haunting memory.

"As for the brother, he stood there in the sunshine, big and strong and happy; and my heart was heavy despite the prospect of seeing him in a week. Was he, too, troubled with foreboding? I knew not. For a moment he took my hands in his as we said farewell. There were gay and cheery greetings. The spring of life and hope and love seemed very full that morning, and my eyes kept turning to the big brother in the sunlight, straight and tall and fit. Was it a warning, that weight at my heart? – a knowledge that never again would I see him standing so, the sun's rays on his dark eyes and cheery smile."

CHAPTER 26

Tragedy Draws Closer

As they drove back to Boulogne in bright sunshine, Grace's sombre mood changed, with Betty's help, and became as cheerful and vivacious as ever. Something else that raised their spirits was the presence of so many British troops in that part of France. Then they lost their way, and, according to Grace: *"through the stupidity of an English sentry we wandered in circles in little by-roads, and didn't reach Boulogne until 12.30!*

"At this point, Betty decided that she would cross, too, and we had a great time Visa-ing our Passports – AND had to borrow money from the Base Commandant!"

This was so typical of the ways of the FANY in those days. They could make a decision on the spot, and act on it immediately, such was their independence. There is no doubt that this characteristic was the root cause of the British authorities viewing them with such suspicion.

Grace took the opportunity of a break away from France to write a long letter to her mother. Dated April 19th, the day before her return to Boulogne, it was full of the last few days, of her adventures with Charlie. It was obvious from the tenor of the letter that she was greatly amused by the whole episode, and loved being with Charlie again. Of the French officers crashing into her ambulance, she said: *"One was very nice and I asked him to come to Calais to see us – so he has promised to come and bring Charlie, too."*

She rattled on in her slightly discordant fashion, about the British troops they had passed as they headed for Boulogne. *"It was rather fun, as we met squadrons of English cavalry on our return journey and they all cheered and saluted – no women are ever allowed here at all."*

She mentioned, in passing, that they had heard the firing of the new 15 inch guns some way away; hastily reassuring her mother that they were 25 kilometres from the Front Line, and perfectly safe.

There were other things on her mind too that she was anxious to tell her mother about. Shortly before leaving Calais to meet Charlie, the Belgian Commandant in Calais, General Clooten, had approached her. Following her proposal earlier, would she go up to Camp du Ruchard for a few days and report back to him on the true state of affairs there?

She was delighted, telling her mother she would be going up next week. It was a vast camp for 4000 or so Belgian soldiers, and about 700 convalescents, the latter being the target of Grace's sympathy. She writes, with obvious excitement: *"I am going there on Thursday, and will probably be five days gone."* Then she adds, almost as an aside: *"I have also offered to start a Soldiers' Club for Belgians at the Front, and my offer has been sent to the King, personally recommended by General Clooten."*

This letter is so typical of the kind of woman Grace was, bubbling with enthusiasm – words and ideas and plans tumbling out of her, often full of *non sequiturs. "I am over here for a weekend,"* she goes on. *"I met Charlie at Boulogne (your wire to me was signed Brown, how was that?) and motored him to St. Omer."* Scribbled at one side of the margin at the top of the letter –another of Grace's hallmarks – she says: *"Charlie gave me a wire to send to you from Boulogne that he had arrived safely – I had not a chance of sending it and forgot it this morning."*

Also at the top of the page, on the other side, was scrawled another snippet: *"Have posted a group of Rhodesian KOYLI with Rannie (her new husband) in it till I get a photo of him. Mine have not come yet."*

So much to write – so little time!

Not quite drawing this rather breathless letter to a close, she dashes off another afterthought at the top of the last page, in her bold, fast-moving, can't-waste-a-second handwriting: *"There is a big photo of me and a whole page interview in the Lady's Pictorial of 3*rd *April also a photo of me in The Gentlewoman same date."*

All this was written towards the close of her weekend, somewhere called The Puzzle, Aston Clinton. But apparently she nearly did not get there, having to pass through Aylesbury. She finishes with a series of fascinating but disjointed sentences, leaving one desperate to know more. She continued:

"I didn't get to Aylesbury till midnight. Rannie had got none of my wires – and the Aylesbury policeman tried to arrest me for wearing an

officer's uniform!! However I soon settled him, AND the Military Police sergeant they had sent for." How one longs to have been a fly on the wall at that particular confrontation! Those policemen hadn't a chance, had they but known.

Finally Grace ends her letter: *"I go back tomorrow and come over again Friday week, d.v."* Still the human dynamo, the whirlwind, rushing from place to place, never pausing for long.

Returning to Calais on schedule, she reassured herself that all was going as smoothly as possible, which, of course it was, in the capable hands of Franklin, and headed for Camp du Ruchard to carry out the survey for General Clooten.

Arriving towards the end of April, her first impression was a real eye-opener. In the lyrical style so typical of much of her writing she builds a picture of the place itself and sets the scene. In mid-April, after one of the worst winters on record, Ruchard did not show up well. Writes Grace: *"In summer there are few valleys so smiling and so prosperous."* She then gets down to the nitty-gritty: *"In winter few places so bleak and damp and bare. In the centre, tucked away, lies Ruchard – a vast place…huts were few and tents were many, and mud was everywhere!"*

It was a depressing place. A huge encampment, where there was virtually nothing to do, nowhere to go. For the 4000 or so troops who were comparatively fit, it was bad enough, but for the hundreds of convalescents trying to recover from a variety of serious wounds and illnesses, it was hell. Grace was appalled. *"I paid my first visit to the Camp, and returned from it sad of heart for the want of comfort, and the monotony of life for these brave fellows."*

It was to be four months before she got back and set the whole project underway. While she was away, everything remained static, in spite of full support for Grace's report from General Clooten. It would no doubt have been a very different story had she been able to remain in France.

Returning to Calais from Ruchard in early May 1915, Grace headed straight to London where she felt there was a possible breakthrough in her constant quest to get the FANY officially working with the British Army. It turned out to be another wild goose chase, being informed yet again by Sir Alfred Keogh that the idea of 'women driving for the British Army was quite impractical'.

While relatively quiet in London, Grace typed up her report on Ruchard, and returned to Calais where she presented it to General Clooten. She started off in her slightly fractured, but fluent, French: *"En suite de mon voyage au Camp du Ruchard je viens vous demander le permission d'installer une 'messe' pour les sept cents convalescents typhiques la-bas."* The poor souls, she went on, were half-starved, and it was intended that the canteen would stock soup, tea, coffee, cakes, biscuits, and other things at reasonable prices, in pleasant surroundings, tables and chairs for them to relax in. The response was a long time coming, but accepted with much appreciation. In fact, it was *'sealed with a closely definite situation'* in the words of the General, proving that French was not the only language to suffer!

Well into May by this time, Grace busied herself, fund and profile raising for the Corps. On her recent flying visit to London she had made one or two valuable contacts, and returned to London to see what resources she could generate through them. There was no shortage of invitations, and when these temporarily dried up Grace was able to issue invitations herself, which many were delighted to accept. It was something of a hectic social round. The British newspapers and magazines were desperate to run stories of British women at war, however far-fetched, and they quickly realised that in Grace they had the genuine article, with real experiences behind her.

Furthermore, there were a great many socialites who liked to be seen aiding the war effort, having their photographs in the press. Grace was happy to exploit all of this for her FANY, and did so very successfully. Funds poured in, as well as gifts ranging from woollen clothing to complete ambulances and cars, beds and hospital equipment. This 'social round' might have seemed out of place for a member of a voluntary medical Corps, but the operative word was 'voluntary'. The FANY was entirely self-supporting and could not exist without external fund-raising.

It was not just the senior officers of the Corps who were expected to become involved – it was an unwritten axiom that every FANY who went home on leave was expected to give talks in her home town to raise what she could.

In this way a great many found themselves rubbing shoulders

with the aristocracy, stars of theatre and music hall, writers, operatic divas and the like. Many of the FANYs themselves were from the upper echelons of Society, and moved effortlessly through these occasions. Grace herself, though by no means among the aristocracy, had been described as a "mixer *par excellence*". And with her gentle Aberdeen accent was accepted everywhere.

With a considerable sum collected and in the FANY coffers, to the relief of the hard-pressed Treasurer and Secretary of the Corps, based in London, Grace returned to Calais. There the letter of acceptance about her Ruchard project was awaiting her, much to her delight.

A couple of days later, her great friend Molly Wilkinson had a surprise visit from her cousin, commanding an Admiralty yacht which had just arrived in Calais with some VIPs. Molly and Grace were invited to dinner aboard. It was beautifully fitted out: rosewood panelling, thick carpets, beds not bunks, the finest crockery and cutlery. The two girls were offered a trip to Dover, a chance too good to be missed amid all this luxury. They were kept out of sight until the official visit part was over.

Once across the Channel, Grace was hoping to catch up with her husband who had just recovered from a bout of pleurisy, but out of the blue came news that Charlie had been badly wounded, and had been in hospital in Boulogne for several days. She took the first available boat back across to Calais, commandeered her Unic ambulance and a driver, and drove to Boulogne.

A sergeant in the Army Service Corps was heard to say about FANY drivers: *"When the cars are full of wounded, no one could be more patient, considerate or gentle than the FANYs, but when the cars are empty, they drive like bats out of hell!"*

Grace lived up to that sergeant's expectations and drove like a bat out of hell. Arriving at the hospital, she handed over to the colleague who had accompanied her, and studied the building briefly. Like most hospitals of that time, it had a grim, almost Victorian appearance. Showing her pass to the sentry, she chafed at the delay as the Corporal in the Orderly Room searched through his file. Eventually he raised a finger. *"Got it,"* he said. *'Lieutenant Charles Smith, 3rd Dragoon Guards?"* Grace nodded. *"Yes, yes,"* she snapped, *"where can*

I find him?" The Corporal beckoned to a weary looking Orderly and told him to take the lady along as quick as possible.

Grace set the pace, the Orderly having to almost run to lead the way. The long stone corridor sent a shiver down Grace's spine. How often had she tramped down corridors such as this, a curious, heavy artificial silence everywhere; the overpowering smell of disinfectant trying to smother those other obnoxious odours of a wartime hospital.

Their boots rang out loudly on the stone floor, echoing down the passage. Doors spaced out on either side, most closed, occasionally one left open; glimpses within of rows of beds evenly spaced out; doctors in long white coats, nurses in VAD uniforms moving swiftly and quietly. In the beds patients, bodies, so familiar to Grace – lying supine, unmoving; men with arms or legs in traction; others with their lower halves hidden under tunnels of raised-up bedclothes. Doors slammed shut with sudden, earsplitting menace, echoes reverberating from wall to wall.

For all her familiarity with scenes like this, for Grace this was a new and terrifying experience. Of all the hundreds of young men, many just boys barely out of school, whom Grace had nursed, so many in their last hours, they had one thing in common: they were all strangers. Now it was her adored brother Charles lying wounded. How badly? She desperately wanted to know, to be with him again. Hurrying along behind the Orderly, her mind couldn't help dwelling on those shattered bodies, severed limbs, blinded eyes, she had met with so often, too often, since this foul war began.

The Orderly's voice broke into her thoughts. *"'Ere we are, Ma'am."*

Grace stopped, closing her eyes for a moment. Then, straightening her shoulders, she marched into the ward. This was an officers' ward, smaller and less crowded than some she had seen on the way through the building.

A nurse approached her. The ward was deeply quiet, just occasional groans, a tired cough. Grace instinctively lowered her voice. *"I'm here to see my brother. Lieutenant Smith, Dragoon Guards?"* She raised her chin fractionally, partly in pride, mostly to give herself courage to face what lay ahead of her. A moment's hesitation, and the nurse nodded. *"Over here,"* she said, and led Grace to a heavily bandaged figure lying in a bed further along. Charlie lay quite still, unmoving, the bandage round his head lightly stained with blood. The rest of him was hidden under the bedclothes. Slow, guttural breathing was the only sign of life.

She bent swiftly and kissed his cheek. Tears came to her eyes. The young nurse reached out and squeezed Grace's arm gently. *"I'm sorry,"* she said. *"You had better speak to the Sister."* The more she learnt from the Ward Sister, and later a doctor on his rounds, the further her heart sank. She had seen the signs, heard the words too often.

The 2nd battle of Ypres was in full swing, casualties pouring in. Charlie had been shot as he 'went over the top' in yet another senseless attack. Falling back into the trench, she was told, he had lain there all day, until night came and it was safe to evacuate the wounded. He had arrived a 'few days ago', unconscious, and been in a coma ever since. He was 'not responding', another dreaded phrase Grace was familiar with. There were so many others in whom the spark of life was stronger, and they got priority. She understood, but it made it no easier for her to bear.

Tears streaming down her face, she knelt by his bedside, and prayed as she had never prayed before. A firm believer in life after death, she prayed not only to God, but to her loved and long-dead father; wildly, grasping at any straw, begging him to step in and help. She knew it was a forlorn hope, but kept on. This was her brother Charlie, and reason played no part in her grief.

All that afternoon and evening she knelt or sat beside him. At last the Ward Sister managed to persuade her that she must eat to keep her strength up. She had had nothing since morning. She returned from the nurses' Mess as the shadows lengthened, and within the hospital, curtains were being pulled across the windows.

As she entered the ward, it seemed to her there was subtle change in atmosphere; the silence of the room was heavy with a sense of foreboding; dark shadows shifted in the dimness of the dusk. A spectral figure stood at the foot of Charlie's bed, silhouetted against the faint light seeping through the curtained window behind. It stopped her in her tracks. She took a quick glance around the ward. Nothing. Nobody. Just a strange quiet stillness.

She moved nearer, and the figure slowly raised a hand. *Don't come any closer.* Grace instinctively stood still. With a gasp of amazement, and a surge of hope, she recognized the figure as her father, standing there before her, just as she remembered him from all those years ago, when she was a little girl. She tried to speak, but no words came.

Then she heard his voice, gentle and kind as ever, tinged with sympathy and sadness. His words were there somehow, all around her, in her head. She was not to grieve, Charlie was going to a better place, the two of them would be together. And later, young Billy, too, would be joining them. But her husband Rannie would survive the war unwounded. She was not to worry about him. All would be well, try not to grieve. Then the apparition smiled, and slowly dissolved in the gloom of the unlit ward.

The silence around was heavy and deep, broken only by Charlie's regular, hoarse breathing. Gradually the unnatural, heavy stillness faded, and the normal sounds of the ward returned. The spell broke. Grace ran forward. There was nothing, nobody. But throughout her life she swore she had truly experienced those few moments. She never doubted the truth of what she had heard, never spoke to Billy of it, only to her husband, but much later when he was able to get some leave.

Now it was a question of 'when' not 'if'. Grace never left Charlie's side. She had not long to wait. Less than 24 hours later, at 2 o'clock the following afternoon, with Grace holding his hand tightly, tears streaming down her cheeks, Charlie, still unconscious, passed on to that 'Great Beyond' as Grace put it.

And only half an hour later, young Billy arrived, having just managed to get leave, racing to Dover, catching a boat across the Channel to Boulogne, rushing to the hospital, only to find he was too late.

They were at least able to share the grief, console each other, be there at Charlie's brief, bare funeral. But now, whenever Grace looked at, or thought of Billy, one word leapt out at her with awful clarity.

WHEN?

CHAPTER 27

Getting There

Charlie's death was a terrible blow to the whole family, but was especially traumatic for Grace and Billy. So they were grateful for the time, brief as it was, that they were able to spend together immediately after his passing: a time in which they were able to console one another..

Billy had to rejoin his unit almost at once, and Grace was left on her own. She was faced for the first time in her life with the dreadfully difficult choice between duty and family. It was a choice that so often faced women, particularly in time of war. It was hard. Grace loved her Corps, her job and believed deeply and sincerely in what she was doing. On the other hand, her family was constantly in her thoughts. Even when torn by this choice, Grace made up her mind quickly and firmly, accepting without any doubts that her strongest bond was to her family.

Back in Calais she handed over everything into the capable hands of Franklin, and went home to comfort her mother and Charlie's young son. It was a difficult time. Her eldest sister, Agnes, always a homebody who remained with her mother, had not been at all well, and was overjoyed when Grace returned home. One of her other sisters was in South Africa, the other in a very busy job as a doctor in London.

Grace spent far longer back in England than she either intended or envisaged, much to her annoyance. When the first distress of Charlie's death had passed, and her mother was back to her old strength, Grace headed for London, to tackle the War Office yet again, and hopefully win them over to her viewpoint, allowing FANYs to drive for the British Army.

On this occasion, however, while still ignoring the offer to provide drivers, the War Office came up with a new scheme to utilize the services of the FANY – and perhaps to keep them quiet? It was not at all what Grace had envisaged, nor was she too happy about it, but she was directed by Corps HQ to work with the Authorities.

The idea was for the FANY to take over the staffing and running of a large military hospital, specifically for British wounded, at Bramshott, in Surrey. The request for this facility had been put forward by the Head of the Anglo-French Red Cross Society.

Asked to draw up a plan, Grace spent almost three months on the project. The scheme itself only partially met the FANY's *modus operandi*, omitting the most important aspect: providing and driving ambulances to transport wounded in war zones. This arduous and sometimes dangerous task was, perhaps, the main attraction of the job for these 'intrepid, well-bred young ladies'!

However, it was a foot in the door, thought Grace, and she persevered, putting all her energy into drawing up a workable plan, and passed it on to the Red Cross Society HQ. By now, it was into August, and she was heartily tired of the inaction of the past few weeks, and insisted on returning to France while her plans were considered.

Once across the Channel, she spent a few days in Calais being brought up to date by Franklin, then headed for Camp du Ruchard to see how it was progressing. She was dismayed to see how little had been done in her absence, but this was the sort of situation she understood, knew how to deal with. She was back in the saddle again. Metaphorically girding up her loins, she went back to Calais and selected a team to run the place as she wanted it. First of all, she called upon her old friend Cole-Hamilton, the staunch and dependable Coley, to be Director of Ruchard. Her close friend Chris Nicholson was next, and a trained nurse, Nurse Lovell, was hired by the Corps specifically to look after the large number of tubercular patients. Initially two other FANYs were included, to complete the team.

Grace, Coley and Chris set off first, to get things organised. It did not start well! 'The best laid plans' certainly went agley to begin with. A boiling hot day, bright sun and blue skies might be thought encouraging, but motor tyres in those days were not as they are today. Grace described the trip with classic understatement: *"The journey was not without its amusements – and its trials!"* In fact it must have been hell, and a lot of people would have given up. They were travelling in a small Ford, named 'Le Petit Camerade', up to now renowned for its reliability. A tyre burst before reaching Boulogne. Soon remedied, another went; then another; and before long both spares had gone, on that long, hot gritty road.

Grace admitted: *"I chafed and fumed and was thoroughly disagreeable."* In her usual way, Chris sailed through it all without turning a hair. Coley's reactions are not recorded, but she was known to have a short fuse on occasions.

Grace goes on: *"Instead of having tea at Rouen, we were yet 12 kilometres from that stately town at 11 o'clock at night."* They dined on coffee and eggs at a wayside café, and did their best to get the car back on the road – this, by means of removing the sacking wrapped round a brand new tent they had bought for use at Rouchard, tying it round the relevant wheels, using rope cut from that selfsame tent. Necessity is the mother of invention!

"We rumbled and bumped into Rouen towards midnight," writes Grace. There was only one garage open, and a drunk driver was arguing with the garage hand, demanding paraffin for his headlamps. The garage hand eventually gave him petrol instead, deliberately or by accident, and moments later the lamps had gone up in flames.

Fortunately, a passing car with three Red Cross men in it, had pulled up to see what was happening. Grace spoke to them, explained her problems, and they offered to give her a lift to the Supply Depot. From then on the whole adventure got more and more bizarre.

On the way, they spotted a small, open Peugeot going in the opposite direction. *"That's the man you want,"* shouted the Red Cross driver, swung around in a swift U-turn, and set off in pursuit. The Peugeot had to stop a bit further on, and the Red Cross car drew up alongside. Grace says: *"I was hoisted unceremoniously beside the pilot [driver] of the Peugeot, and the Red Cross car sped into the darkness and vanished."*

When Grace recovered her breath she glanced at her companion. He was an officer, immaculate in khaki, Sam Browne belt, face totally without expression. He looked as though he was used to this kind of thing happening all the time. Grace remembered:

"Can I do anything for you?" he asked.

"Yes," I answered frankly. *"I want at least two Ford tyres and two*

inner tubes, and I want them tonight."

At that he swung the car around, and drove off in a new direction, chatting amiably as he went. And, quite incredibly, Grace recalls that in the course of that conversation: *"so small is the world that he knew well friends I had visited in New Zealand!".*

"Here's the place," he called, and blew the horn at the great gates looming in front of them. When there was no reply, the young officer got out and scrambled over the top of the gate. Grace says: *"I sat in the car and waited for a shot to break the stillness, and for myself to be arrested as a spy!"*

But apparently all was well, the gate swung open, and they drove up to a long, covered building. A sleepy Corporal appeared, and urged on by the officer, sorted through the piles of tyres and tubes, eventually producing all that Grace wanted. Within half an hour they were back at the garage. Chris and the subaltern began to replace the tyres and tubes, while Coley slumbered in the back of the car, until waking, and practical as ever, brewed Bovril on a small 'Tommy cooker', and "saved our lives" according to Grace.

At last their troubles seemed to be over, and at about 4 o'clock in the morning they headed, once more, for Ruchard. Stopping on the way for breakfast and an hour's sleep, they finally arrived at around midday. It had been a traumatic journey, leaving them all weary, wilting, and pondering over the astonishingly improbable events of the night before.

But not for long.

CHAPTER 28
Setting Up Ruchard

Grace was never one to let the grass grow under feet. Off she went to the Office to report in, and fix an appointment with the Officer commanding the Ruchard area, a General Paulhan. Based not far away in Tours, he was anxious to meet them, and Grace and Coley were driven there immediately. She was much taken with him, describing him as: *"courtly and kindly to a degree; his words of gratitude were eloquent, and he did not stop at words"*.

The expense of building a hut large enough to meet demand was weighing heavily on Grace's mind. In her usual cavalier manner she had accepted the challenge of running a canteen in Ruchard, without consulting anyone. There had already been grumbles of discontent and irritation from the Treasurer, The Rev Cluff at HQ, as well as Janette Lean, the Secretary. However, Grace's fundraising tour earlier in the year had yielded much of the requirements, but there was still the problem of the building itself.

She need not have worried. The General was magnificent, needing no urging. He gave them two large semi-detached, stone-built 'huts', and directed that the dividing wall be knocked down, creating one very large space, ideal for what they planned. *"We had our Barrack,"* said Grace.

In the following weeks an amazing transformation took place. The Belgians supplied soldiers as labour, and all the basic materials. A small separate dining and rest room for the staff was constructed inside, followed by a large service counter in the main hall. The walls were whitewashed and painted with the Colours and Arms of Belgium and her Allies. The *piece de resistance* was a large painting of the FANY badge above the door.

For decoration and pictures round the wall, shipping company posters were framed and hung, along with some of the more artistic advertising illustrations. Next came curtains at every window; and finally, decided by the men themselves, a large stage erected at one end, ideal for concert performances of every kind, most of which were put on by the troops and patients.

Grace was delighted, as were Coley, Chris, the General himself and all who saw it.

The next step was to make it habitable, and chairs and tables were provided to meet the demand. On sale, at very low prices, were coffee, tea, hot chocolate, soft drinks, cakes, pastries, a large variety of chocolate, and, of course, cigarettes.

Cakes were especially popular, and it was always an uphill struggle for the FANY to provide enough. Janette Lean, back at HQ, had an astonishing ability for sweet-talking often reluctant cake manufacturers into parting with large quantities of their product for free. She also organised a hugely successful 'Ruchard Cake League' at HQ, which kept the customers in France well supplied with every sort of *gateaux* or *bon morceau*.

Newspapers and magazines were also available, to buy, or to be picked up and read over a drink. As time went on, packs of cards were provided, along with various boardgames.

Once the stage was finally in place, and equipped, the FANY hired a piano for 12Frs a month, perhaps the best 12Frs worth ever. The men loved it. Even with an ever-changing community there were always piano players available. Concerts, as well as impromptu sing-songs, were hugely popular.

The Canteen was opened with an inaugural concert playing to a full house, and attended by some top brass, as well as hundreds of happy convalescents. It became an unqualified success, and no more was heard from HQ about Grace's failure to consult anyone before getting involved. Had she done so, the scheme would almost certainly have not gone ahead. Others were equally pleased with the project.

The Military Police were delighted, too. In this God-forsaken place, miles from anywhere, no transport, and nothing to do, arrests for various misdemeanours and crimes had been running at 20 a day, or more. Within a very short space of time this dropped to fewer than three.

If the men were over the moon about the place, alas it wasn't the case for the FANYs staffing it. Their living conditions were hard and uncomfortable. Often rushed off their feet while on shift, any time they had to themselves was boring. They were in the same position as the men they were looking after so well had been: nowhere to go and nothing to do.

Janette Lean visited the Camp on one occasion and was horrified at the living conditions. More so, as she felt that with the girls putting up with it so stoically, the Belgians would think that was how they lived at home! It was often difficult to get staff for the Camp for those very reasons: harsh living conditions, and being cut off from the sort of life they were used to. But while there they did a magnificent job.

One who did stay was the indomitable Lady Baird who arrived at Ruchard and became something of a legend throughout the Corps, for the hip flask which she always carried, and which, in some miraculous way, was always well-filled with brandy. Lifting spirits was her speciality, which she did on innumerable occasions with sick and wounded soldiers. Mainly she concentrated on helping out Nurse Lovell with the tubercular patients.

Under Coley's inspired leadership as Director, the enterprise thrived, but the time came for her to move on. Her place was taken by an Australian girl, who turned out to be equally memorable, Adele Crockett. Shortly after her arrival, Grace managed to obtain a cinematograph projector; yet another gift from the ever-generous citizens of Aberdeen, after one of her regular fund-raising expeditions.

This lifted the interest in the Canteen to a whole new level. It did the same, also, for the administrative load upon Adele's shoulders. Costing 145 Frs a week to run, its own generator was heavy on petrol, noisy, and a fire risk! However, the upside was that it also supplied the Canteen with electric light.

Various other helpers were required whose services were usually obtained free from professionals among the 'congregation'; a mechanic to work the generator; a cinema operator plus an assistant in case the film caught fire. But it worked – most of the time. Hundreds of desperate convalescents poured in night after night, paid their 5 centimes entry fee, and for a while were able to drift away from the reality of war and disease into the make-believe world of cinema.

Already a great success, this latest innovation, the

Cinematograph, was the final seal of acclaim, in the bleak and barren camp-scape that was Ruchard.

It was indeed Shangri-La!

CHAPTER 29

From The Heights To The Depths

With Camp du Ruchard up and running under Cole-Hamilton, Grace was free to concentrate on her main themes – expansion of the FANY operations, and, most importantly, working for the British Army. In the former she had some successes, but with the latter the Establishment stone-walling was as solid as ever.

She tried once again, putting forward a new plan to the War Office. Once again the monotonous rejection: 'women will never be drivers in the British Army'. However, there was a ray of light – an episode in Calais back in June, when Grace was in England. The battles at Ypres were still going on, when the British launched two disastrous offensives at Festubert and Aubers Ridge.

These generated thousands of unexpected casualties, and the BRCS was unable to cope. The Assistant Director of British Medical Services approached Franklin and asked if the FANY could help. They jumped at the offer. The drivers were specially selected, mostly old hands, and instructed to give even better than their best. These were British wounded they would be dealing with, and they needed no urging. The service had to be second to none. It was.

They received lavish praise for their work from all sides, including the British Administration in Calais. Though Grace was absent, she heard all about it, and tucked it away in her memory for future use. She got together with Franklin and they decided to wait for a time before making yet another concerted effort on the BRCS and War Office.

Grace worked hard on this, using her various contacts shrewdly, and over time arranged a series of meetings at HQs in Boulogne, Abbeville, and finally GHQ at St. Omer. It was a tactic of slow infiltration. She first approached Major Smallman, a long-time friend and ally of the FANY; Surgeon General Woodhouse, he who had been so impressed by the Corps at their last pre-war camp; Colonels Dadson and Barford; and her old fencing master Felix Bertrand, all of whom she had won over previously.

This all took time, and the end of 1915 was not far off. Grace and Franklin were putting the finishing touches to the new plans for the employment of the FANY – even though indirectly – as drivers for the British Army.

The biggest hurdle was still the insistence by the FANY on retaining their independence. This was something the British could not – would not -agree to, even though some of the Top Brass concerned were sympathetic to the Corps.

After Grace's attempt in August to win over the Army, Sir Arthur Keogh, Director General of the Army Medical Service, wrote to Sir Arthur Sloggett Head of the British Red Cross [BRC], saying in effect, how much simpler things would be if only the FANY would affiliate with the Red Cross.

This, of course, was anathema to the FANY. Sloggett sent a copy of the letter to Grace, writing on the back of it: *"Dear Mrs MacDougall [sic], you see what the IGC [Imperial General Council] think – wouldn't you like to join the Red Cross?"*

Grace realised it was going to be a time of difficult decisions, and compromises would have to be reached. The plan she was now about to bounce off the Authorities needed very careful thought and absolute clarity in her own mind just where the lines were to be drawn: Independence of Command Structure; Title; Uniforms. She would have a fight on her hands.

She and Franklin went into action. They had the advantage of sympathetic contacts in high places, and proof of the outstanding ability, discipline and dedication of the FANYs, sometimes under extreme conditions, from the desperate weeks in the middle of the year working for the British Army in Calais.

Over the following weeks – months – an agreement was thrashed out. Towards the end of the long drawn out negotiations, which themselves put Grace under great stress, disturbing news arrived from her mother in Scotland. Her sister Agnes had gone down with a virulent form of flu which looked like becoming an epidemic. Grace was in a dilemma. Should she abandon the negotiations, hand over to Franklin, risk losing that prize for which she had been striving for so long? It was something very dear to her heart, the thought of the Corps working for the British Army.

After the exchange of more wires with her mother, she decided that she should stay. Agnes was in good hands, getting the best medical attention money could buy. If she went, there was little she could do. Earlier in the year when Agnes had been unwell, she had recovered completely, seemed fit and strong.

Grace stayed at the helm. Rightly or wrongly she believed she needed to be there; only she could break down the opposition and win the right terms.

The compromises were worked out over countless meetings. There were three parties involved – four if you counted the British Army in the background. There were the FANY, of course. At the other side of the table were the BRC Joint War Committee, along with the Order of Jerusalem, who had aligned themselves with the Red Cross for the war.

It was a pretty complicated scheme. The FANY would be 'commissioned' by the BRCS to provide drivers to transport British wounded wherever and whenever required, in Calais. The BRCS would supply the ambulances, stores, tools and other logistical requirements.

The FANY would retain their *own* title, and wear their *own* uniforms – a concession Grace had to fight very hard for – and would be treated as all other BRCS employees in terms of employment.

Eventually, at the end of November, Grace received a letter from Sir Arthur Lawley, heading the BRCS in Calais, asking her to go and see him. The conditions had at last been accepted. He had signed and forwarded the Agreement to London. This was the news she had worked for, striven towards, for so long. Now at last her efforts were coming to fruition.

After that meeting, Grace and Franklin lost no time in crossing to London to contact Sir Arthur Sloggett, the Head of the BRC, who showed them the draft Agreement, which they read and agreed with, after making quite certain about the FANY title and uniform. It was a time of great excitement for them both.

While over there Grace took the opportunity to visit her mother and Agnes in Edinburgh. Her sister appeared to be holding her own well, and Grace returned to London greatly reassured.

There, on December 6th, Sir Arthur Sloggett and Grace signed the historic agreement. For her it was one of the greater moments in her life. Her FANY Corps was to be in the service of the British Army at last, now transporting, nursing and succouring not only Belgian and French, but British wounded as well.

A day or two later reality intervened, highlighting the degree of ill-feeling which could develop between similar organizations, purportedly on the same side. A group of FANYs were assembled ready to travel to Calais, under the auspices of the VAD, who themselves were under BRCS jurisdiction, but whose hierarchy was perhaps jealous of FANY independence. The VAD official in charge of the group refused the FANYs permission to proceed, unless they wore VAD uniform! The FANYs were decidedly unhappy with this, and phoned Janette Lean at FANY HQ. She was furious, but could get nowhere on the phone to VAD or Red Cross HQ.

Grace, who had not yet left for France, was just as angry, but much more able to deal with that sort of confrontation. She stormed over to Devonshire House, VAD HQ, and demanded to see the VAD Commandant. This was smugly refused by the rather supercilious second in command on the grounds that the Commandant was out, and it wasn't known when she would return. The second in command then added rather maliciously that 'no FANY would be allowed across the Channel, unless in VAD uniform'.

Grace relates the incident in detail: *"I looked at the lady. 'Please ask one of your staff to look up the next boat to Boulogne.' I began to buckle my coat. She looked startled.*

"Why? Are you crossing?"

"I'm going over to tell Sir Arthur Lawley that his signature has no value in England!"

"What do you mean?"

"What I say. I have a copy of the Contract here – see for yourself – there's Sir Arthur's signature, and THERE is the clause. 'Drivers will wear FANY uniform and be styled First Aid Nursing Yeomanry'!"

"May I have the Contract to show the Commandant?"

"No! I don't have time to wait. You've already told me she is out and you don't know when she will be back. Good afternoon."

She continues: *"I went straight to Sir Arthur Lawley at BRCS HQ.*

He was extremely angry, phoned through to VAD HQ immediately. After some very plain speaking, he turned to me and said, 'Mrs McDougall, your people will have their passes this afternoon!'."

They had!

Grace thoroughly enjoyed that kind of encounter, and was well practised.

Setting off for Calais once again she was cheerful, but feeling very worn out after the stress of the past few weeks. Travelling back and forth across the Channel added to the pressures; while at home, Agnes being ill and her mother worrying over both of them made things worse. It was all beginning to affect her general health. It dawned on her with some surprise, that Christmas was fast approaching, their second of the war in France, and she wondered just how many more lay ahead. Would it be as enjoyable as the last?

The shocking answer to that came very shortly after her return to France. A frantic wire from her mother reached her. Agnes, her sister, was dying, please, please come home.

That plea pulled at her heart and conscience. She packed once again, headed back across the Channel, and took the train straight up to Edinburgh, a long, wearisome journey at the best of times. The next few days passed almost in a haze of disbelief. Sitting by Agnes's bedside, with her mother and Isabel, she agonized at her helplessness. In mid-December Agnes passed away, as she had lived, quietly and gently.

It was a sad, difficult time, with her mother particularly hard hit. This strong, proud woman was struggling to keep her composure, grieving for the loss of her eldest son, and now her eldest daughter.

To say that Grace was devastated, as when Charlie died, would be wrong. She loved Agnes as a sister, but they had never been close. Ten years separated them. Grace was a restless, adventurous tomboy, while Agnes was a quiet, stay-at-home person, happy to be with her mother and live quietly at home.

Nevertheless she was deeply saddened by her death. Her mother was affected a great deal more, as would any mother losing a child. This was the second child whose death she had had to bear, within a year. In Agnes, she had not only lost her firstborn, but someone who had become a friend, confidante, and companion. She needed help, and Grace stayed on to give it as best she could.

She could not stay indefinitely. Grace knew that, and her mother realised and accepted that Grace would have to go back to her FANYs in France. She was a strong woman, could stand on her own feet, and urged Grace to return. She could manage.

Another sister, Carolyn, who had just lost her husband from illness in South Africa, had decided to come home and look after her mother. In the interim, Grace and Isabel would do their best to visit regularly and keep an eye on her. It added yet another dimension of strain to Grace's already rather frenetic lifestyle.

During this difficult time, they heard from Billy that he had transferred from the KOYLI to the Cyclist Corps. The job of this Corps was particularly dangerous. They were faced with carrying out reconnaissance of enemy territory and No-man's-land. They had to provide useful information about trenches, layout, defensive screens, anything that might help Higher Command, when planning localised attacks or major offensives. Mounted on bicycles they could move quickly and quietly, to an area, but once near their objective they proceeded on foot, under the nose of the enemy, and casualties were heavy. It was an essential job, and typical of Billy to volunteer for it.

It did nothing, however to allay his mother's fears for his safety. He was in his element, so much so that he gave up leave that was due to him in January of 1916. He wrote home to his wife,

"I have postponed my leave to carry through a scheme. Everyone says I'm a fool. But what's the good of leave if you haven't done something worthwhile? If I come through this, it may mean a Military Cross."

This, too, was typical of Billy. Always chasing new thrills and adventures. The family were proud of him for that, but it added to their ever present worry.

Grace returned to France early in January 1916, and in spite of the grief of losing her sister, and the general feeling of stress she was undergoing, she was also filled with a great sense of triumph, especially when she saw the FANY transporting British soldiers to British hospitals. At last, the Corps were working for the British Army officially – a dream fulfilled.

The Convoy began its new task on January 1st, with 18 members specially selected, mostly old hands. The Corps were not taking any chances. Lillian Franklin was in Command, a choice nobody ever regretted. She was always strong, fair, approachable, unflappable and above all, competent.

Add to those traits – courage. When an ammunition dump just outside Calais blew up in the middle of the night, the FANY were immediately called upon. As usual they responded magnificently, dealing with casualties on the spot, among exploding shells and bullets. One British officer there described Franklin as *'the bravest woman he had ever seen'* calmly standing for hours amid the carnage directing drivers and ambulances!

Grace was a major contender for the chance to run that convoy, given her admiration and respect for Britain's army, and the very large part she had played in finally winning an agreement. But she loved the Belgians too, and knew that without their unstinting support in the early days of the war, the FANY would have got nowhere. She was away a lot, using Lamarck and Calais mainly as a base, visiting FANY units scattered around; and fighting for a place in the British military both in France and back home.

Franklin, however, had remained static, battling away against all the problems surrounding the hospital, making it a huge success, with thousands and thousands of sick and wounded Belgian troops passing through their hands. She knew all the FANYs there; they knew her. Not only that, but she had a good working relationship with the British authorities in the town.

Grace decided that she would stay with her Belgians, a decision neither she nor the Belgians ever regretted; Franklin took over the English convoy, and went from strength to strength, eventually becoming Commandant of the Corps in 1920 and being awarded the MBE.

Her decision made, all doubts that Grace had had cleared, and she was once more back in the saddle. She swept around inspecting FANY units and reassuring herself that all was well. As one of the FANYs in charge of a unit near the Front Line put it: *"Whenever Mac* [Grace] *pays a visit, things always get more lively!"* There's little doubt about that.

It was all going too well.

On a trip to Boulogne on the 27th January, the bubble burst. Grace's world came to an end. A telegram caught up with her. It read: *'Billy has been killed in action. Please come home.'*

CHAPTER 30
Pulling Together

The words leaped out at her, struck her an almost physical blow. She had loved Charlie, but Billy had been her favourite. She adored him. Ever since the vision of her father, and his prediction, at Charlie's bedside, the memory was there, hidden at the back of her mind. She almost convinced herself it would not happen; how wrong she was.

The reality hit her. She couldn't believe it. First Charlie, then, so recently, Agnes; and now, her beloved Billy. In less than a year three of her family had gone. Through her tears, fingers twisting, she read the fateful words again. Billy, killed in action. They would be imprinted on her mind forever. Some indication of how deeply she felt about her younger brother, can be gleaned from an entry in her diary, more than a year later. Visiting Billy's wife and children she wrote: *"Billy's children are beautiful; fat, sturdy. Sonny with Billy's chubby cheeks and laughing eyes; Bea with her dainty, coaxing ways."* Then she bursts out into unrestrained grief, overwhelmed by memories: *"Oh my God, Billy is gone…Billy, my Billy."*

Torn apart once more – family or duty. She remembered later, writing: *"Again duty had torn me in two directions. It was the old struggle women have – families versus work."*

Numb with grief, she made the only decision possible, and rushed home as quickly as she could to help her mother, as well as Billy's wife and two young children.

Her mother, a proud, feisty woman, had nevertheless suffered three hammer blows in less than a year with the deaths of her two sons and a daughter. Unbroken, yet getting on for 70 years of age, and suffering, she desperately needed the support of her remaining children. Isabel and Grace gave her all the support they could manage, as did Carrie when she arrived back from South Africa in February, though she herself was the victim of a recent bereavement.

Both Isabel and Carrie were in good health, which is more than could be said for Grace. Her frenetic lifestyle, the constant, arduous travelling, often in great physical danger while visiting her frontline units, living under very basic or dreadful conditions, were all taking their toll.

Being the sort of woman she was, Grace refused to acknowledge the approaching disaster. Once her sister Carrie had settled in, Grace decided she must return to France. Things were happening there, new FANYs arriving every week, and she needed to be there. Duty was pushing at her conscience. She felt she had to be back at the helm.

It wasn't to be.

Saying her goodbyes once again, she set off south on the first leg of her journey. By the time she had reached London, she had collapsed several times, and developed acute abdominal pains. In London she was diagnosed with appendicitis, and a nervous breakdown. Absolute rest for at least three months was ordered. After what she had been through in the past eight months it was not surprising.

Franklin was consulted, and sympathetic, in her clinically frank way. She agreed that Grace needed a long break. In a letter to Cole-Hamilton, she wrote: *"Naturally all this trouble has completely unhinged her, and she cannot see things as clearly as she would under different circumstances."*

Grace finally accepted that a thorough rest was inevitable, and that she had pushed herself beyond her limits. Her cousin Elizabeth invited her to stay with her in the peaceful old rural Kentish village where her husband was the local vicar. It was ideal, but first she had to have a burst eardrum seen to, the legacy of a shell exploding near her in Antwerp, in those early days of the war.

After that she was able to relax utterly. But it wasn't long before she was chafing at the bit once more. It wasn't in her character to sit and do nothing. She delved into her precious diaries, filling them out a bit, where she had not had the time to do so previously. Always fond of writing, she decided to develop them into a full-blown book, and, once decided, gave it her full attention.

The weeks flew by, and she finalised her manuscript, calling it 'Nursing Adventures'. Writing it proved to be the best therapy ever. From the physical point of view it put little strain on her body; more importantly, writing it became a great release for all her pent up feelings and fears and grief. She got enormous personal satisfaction from finishing it, and more so when one of the top publishers, William Heinemann, accepted it for publication without demur. Although, as she has scribbled inside the cover of one of her own copies, it wasn't printed until 1917 due to 'shortage of paper'!

Although it was almost entirely about her own adventures, it was not for her personal aggrandisement. She wanted to highlight and publicize her FANY Corps, the work they were doing and the conditions they had to endure. Written anonymously in a bid to reflect on the FANY as a whole, rather than herself, few names are mentioned, and at times it appears slightly disjointed. What comes across strongly though, is the dedication and cheerfulness of these 'high spirited young ladies' in difficult, dangerous, and life-threatening situations.

She felt strongly that if she could succeed in doing that for her girls, it would all have been worthwhile.

And, in fact, she had.

It was time to move on.

CHAPTER 31

Back In The Saddle

She said a fond and grateful farewell to Elizabeth – who was years later to become Godmother to her younger son – and returned to Edinburgh to see her mother, who, largely due to the care of Carrie, was now much recovered. It was then that the three girls decided it would be best if their mother moved south, to be more accessible to all of them. Their mother agreed, albeit reluctant to leave her beloved Scotland.

Grace and Isabel travelled back to London to begin the arrangements. By now Grace was desperate to get back to France and find out what was going on. Rannie's regiment was back across the Channel again, something else for her to worry about, for she had heard little from him since then. Millions of wives were in the same position. There was nothing she could do but accept it, and get on with her own life as best she could.

France beckoned, but first she spent time at FANY HQ writing up where they had been operating and what they had achieved since the war began for The Gazette. Then, satisfied, refreshed and eager, she once again set off across the Channel.

There she lost no time in catching up with what had been going on. Lamarck, their 'flagship' if you will, was still going strong, but with the shadow of possible closure hanging over it.

The first British Convoy, also based in Calais, was highly regarded now, after being inaugurated in January with so much trouble and Establishment opposition.

Camp du Ruchard was still meeting the needs of the hundreds of Belgian convalescents based there. The Belgian Military were finding it difficult to believe just how well the patients responded to the care and dedication of the five FANY staff who ran the canteen. It was a huge success.

Glad as she was that all these established units were doing well, Grace was slightly disappointed to find that in her absence no new initiatives had been implemented. However, now she was back she decided that would have to change.

She wasted no time. In view of the success of the new British Convoy, she determined she would have the same sort of set-up for the Belgians. Her energy and tactical approaches to Authority were in no way diminished by her recent indisposition, and it wasn't long before she got the green light from the Belgians to go ahead and form a new unit.

Apart from Lamarck, the Belgians had another hospital in Calais at the Gare Centrale, known as L'Hôpital de Passage. This was a sort of clearing station for wounded arriving by train, canal barge or ambulance from other hospitals.

It was October before all the details had been worked out, and the new FANY Unit 5 was set up, and was the best equipped FANY unit of the war. The housing for the drivers was the most comfortable and well furnished of any; the vehicles were all brand new, supplied by the Belgians; there were well equipped workshops, and a washing bay. It became Grace's pride and joy, and she regarded it as 'hers' for the rest of the war.

It was this Unit that was involved in a face-to-face standoff with the British Army backed Red Cross the following year, in an attempt to stamp out the FANY for good. But it hadn't come to that yet.

During the negotiations for her Belgian Convoy, she became involved in a request by the Belgians for girls to help out in a Field Hospital at Hoogstadt. As this was only four miles from the Front Line, special permission was required for women to work in such a dangerous environment. Hoogstadt was unsafe at the best of times, but there was a good deal of extra military pushing and shoving along the Front, and in theory women were no longer allowed to work so close to the firing line.

Being the sort of woman she was, Grace looked on this as just part of the job. She checked it out personally, as was her way, and chose Doris Russell-Allen as one of the staff, 'Bobs' Baillie, and Nora Cluff, who was to become her life-long best friend.

The posting was to last six months – six months of "cold, wet and rats" according to the girls. The work was pretty hard too, and dangerous. They drove camouflaged Army vehicles to places like Dunkirk and La Panne to collect food and supplies for the hospital.

There were air raids almost every night, and the 'coffin cart' was a frequent visitor.

Unfortunately things did not run smoothly. The Commandant of the hospital was apparently thoroughly obnoxious and rude. The girls thought they weren't appreciated. Two of them applied for transfer. This upset Grace slightly. Getting permits to work in that area had been difficult, and required special sanctions. The Authorities were not happy, now, at having to replace them. As a result of delays involved there was apparently some ill-feeling. Grace wrote later: *"[the girls] felt they were not wanted and thought I was riding roughshod over them in expecting them to stay"*.

Eventually, it all blew over. The girls were withdrawn in December, when the hospital was closed. Grace was upset over the whole episode. She was angry that 'her' girls had been treated badly by the Commandant of the hospital. She was disappointed – in fact she herself described it as *"a bitter blow"* – when as a result, barriers were put up against Convoys being allowed to operate so close to the Line. In spite of the problems, however, the girls had been a tremendous help, and carried out a huge number of trips to and from the supply depots, in dreadful weather and over appalling roads.

It also highlighted the versatility and adaptability of the FANY to undertake any sort of duties at short notice, a flexibility completely lacking in any of the Services attached to the British or French military.

Another instance of this capacity for swift reaction arose when the YMCA suddenly found itself unable to staff a major canteen serving over 4000 British troops. It was known as the 'Dundee Hut'. Staffing arrangements had fallen apart, and the FANY were asked if they could help out. The 4000 customers were living under canvas surrounded by 'a sea of mud', and were desperate for any sort of haven.

Grace agreed immediately; where their own British soldiers were concerned they would seize any opportunity. With her record of competence, ability and experience there was only one candidate to take over and run something of this size – Cole-Hamilton, or 'Coley', currently running Ruchard with such success.

Handing over to Australian FANY Adele Crockett, she and FANY

Ida Lewis took on the daunting task of catering for 4000 unhappy Tommies, and became known to all and sundry as 'The Sergeant' and 'The Fair Corporal' respectively. Between them they soon had the place under control, largely through cheerfully dispensing vast quantities of tea!

The duties at Ruchard and the Dundee Hut may not have been quite the kind of service that the FANY had been trained for, and expected to be doing, but they were not only being of great help to Allied troops – more importantly, they were making a name for the Corps for their flexibility of decision making, and expertise and competence in anything they took on. Not to mention unfailing cheerfulness.

But in a way, these projects, however effective and useful, were in effect only sidelines. The large British and Belgian ambulance convoys, and hospital running, was the way ahead. Unfortunately, it was now definite that Lamarck was to close, and Grace was determined it must be replaced by something equally stretching and high profile.

Lamarck finally closed on October 30th, almost 2 years to the day from the time that first small contingent of FANYs, the Band of Hope, marched through the imposing gateway to see the scruffy, malodorous buildings that awaited them. Vastly different now, it had been a huge success for the Corps, and over 4000 sick and wounded had passed through it.

In the summer Grace had written in The Gazette, *"As progression is our watchword, new developments must be looked for."* It was increasingly obvious that this hadn't been done while she was away ill. Hoogstadt and The Dundee Hut were useful, but Grace wanted something really worthwhile to replace Lamarck.

With FANY Units working for the British and the Belgians, Grace approached the French in early autumn. She had recently been decorated with Chevalier de L'Ordre de Leopold II, a very prestigious Belgian honour. Aware of the French fondness for medals and decorations of any sort, she made her way to Paris and called on the The Societe de Secours aux Blesses Militaires (SSBM) at their HQ, and persuaded them that the FANY had something to offer.

It was too much to expect an immediate reaction. They had an almost pathological objection to Frenchwomen doing this kind of war work, but as Grace pointed out in her very persuasive way, the FANY were all British. She also reminded them that in Calais FANY convoys were carrying all British, Belgian AND French casualties, and ferrying their doctors and nurses from hospital to hospital. Not only that, but during air raids and naval bombardments, it was the FANY cars and ambulances which provided all transport for both French and Belgian civil and military authorities, in Calais, a French Port.

This was a successful ploy, and before she left she had got grudging approval for the employment of the Corps by the SSBM, details to be worked out and discussed later.

To Grace's surprise, the SSBM came back to her quite soon, with a proposition. They would give the FANY Corps a 200 bed hospital to run, 20 miles from Reims. It was a Cistercian Monastery in a place called Porte à Binson, part of it still occupied by members of the order.

The Corps would supply staff for nursing, as well as drivers and transport, medical equipment, and beds. The SSBN were providing lighting, heating, food and, most important, doctors.

This really was a major breakthrough, not only with regard to the size of the operation, but the fact that Grace had managed to overcome the French Establishment prejudices and objections. It would be some time before it opened, but the walls had been breached. It was theirs.

Though it had been used by the French as a hospital since 1914, they had recently evacuated it completely. When Grace arrived there with Coley and her advance party, they found it in a filthy condition. That wasn't until January 1917, the cold bitter, the whole place bleak, unwelcoming, unfurnished and desolate.

In her usual cavalier fashion Grace had agreed the terms and signed up for it, without properly considering the costs involved, and the staggering amount of work and investment ahead.

But before that could be tackled, Grace faced a more immediate, and bitter, series of battles within her own bailiwick. At FANY Headquarters in London, Mr Cluff, the Treasurer, and Janette Lean, the Secretary, were out for her blood. There were fierce, venomous hostilities ahead.

But, up on Cloud 9, she celebrated, if that is the right word, while visiting old friends in a Belgian Field Artillery unit in the Front Line. There, after a warm welcome, good food and wine, the Officer Commanding allowed her to fire two 75mm shells at *Les Boches*, while the whole crew watched with a mixture of elation and admiration, as she sent the two deadly missiles hurtling across No-Man's-Land into the German trenches, one for each of her brothers they had killed.

She always said it was the most satisfying thing she had ever done!

A week later a large cardboard box was delivered to her in Calais. It contained the two shell cases from her exploit, one neatly engraved:

'Tiré sur les Boches par Madame McDougall 5 Septembre 1916'.

What she didn't realise then, was that the explosions at the German receiving end would be insignificant beside the explosion at FANY HQ when they heard about Porte à Binson!

CHAPTER 32

Storm Clouds Gather

For some little time there had been rumblings of discontent at FANY HQ in London at the manner in which Grace relentlessly pursued her target of 'progression'.

Way back in 1914, her promise to the Belgian Surgeon-General that the FANY would provide a Convalescent Home by Christmas, was made on the spur of the moment. It made life very difficult for Mrs Morris, the dedicated and hardworking Secretary/Treasurer/Storekeeper struggling to run HQ single-handedly.

At that time there was virtually no equipment and very little money available. Grace, realizing and accepting that the problem was of her making, had embarked on her hectic and very successful fundraising blitz in Scotland and London, collecting enough in the way of both money and equipment to get St. Inglevert up and running very successfully.

In July 1915 a Rev William Cluff took over as Treasurer, relieving the pressure considerably on Mrs Morris. But in early 1916 she resigned, and Janette Lean became Secretary. As time went on, Cluff and Lean combined in an increasingly fierce opposition to Grace's way of doing things, which eventually became almost a personal vendetta.

Looked at from their viewpoint, their objections were, perhaps, understandable. Grace was headstrong and determined, time and again making decisions off her own bat, which closely involved Cluff and Lean at HQ in increasing worries about the ability of this purely voluntary organization to cope financially, and meet the obligations Grace so blithely committed them to.

On the other hand, Grace believed she was the only one capable of expanding the Corps, prepared to do all the footslogging, taking all the rebuffs, fighting to break through red tape and entrenched convictions. After all, during the two occasions she had been away – the months following illness and bereavement, first in 1915 and then again in 1916 – everything had stood still.

Grace had been solely responsible for the absolutely vital and indispensable help and support from the Belgian Army in those first weeks and months of the war, without which the FANY would have foundered. She alone pushed through Lamarck, their highly successful flagship enterprise, so well run by Franklin; then, later, other projects such as Oostkerke, St. Inglevert, Camp du Ruchard, the Dundee Hut, Fismes, and of course, Binson, agreed, not yet opened, but a ticking time bomb about to create mayhem in the ranks!

Both the English and French successes were won against long and dogged stonewalling by both these nations, refusing to accept the idea of using women in any capacity other than the idealized image of Florence Nightingale–type nurses.

Grace was also very largely responsible for the formation of the English Convoy, Unit 3, in 1916; wholly responsible for the large Belgian Convoy, Unit 5; and she had just broken through the French resistance and signed an agreement with their SSBM to take over Binson Priory Hospital. On every front, she led and the others followed. Unfortunately, essential as these projects were to the future of the Corps, the way in which she took them on, giving little or no thought to the costs involved, only informing HQ at the last moment when already committed, made life very difficult indeed for Cluff and Lean.

Sadly, instead of sitting down together and sorting out their differences before they escalated into disputes, the main protagonists became somewhat embittered, and much ill-feeling resulted. Faults lay on both sides.

Although during 1914 and 1915 there had been spasmodic upsurges of annoyance and irritation with Grace from the HQ staff, by and large these subsided very quickly when the various schemes worked out and were successes, through the efforts of Grace and others involved. It was during the latter half of 1916, and into 1917, that trouble really began to brew, principally over the French hospital at Binson, although this was not the only gripe.

When Grace persuaded the Belgians that they needed a strong motorized Convoy in Calais, on the same lines as the English one, already proving its worth, the response was gratifying. Eight staff were transferred from elsewhere immediately to form the nucleus, but new girls were also required from England. Lean claimed that Grace requested that these new drivers should sign the contract in *her* name as Commandant of the new Corps de Transporte Militaire Belge, FANY Unit 5, instead of the standard FANY enrolment form. Lean saw this as a 'gross infringement of FANY Rules & Regulations', and proof that Grace was Empire-building for herself. It is difficult to ascertain the true facts. It seems very unlikely that Grace would do this, but possible, as she was immensely proud of Unit 5, and always considered it *her* convoy.

Grace also came under attack, again from Lean, on her decision to send FANYs to work in a YMCA Centre Canteen at La Brouck, too close to the Front Line. In fact, so incensed was Lean at this decision that she actually took the very serious step indeed – as far as is known, of her own accord – of writing to the YMCA to warn them, rightly or wrongly, that employing FANYs in a 'Military Centre' was contrary to the Geneva Convention. That really does seem to have been carrying things too far, but is an indication of just how high feelings were running – Lean's, at least.

In the event it had little effect. The two girls went up there, helped the YMCA out of an embarrassing hole and created a deal of goodwill. The FANY became known to increasing numbers of British troops for their efficiency and cheerfulness running this busy canteen, though not perhaps in their primary role of driving and nursing. However, it all helped. On one of her visits to La Brouck in January 1917, Grace noted that *"Coley and Lewis were busy and happy, their work a great success!"*.

It was Grace's breakthrough with the French that caused the greatest furore. It really got the chests heaving with indignation at HQ. She had casually agreed to staff and equip a 200 bed hospital without any reference to Headquarters, little idea of costs involved, or the amount of work entailed in setting up and running an enterprise as large and important as this.

She herself was delighted. She had broken down French resistance and expanded her Corps. The FANY were now directly supporting all three Allies – British, French and Belgian. Grace felt she was getting somewhere. That was what really mattered to her. Anything else was by the way, nothing that a bit of hard work wouldn't sort out. It had always happened that way before.

This bland acceptance of the French terms triggered off a veritable volcano of resentment. Verbal lava of recrimination and accusations flowed fiercely from Cluff and Lean at HQ. Once again Grace had left it very late indeed before informing Headquarters of what she had done and agreed. It has to be said that this was typical of her rather high-handed disdain for Authority, and infuriating for Lean and Cluff, whose earlier strenuous efforts to get Grace to toe the line had apparently failed.

According to Grace, Lean 'bombarded' her with letters. Not only that, but she resorted to a previous dubious tactic, writing direct to the French Red Cross official in London, a Mr Illingsworth. In the letter she strongly opposed Grace's plan for taking over the running of Porte à Binson Hospital. The ploy had as little effect in this case, as had the letter to the YMCA about La Brouck.

There came a time when Cluff and Lean felt that all the work they were doing was not appreciated – no doubt connected to their ongoing disputes with Grace. They both threatened to resign unless they got the support of all members of the Corps, especially the officers.

In a move calculated to improve their position, they produced a Paper as early as July 1916, calling it 'Suggestions for the Future Government of the FANY Corps'. In it they laid down various rules, basically aimed at controlling Grace's often impetuous ideas. Cluff was to have the power to refuse funding for any new scheme not approved by the Board of Officers, or at least the Treasurer and two other Officers, *including at least one of the Senior Lieutenants*. That last was put in, no doubt, to underline the point that the two, Franklin and Grace, ranked equally. That was really self-evident, but tends to support the hypothesis that Franklin resented Grace unintentionally usurping her position as Senior Officer, through her single-minded and successful efforts to expand the Corps.

As a corollary to this Paper, Franklin had written a short eulogy, praising the strenuous efforts of both Cluff and Lean, adding that from now on they would be made Honorary Lieutenants, in full control of Headquarters and Funds.

Both Franklin and Grace signed beneath, and peace reigned in the land. But only temporarily!

Some months later more conflict surfaced, with the Minutes of a Board Meeting in November indicating that Grace had threatened to fire Lean. A resolution was passed at that Meeting ruling that no Officer had the power to dismiss another on her own. There must be consultation with at least one other officer. It would appear that this, too, was directed against Grace, as was another passed at the same Meeting.

Aimed at putting the brakes on her solo activities in pursuit of 'progression', the timing of this, November 1916, points once again to Grace's Binson project. The Minute lays down that no new Unit could be formed unless it had been discussed and approved at Headquarters.

Grace ignored this, apparently, and continued with her preparations for launching Binson Hospital.

Apart from Cluff and Lean, others appear to have been dragged into the disagreement, particularly Franklin. Her part in it is perhaps a trifle enigmatic. All Grace's references to Franklin in her fairly extensive writings, were complimentary and supportive. Franklin herself left few records of that period, at least in the public domain, and her opinions expressed about Grace were sometimes ambiguous, and often directly critical. Never, as far as can be ascertained, directly to Grace herself, usually in letters to others.

For instance, in December 1916, Franklin wrote direct to Miss Lean: *"I am sincerely sorry to find that Mrs Mac (Grace) is taking up this impossible attitude."* She then hedges her bets. *"There is no question of any one of us wishing to crush any forward movement of the Corps, but as anything undertaken by any unit of it concerns all the others it is absolutely imperative that Headquarters be fully informed of any fresh responsibilities undertaken."*

She continues, saying that there was plenty of time for them to have been given at least an outline of the scheme. This was with reference to taking on Binson Hospital. Then she adds, *"I am writing to Mr Cluff and suggesting that he, as Chairman representing the Committee, should write and inform Mrs Mac that she must conform, or her unit must be considered no longer part of the FANY and no help appealed for it under that name.”*

Finally, and significantly, she writes: *“Joynson, Thompson and Wicks are quite of the same opinion”*. This last clearly indicates that she had been discussing Grace's conduct with at least three other FANYs, all junior in rank to Franklin and Grace. As Co-Commandant, even in a quasi-military unit such as the FANY, this is something she should really not have done, without speaking to Grace first. On the other hand, the FANY was a very independent bunch, and followed their own rules.

It would have been so much better for Franklin to have approached Grace herself, and talked the matter over as equals, but there is no mention of this from either of them. In her letter to Lean, Franklin makes the point: *“Why did not Mrs Mac put in even half an hour at the meeting to give us some idea of the scheme? No one wants to interfere with it, only to ensure if possible its complete success. She cannot work everything herself therefore she must trust others to help her.”*

This was a sensible and reasonable stance to take, so why didn't she take it up with Grace, instead of writing to Lean or Cluff? She was a woman of great personal courage, so would not have been afraid of Grace. Could it have been an underlying irritation at the way in which Grace had usurped Franklin's originally dominant position? After all, she was senior to Grace in length of service; had been made Sgt. Major while Grace was still a Corporal; and Lieutenant while Grace was still Sergeant. But now, not only was Grace of equal rank, but calling all the shots and getting all the applause. That must have been supremely galling for someone like Franklin, quiet, self contained, supremely efficient.

In reply to Franklin's long letter, Lean wrote back a few days later, *“Mr Cluff and I are quite determined that unless Mrs McDougall conforms to the rules of the Corps she will forfeit all right to the name, money, stores and personnel of the Corps.”* Strong words indeed, many of them very similar to those used by Franklin informing Lean of what she was going to suggest Mr Cluff should say to Grace.

Of course, Franklin would have been aware of her shortcomings in the field of expansion of the Corps. This was Grace's most outstanding contribution, her forte, and without it the FANY would almost certainly have faded away in the early months of the war.

On the other hand, Franklin's competent, capable and businesslike running of Lamarck, and the excellent relationship she built up with the British authorities in Calais, contributed very largely to their acceptance by them of the FANY English Convoy.

Writing in The Gazette in 1916, in Grace's absence, having negotiated a new Agreement with the Red Cross for FANY Unit 3, the English Convoy, she said, *"This new Agreement is a rather great achievement when one remembers the old one –* [negotiated by Grace] *– and the very great monetary responsibility under which the Corps was placed."*

Another dig at Grace in her absence? Or a perfectly reasonable statement of fact with a touch of hyperbole thrown in? Grace herself was no stranger to a bit of trumpet blowing. There is no doubt that she was facing a great deal of criticism, sometimes well-deserved, from both Lean and Treasurer Cluff.

Whatever Franklin's real objectives were in this internal struggle within the Corps, it never crossed Grace's mind, as far as her diaries at the time are concerned, that Franklin was involved against her. There is no doubt that she saw her main adversary as Janette Lean, backed up possibly a shade reluctantly at times, by Mr Cluff. In fact, in her memoirs she referred to Franklin as a 'life-long friend'.

The New Year brought an early renewal of the assault from HQ. A letter from Cluff arrived on January 5th, threatening, as Grace wrote in her diary, *'to disavow me to the British, Belgian and French authorities'*.

The battle was hotting up!

CHAPTER 33

The Lull Before The Storm

It couldn't have come at a worse time, and Grace ignored it.
Not only was she too busy to really give the challenge her full attention, but she was suffering from a *"throat too sore to swallow, discharging from the eyes, feeling sick and giddy, with fearful headaches"* she writes in her diary. On top of that they were enduring the worst winter since 1870! Towards the end of January she records: *"It is intensely cold – the water freezes on one's fingers as we wash in the mornings."*

It was a time of change, comings and goings, and a lot of worry for Grace. Staff were going on leave of one sort or another; she had to visit outposts like La Brouck and Hoogstadt which had recently been handed back or closed, tie up loose ends, and organise the packing and despatch of some staff's personal belongings and equipment.

By the middle of the month she was feeling much better, and was at Binson, preparing it as best she could for opening. The place had been cleared of patients and equipment by the French.

Belgian General Thooft came to congratulate her on her Leopold II decoration. Around this time she was having her portrait prepared for an exhibition by 'Artists on Active Service', by someone she refers to only as 'Mr George'. What became of it was never revealed.

It was a hectic time, a lot of travelling involved in setting up the transport facilities for Binson. On one occasion she and Anderson drove through the night to collect a vehicle, but theirs broke down in a place called Chamblis at 4 o'clock in the morning. Grace's brief and succinct account states: *"Clutch gave – stayed there till daylight."* This sort of thing was commonplace, but induced constant worry and weariness over time.

On another occasion, broken down far from a town, she was given a lift by a French Colonel, eight miles to the nearest place with a garage. It was of no use, and she had to walk the eight miles back to the car.

Towards the end of the month three truckloads of stores and equipment arrived from the now closed Lamarck, and the unloading began – by Coley, Lewis, two others and Grace. Heavy, tiring work. They managed to clear one and a half trucks, she records, with the remainder the next day.

There was so much to do. She spent a lot of the time writing letters to HQ, the French Red Cross in Paris, French Army Medical people. So many loose ends to tie up. The place was absolutely filthy, floors thick with ingrained dirt. Used and festering bandages and dressings were tucked under grimy mattresses. Some were actually wrapped in old newspaper dated as far back as 1914! A major clean-up operation was needed, and the small advance party got down to it in true FANY fashion. Once Lamarck finally closed, the staff were transferred to Binson. The expected French casualties had not yet arrived – a blessing in disguise, considering the appalling state the place was in.

On one occasion, while she and the FANYs were having tea, the head of the Priory, Rev. Pere Econique and some of his Peres Blancs unexpectedly called on them. Grace immediately welcomed them and offered them tea. She writes: *"They ran away horrified. Their rules do not allow them to eat in the presence of a woman."*

The cold, the worries about Binson, the letters which kept arriving from Lean or Cluff, all these were getting her down. As the month drew to an end, she wrote, almost despairingly, *"so many things to worry about"*, and again a few days later, *"Still arranging and worrying! If only people at home would help instead of hinder"*.

One of her worries was the sorting out of the rooms available to them in the Priory, where everything should be put, the allocation of areas for wards, offices, mess rooms etc.

Grace arranged a meeting with the Peres Blancs, carefully avoiding any mention of tea or coffee. On this occasion it was she who was shocked. She notes in her diary, *"The Peres Blancs explained politely but firmly, 'no agreement is signed for the building, and you have no right to be here at all!' She adds wryly, "Nice, eh?"*

This extra and very serious worry sent her off as quickly as possible to see the local Medecin Chef to tell him about it, and see what he could do; why had nothing been signed between the French

Authorities and the Priory?

Finally, perhaps as an afterthought in a moment of acute frustration, she scribbled underneath it all: *"Still no staff from England. D---n Lean."*

Next day, she, Coley and the others set off for Paris, knowing nothing would be dealt with over the weekend. They were worn out mentally and physically, and needed a break. They began to unwind immediately, meeting up with a "little French airman" on the train. How relaxed Grace was able to become shows in her diary entry. No doubt it did her the world of good. One can imagine her having a quiet chuckle to herself. She wrote: *"It is amusing for me to be a chaperone – I know exactly when they are playing footie (sic) under the table and looking innocent above it. What a chaperone I make – and they think I don't see!! Tiens! Tiens!"*

The brief time away did them all good, recharged flagging batteries, and set Grace up for the tussles ahead. It would be needed.

On the Monday a letter arrived, and her short interlude of peace and pleasure came to an end. The letter gave notice that a Board of Officers' Meeting was called for January 31 – only two days ahead – *"To Consider Mrs McDougall's Position"*.

This she could no longer ignore.

Handing over to Coley, she headed for Calais. There she had a hectic round of visits to transport depots, organizing car replacements involving lengthy discussions. There is a cryptic and intriguing entry for February 2nd: *"Vice Consul came to tea and brought my new Passport – my third since the war. He had changed my description as he said I had libelled myself!"*

On the 4th February she crossed the Channel; a Capt Synge attached to Army HQ had got her a cabin to herself where she *"lay and read and ate chocolate, cold even in cabin with heater thing on"*. Arriving at Victoria she was not in a good mood, and recorded *"no porters, had to trail my bag along. No taxis"*.

But the real measure of her mood, stepping onto English soil again, was what she wrote furiously in her diary the Monday the notification arrived about the Board Meeting to ' consider her position'!

Her comments were typical of Grace. Her Highland blood was on the boil. Accept this? Nae chance!

She wrote: *"D___d cheek – however I'll fight them – but I wish I could get the staff out. God knows, we want help for the wounded, not kudos for ourselves."*

CHAPTER 34

Grace Fights Back

The following day she went into action. She swept into FANY HQ and confronted Mr Cluff. Grace records: *"*[Cluff] *admitted that two rules of the four were absurd. Climbed down and said he wanted to work on with me."*

After settling with him, she went straight along to see Janette Lean who, according to the entry in Grace's diary that day, agreed with everything Cluff had said – adding that *"they would see Grace got the money, the staff and the buildings etc"*.

Satisfied that she had quelled the opposition, she wrote in her diary: *"Lean's game is so plain. She thinks if every unit has to report to her, & she is the only person with the authority to enrol people, she will make herself C.O. – she calls herself O.C. Headquarters."*

The next day she went to see Mr Illingsworth of the French Red Cross at their London HQ and showed him her plans for Binson. He was very welcoming and supportive. He told her about Janette Lean's letter to him, and promised her all the help he could give. *"Tell 'em to go to blazes,"* he is reported as saying, *"only don't tell them I said so! I'll get your people out for you."* She left that meeting happy and satisfied.

There was more trouble ahead. Grace returned to HQ and read the minutes of the Meeting held on 31st January, at which neither she nor Franklin were present. She came in for strong criticism from all the members of the Board for the cavalier manner in which she ignored previous resolutions and continued with the Binson project; and in spite of repeated requests had failed to provide the Board with any information about it.

They all passed the Resolution that if full details of her plans were not submitted within 14 days, the Board would repudiate all liability for any Agreement she may have entered into.

That was pretty damning on its own, but not enough apparently for Lean. She campaigned forcefully for a resolution that Grace resign from the Corps immediately, 'since she had been repeatedly warned as to the folly of her actions'.

The rest of the Board, however, refused to support or accept that particular motion, settling for being opposed to anything which might land the Corps in legal difficulties.

After she had digested these resolutions and accusations, her reaction was much the same as when she got notice of the Board Meeting to discuss her position "D—d cheek!" She had already confronted Cluff and Lean, who, according to her, had backed down.

On the day she had been to French Red Cross HQ and spoken to Mr Illingsworth, she had received an urgent wire from Lean asking her to go and see Mr Cluff. She went along to the office to see him, but noted in her diary *"he had nothing to say. I felt that Lean had been trying to get him to make me sign things – he hadn't the caddishness to do it"*. She added ominously: *"If I sign they sign, too!"*

The following day she received a letter from Cluff which she described as 'rather rambling'. She goes on: *"I'm sure Lean is trying to upset him and he doesn't know what to do."* It was all a bit irritating and time wasting.

She was going through a busy time – Foreign Office to get her new Passport back; then on to French Red Cross HQ; interviewing possible recruits; looking for a good Matron for Binson.

Here she enrolled the help of the Chief Matron of the Anglo-French Hospital Committee in London, a Mrs Watson. She appeared to be very helpful; Grace was very impressed by her. In fact, more than impressed, she became quite lyrical about her, describing her as *"a very beautiful woman – I admire her more each time I see her"*, adding *"I would like to be like her. She is the only woman I have ever felt like that about."* A quite astonishing admission from a strong-minded, independent woman like Grace!

Yet a few months later Irene Cowlin, who had taken over from Lean, was writing to Grace about Mrs Watson, saying she was the most disagreeable woman she had ever met, who kept delaying FANYs who wanted to get across the Channel. It would be interesting to know Grace's reaction to the strong criticism of someone she had obviously placed on a pedestal. Suffice to say, the log-jam of FANYs waiting to go was quickly cleared once Grace became involved.

Then, with a very hectic and rather disjointed programme ahead of her, and not very happy, Grace had some good news from her husband – he was coming home on leave. It obviously set her heart racing, although she tried valiantly to keep her 'service' and married lives separate. She scribbled excitedly in her diary: *"Ronald is coming and should be here tomorrow. I dare not hope. I am going to Canterbury* [for her god-daughter's weekend christening] *I am sure if I don't he won't come. Oh my darling, I am so excited.*

"Oh God, don't stop him, don't stop him."

The following day she writes with an almost tangible sense of disappointment. *"Went to Canterbury Saturday night, Barbara's christening. I went to early Communion, morning service, and afternoon."* One can guess what she was desperately praying for.

Then the disappointment: *"I rushed up to Town to meet Rannie – He didn't come."*

For Monday there was only one brief entry. *"Letter from Ronald – leave all off."* That probably meant just one thing – back to the trenches.

To get her mind away from the immediate past, she opted to take lessons in basic car servicing. Never one to waste time, she went along to 'Mansions Motor Garage' where she booked a course of hands-on lectures starting the next day. For the next few days she wore herself out *"changing wheels, tyres, adjusting valves"* – the latter a *"stiff job and was left dead beat"*. Maybe that was the point of the exercise: trying to forget her disappointment.

These courses were morning or afternoon, and she was also busy at HQ seeing Cluff and Lean; going off to inspect a Buick chassis; buying it. *"Mrs Allen,"* she writes, *"sending money and went to see about body at cheap* [body] *builders."* She made time again. *"Saw Lean at office."* Lean was certainly paying the price for 'bombarding her with letters'. In between times she was recruiting and interviewing, once more back into 'full steam ahead' mode.

In spite of all that had happened, there was still a deal of ill feeling and worry at HQ about the costs involved in the Binson project. Grace decided to get the matter out of the way once and for all, using the same sort of barnstorming tactics that she had used so successfully in 1914, and to a lesser degree over Camp du Ruchard. This time, rather than a solo effort, she co-opted the willing help of another FANY stalwart, Mary Baxter-Ellis, who had strong connections in the North of England. Grace would cover Scotland.

Now the talking phase was over, Grace was itching to go. She had decisively evened the score with Cluff and Lean; now she was into the end game of her fight back against all those who had sought to bring her down, or at least harness her. It was to be a hard, wearying slog, but she was a tough Aberdonian shortly to be back among her own folk, and looking forward to it. Mary Baxter-Ellis was of the same mould.

Provided with tickets by the British Red Cross, the two girls met up at Kings Cross, and headed for Newcastle, the heart of Baxter-Ellis country. Next day they swung into action, starting at the top!

Grace remembers: *Went to the Lord Mayor he started our list with £10. The Sheriff gave £10 and Sir Joseph Baxter-Ellis another £10. Mr Berry, Secretary of the Working Men's War Relief Fund (WMWRF), came to tea and promised heaps of bandages, and gave me some tips. Dick (?) and I had to go to the Committee Meeting – and I had to address them – Ye Gods! I got through it somehow & they seemed to like it. They were nice to talk to – one jolly old man with a very dirty face laughed and cheered and that helped me! They voted us £140 worth of things for the hospital, and there is a chance of a car."*

(Mary Baxter-Ellis was later presented with a fully equipped ambulance!)

They also visited three newspaper Editors – The Journal, The Chronicle and The Northern Mail – all of whom promised their full support. "Lady Ellis came with us and helped."

It was a great start to the quest for money and equipment. Donations poured in. Both girls had tremendous pride in the Corps, and managed to convey the impression that what the FANY were doing in France was of vital importance to the war effort.

It didn't come without a lot of physical effort and exertion by the two trailblazers. Travelling long distances from place to place; attending meetings; and calling on likely donors personally. The focus then moved from Newcastle across to Cumbria where the Baxter-Ellises were well known.

There they were taken to the Gosforth War Hospital by Mr Berry of the Working Men's Fund, and a charming Mr Young, where they got "£47 worth of tobacco and cigarettes".

At the hospital Grace recalls: *"the poor old wounded doing lovely embroidery – Regimental badges in silks etc"*.

In between this frantic fund-raising, they somehow found time to write innumerable letters asking for help. They both had good social connections which they exploited unashamedly, and donations kept arriving. For instance, Baxter-Ellis wrote personally to Princess Louise, Queen Victoria's daughter, who sent her a cheque for £5. Grace used her for a bit of judicious name-dropping soon after in Edinburgh, with good results. A Lady Allandale sent £10 and another gift arrived from Lady Londonderry. These sums may not seem a lot today, but in those days were sizeable offerings indeed.

When the first FANY convoy, for instance – The Band of Hope – landed at Calais and set up 'shop' at Lamarck hospital, they had a total of £12 in the bank to see them through those first weeks. Binson was going to do very much better.

Following their joint successes in Newcastle and Cumbria, Grace and Mary Baxter-Ellis split up, each to cover their own familiar areas. It was nearing the end of February, a year since she had been home after the death of Billy. Her mood was one of excitement tinged with sadness.

The constant pressure on her since coming back to England, to face recrimination and accusation from her colleagues; rushing about in London trying to sort out recruitment problems; and this latest load on her shoulders raising enough money to justify her acceptance of Binson, were beginning to take their toll once again, inducing a depressed introspection unusual for her. In her diary at the end of February, she wrote:

"I wonder if this is my last time home? I feel uncanny. I am so loth to leave it all, I do love it all, the rivers & the hills & the brown leaves & fields – if only I could live in Scotland again – just in the country with a nice little property & Ronald – the boy – is it to be?

"I feel there must be a Charles Ronald [the son she yearned for, names already chosen] *and yet I feel I haven't much longer to live.*

"And after all I've had a lot out of life & wouldn't mind going now if it weren't for Ronald."

Things really must have been piling up in her mind for her to think like that. Almost certainly the charges and complaints made against her, or supported, by fellow FANYs must have hurt her much more deeply than she ever let on. After all she had done, striven for, to build her beloved Corps into a group admired by all, it was akin to a stab in the back .In spite of her tough, no nonsense exterior, inside she was a sensitive woman.

Again, it was clear she was missing Ronald. Possibly as a result of her inward feelings, back again in Aberdeen, the following night she had a shocking dream, nightmare almost, writing about it in stark detail:

"Awful dream about Ronald that someone shouted 'here's your husband' and I flew out with a yell of joy. He stood quite still on the stairs & never spoke nor moved.

"Oh my God, keep my Rannie safe for me."

Millions of wives were going through the same trauma of separation and fear for loved ones. Still obviously upset, a few days later she scribbled into her diary: *"More collecting. Got fed up with it and left it."* She had been pretty successful, it was the weekend, and she headed for Broughty Ferry to stay with Billy's widow, Bea, and their children. The visit brought back to her the pain and grief of Billy's death, and knowing how much he adored the children, she wrote: *"Oh my God. My Billy is gone – never to see them & play with them & love them."*

She was experiencing an agonizing time, and memories tore at her heart. She still had that inner strength and humour with which she could and would bounce back. Bea showed her the pitifully few possessions of Bill's which were sent back to her from France. One large item eventually had both of them in fits of laughter, a welcome release from the tight grip of grief. Grace tells the story:

"Very little. Only his 'jerry', a big china one carefully packed! We laughed with tears rolling over our faces – for Billy would have laughed so at that. No diary, no letters, no revolver, hardly any clothes. Poor Billy."

Grace spent another day with Bea and the children, then tore herself away to get back to fundraising. Aberdeen had produced substantial donations, including a fully equipped ambulance!

She headed for Edinburgh. Again going straight to the top. The Lord Provost had a niece in the FANY, and that was enough for

Grace, but she had already met him. When he was a JP, she had had to get some papers signed at Colinton after Charlie's death. She remembered the occasion: *"He was awfully nice to me."*

She went to the City Chambers to beard him in his den, and records how she got round him.

"Saw Lord Provost. He was very nice but afraid to do anything without the City Chamberlain, a dry old stick.

"It was great fun manoeuvring around him. I broke down all the barriers one by one and at last he read my letter to the Scotsman, & the mention of Princess Louise's donation did it. He gave in – & even offered to accept donations.

"I went straight to The Scotsman office to have it put in. [A letter she had quickly written about the Lord Provost accepting donations]

"Lord McLeod, the Provost, is such a nice man – not a bit dusty & pompous."

The next day she returned to London, where her mother was alone, Isabel and the boys having gone down to Eastbourne while Bertie was recovering from his bout of pneumonia. In a mood of constantly changing feelings, she writes, *"Am fed up with collecting."* Then right after this statement, she goes on: *"My letter in Scotsman this morning. I hope will have some effect."* In fact, it had very considerable effect, raising a lot more money and much needed supplies of every sort.

The fund raising trip was virtually over. Grace and Baxter-Ellis had spent 17 days 'on the road'. Between them they had produced an incredible amount of money and hospital equipment of every sort, from scissors to ambulances – three of them! – beds, mattresses, sheets, blankets, medical instruments, bandages, dressings.

Grace, with Baxter-Ellis' help, had saved the day for Binson, and paved the way for a successful setting up of the hospital.

Once again she had won through with her energy, scorn for red tape and 'office-wallah' officialdom, and her single-minded determination.

Janette Lean resigned shortly after, not waiting for the final scenes in the drama of Binson. In the same issue of the Gazette which published Lean's resignation in the back pages, the front page expressed appreciation of the transfer of the title FANY Unit 1 from the successful Lamarck Hospital to their new L'Hôpital Auxiliaire 76, FANY Unit 1, Porte à Binson.

It stated: *"Mrs McDougall must be congratulated on this achievement as it is particularly difficult for women to get into this area, and the French Red Cross own that it is a very important piece of work."*

Another battle won, but the war still went on. There was a lot of 1917 left, and ahead lay successes and disappointments.

Grace had a busy time in front of her, shortly to be faced with yet another confrontation, this one putting not only Grace's future at risk, but the FANY Corps as a whole.

CHAPTER 35

All In A Day's Work

The February issue of the Gazette must have been late coming out, as Grace didn't return from her fund-raising marathon until March 10th. With a very good idea of just how well the tour had gone, she lost no time in making straight for HQ and ...."*saw Mr Cluff and told him about the collection etc*". She wasn't one to let an opportunity like that go by! She was careful to note: "*Also Headquarters!*"

Though very anxious to return to France, there was still a lot to be done in London. Top of her list was to see Mrs Allen, the FANY benefactress *par excellence*, to settle details of the de Dion ambulance she was presenting to the Corps.

Added to that there was recruiting to be done, people to interview, letters to write, and various Red Cross and other officials to meet, pacify and get round. "*A genius at organizing*" as Grace had been called, she hated the nitty-gritty of administration. Her diary at the time was full of entries such as: "*Busy all day, too tired to write – just the usual scrum*". Or "*Busy again, interviewing, writing, seeing people*". And the next day: "*Same old story!*"

It all had to be done, and she got on with it.

On 17 March, she and Mrs Allen set off into the country to Wargrave, to collect the de Dion. 'Uncle' went with them. Unfortunately, things didn't go smoothly. Cars in those days were not as reliable as today. Starting out in 'the Napier', Grace remembers, "*the rim came off the wheel*". An hour later, repaired, they tried again. The same thing happened.

They took a taxi instead, got there, checked the vehicle, accepted it, and set off back to London. Grace and Mrs Allen drove home in it. "*A lovely day,*" said Grace, "*quite a rest to be out in the country.*" She also recorded: "*Car went beautifully. Lost taxi man!*" It had already been said of the FANYs that they drove like 'bats out of hell' when their ambulances were empty, and Grace wasn't going to tar their reputation.

The following day she recorded: *"No news of taxi man!"* He wasn't mentioned again.

By this time Grace was getting really fed up, not feeling well either. *"Sick of little things that all have to be done and so sick of Town. Will be glad to get back, but feel rotten."* The stresses and strains of her life were once again beginning to take their toll on her health. Even so, she kept going – a characteristic of hers, to finish anything she had set her mind to, come what may.

At least she felt now that things were coming together, and she was very pleased to be spending a good deal of time with her mother, now back to her old, strong self, happily set up with Carrie and Isabel, and the two grandsons. However, there was to be no immediate let up. Meetings with Mrs Watson at Red Cross HQ, and Mr Illingsworth of the French Red Cross. *"Palaver!"* she scrawled contemptuously in her diary, heavily underlined. She goes on: *"Packing – getting letters off & a/cs – INTERVIEWS AT HQ."* She finished in capitals.

As time grew shorter, she moved into top gear. *"Was out from 9 a.m. to 7 p.m.. Cdn't [sic] get off sooner. Feeling tired."* She was desperate to get back out to Binson, where Coley was in charge. So far no patients had arrived, and Grace wanted to find out from the French just what the delay was about.

At last all the preparation was over and on the 23rd March her small contingent took off, four FANYs and Mrs Allen. They had with them the three cars/ambulances that Grace and Baxter-Ellis had managed to obtain. Unfortunately Baxter-Ellis was ill, and didn't return until mid-April, so missing the triumphal procession!

The party drove down to Folkestone where they stayed the night. Next day they crossed to Boulogne, complete with their Buick, Overland and de Dion – very welcome additions to the growing fleet of FANY vehicles.

Met by Captain Synge, who had got Grace a cabin to herself on her way home, they phoned Calais and two FANYs, a mechanic, and a Dr Fete came to join them on the trip to Binson. It was not to be an uneventful journey, but as usual they coped.

The hospital wasn't far from the Front Line, and as they approached they drove into an air raid close to a nearby Cavalry

Remount Depot. A stray horse in the road panicked and kicked out at the Buick. A young FANY called MacKenzie was driving, with Grace beside her. The windscreen was smashed. Not a good start. They drove on to an Army Transport garage to get it seen to, and while there the Germans launched another raid with *"bombs dropped all round"*.

Back at Binson, Grace carried out a swift check all around with Coley, though she had developed a *"fearful throat & cold. Was quite warm crossing can't understand it"*.

There was a Musical Evening being held that night, which Grace attended in spite of feeling very low. A surprise twist to the evening was the arrival of the Belgian Area Commander, General Thoof, to present her with the actual medal of the Chevalier de l'Ordre de Leopold II. He then made an impassioned speech – at which the Belgians were very good – praising the work of Grace and her FANYs .

A little later he broke it to her that Ruchard would definitely be closing, but wanted the Corps to take up other work for the Belgians. There had been rumours for some time, so the news was not unexpected.

However, what was unexpected, and not at all welcome, was a note from the Assistant Provost Marshal (APM), Vice Chief of the Military Police. Three of her FANYs – Marples, Moses and MacKenzie – had taken in a deserter, given him food and shelter, and warned him that the Military were looking for him. This was a very serious offence indeed in wartime. Moses, along with Mackenzie, was one of the younger FANYs; both were very capable and helpful. Marples was older, more experienced, and should have known better. Human nature being what it is, they had all felt sorry for 'the boy'.

Grace played the delaying tactic game, but unsuccessfully. A few days later she was again approached by the APM, "still flapped" as she put it. The APM was deadly serious. Grace finally agreed to have Marples sent home, if necessary, to save the other two.

Part of the problem was solved soon after, when MacKenzie elected to go home. Grace wrote: *"MacKenzie left us. I am so sorry, she is such a nice child – she is the first to go – wants to work for money now."*

A week after that Marples was sent home after all, for "two

months or so", to assuage the APM. She was accompanied by another FANY, Celia Meade, who had already stepped out of line when Lean resigned, writing direct to Belgian General Clooten. Grace recorded the incident soon after her arrival back in France: *"Row about letter to [General] Clooten got up by Meade for Lean to stay on."* But now, she had, according to Grace *"smashed up the Argyle [lorry] through laziness and carelessness"* and was sent home for good.

One of the other seemingly trivial incidents which took up so much of Grace's time and energies – what she referred to earlier as being *"sick of the little things that all need attention"* – was a shaft going in the new de Dion just after they arrived at Binson. She had since constantly badgered various Army Transport units and garages to get a replacement, but with no success.

However, in the way that fate works, at one of their Sunday tea parties, she noted an Air Force guest, *"an aviation ground crew Chief, promised to make a de Dion shaft for us – funny little man"*. Funny little man he may have been, but he delivered on his promise within a week, which was more than the Belgian and British armies had done in almost a month!

Although the FANY had taken over Binson in January, it was not until the end of March that the first patients, some sick, mostly wounded, arrived. This was with practically no notice at 2 o'clock one morning, when over 100 were unloaded, creating major problems. However, the redoubtable Cole-Hamilton dealt with it in her usual determined and dedicated way, and when another 70-odd arrived a few days later she and her staff were ready for them. In the month following there were 30 serious operations, but only four deaths.

It wasn't a good time for Grace, constantly shuttling between Binson and Calais, with trips to the French Red Cross Headquarters in Paris from time to time. Calais was under almost nightly bombardment from the air during that period, and to add to her problems, the "wretched throat and cold" had got much worse, and was constantly troubling her.

Being a true FANY she took all this in her stride. A brief entry in her diary records succinctly: *"Train of French wounded arrived. Up all night"*. And the next day, *"Fenced at night with Devienne. Got rotten cough keeps me awake at night never had cough before like this"*. Devienne was a French Fencing Master, and Grace happily took the opportunity to brush up her skills.

There were not only air raids to cope with. Calais from time to time was shelled by submarines. She describes one event in some detail:

"Busy day. About midnight terrible noise began – whole barrack shook. I jumped out in dark and got a black eye on edge of marble table. Most terrible noise I ever remember, then silence.

"We dressed and walked up and down – then went back to bed thinking it was aeroplanes but seeing no searchlights. Had just tumbled back into bed when cars ordered out to bring in casualties and dead.

"It was submarines! I went with Bowles-White & Moses – Hoole & Faulds & de Buisson. We came in about 3.30, Ellis and Mason had a fire going and hot tea for us.

"Citadel wall smashed, also the house next to General Clootens Etat Major. I went all over it, awful mess up. Very few killed & wounded, 4 at Baraques.

"Hasn't done my cough much good!"

That last remark was typical of the sort of sardonic, self-deprecating humour with which the girls shrugged off the dangers and ailments they faced almost on a daily basis.

Next day she was "frightfully tired" but had to go to French Headquarters about Passes. These were a constant problem for the FANY, being an independent unit. There were so many varieties of Passes, all considered important by the differing administrations and organizations they worked with. Later she recorded: *"I wish this d____d cough would go & let me sleep. I am so tired of sitting up to cough under the blankets every half hour it makes me feel so cross."*

She didn't realise, or refused to acknowledge, that she was becoming seriously ill.

A short time before this brush with a submarine, she had been involved in another bombardment by submarines. At the time, a particularly heavy flow of casualties was going through Calais. The FANY were working day and night. A shell landing close by enveloped her ambulance in a mass of falling overhead wires, sparks flying everywhere. Grace leaped out of the ambulance, and *"a queer serpent-like thing coiled up all round me, and a flash of flame wrapt [sic] round me"*. Fortunately she was well insulated by her bulky leather and rubber clothing, and all was well.

It wasn't doing her health any good. Towards the end of April a dreadful pain in her side and back developed, she could hardly move, and coughed all the time. She finally accepted she should see a doctor, but only asked for cough mixture!

Despite feeling terrible she insisted on going to Beauvais about Passes again and then on to Montreuil. There she walked into the Military Police HQ, and asked for the Provost Marshal, General Howood. That caused *"an awful flap"*, she says, and she was escorted to the Base Commandant, almost under arrest, because she had not got the "Adjutant General's White Pass".

It was 3 o'clock before she got away, *"dead beat with hunger, had no breakfast"*. Despite being "dead beat" she insisted on going to Paris to see about "those wretched" Passes again. Then she was off to Binson once more, a trip which bucked her up no end, it seems. She recorded: *"Lovely run, trees not out yet. Filled up with petrol at Chateau Theiry. Troops all cheered wildly."* Grace loved any demonstration of this nature.

She had heard that Reims, was under bombardment, but being determined and obstinate, she headed for the town to see for herself. It was being shelled as they approached. At the time she was with one of the senior nurses, and Moses, their youngest FANY. She was all for driving in, but the nurse was very upset so they stopped at the outskirts. Grace wrote excitedly: *"I never saw such shells in my life, great columns of black smoke, like a great building sprung up & vanished – I was rather scared, too, but of course I pretended I knew all about it."* She finished that entry with *"Got awful pain in my side still"*.

The following day it came to a head. At a small local French HQ in Dormans not far away, a fit of coughing ended with *"something seeming to burst inside me. It was agony. I wanted to scream. I don't know how I got to the car or home in it. It was torture"*. Finally she had the sense to send for a senior doctor. He took her straight to an operating theatre, and *"cupped me six great glasses full of blood"* and sent her to bed immediately. She had had a bad attack of pleurisy, but now the pains slowly subsided; she was being properly attended to, relaxing, resting and recovering.

She was going to need all the strength she could get. Ahead lay a pleasant surprise, despondency, and further confrontation with the British Administration office-wallahs protecting their territory!

CHAPTER 36

A Week Can Be A Long Time In Paris

Lying in bed all day recovering just didn't suit her. It is possible she took things at a slightly slower pace, but that would have been about the limits of her concessions to doctors' orders. Two days later she was up and about: *"Got up in the afternoon. Pain still there, but cough improving."*

Those wretched Passes were not to be denied, and the next day, under the watchful eye of Cole-Hamilton, she was off to Chalons-sur-Marne to get her Pass renewed. Rather gruesomely she reports that they *"saw an aeroplane taken away after an accident – all blood and bits of flesh"*.

The 1st of May saw her 'unpacking cases' again, just four days after her blood-letting! Some tents had arrived, and after several nights of constant bombing around Epernay, not far away – *"awful noise, flashes all night"* – they erected them in a field nearby so that they could sleep out. *"Much fresher and nicer."* It was going to be a very hot summer. As fate would have it, the night after the tents had been set up, all the FANY ambulance crews were called out to air raids on Troissy a few miles away, from the early hours of the morning until well into the afternoon. Grace noted that she slept for an hour in the tent. Presumably before the call-out.

About that time she also mentions *"two Boches in – one dying with sunstroke – quite delirious"*. She rounded up this entry next day with just two words: *"Boche died"*. The entries carried no word of pity, far removed from the loving, caring Grace she really was. For the rest of her life she never forgave the Germans for the deaths of her two brothers.

The next day she and Doris Allen set out for Paris. In no hurry, they hitched a lift to Chateau Thiery, and after a leisurely lunch finished the journey by train. Grace was relaxed and happy, writing: *"country gorgeous – masses of blossoms on every side"* – although one of her reasons for going to Paris was, as she wrote rather ominously *"I shall see Boutiron and have it out with him!"*. He was a senior official in the French Red Cross HQ with whom she had had many brushes, particularly about Passes.

It was to be the start of a rather bittersweet week, had she but known it. In Paris the Metro had broken down. Grace and Doris booked into a nearby hotel, unaware that Grace's husband was staying the night at the Grand Hotel, not far away. He was heading for Binson to see her, thinking she was still in bed with pleurisy.

More relaxed, Grace called on her old friend Baroness Mannerheim the following day, went shopping, and managed to see M. Boutiron briefly at about 6 o'clock, who fixed an appointment for the following day.

Meanwhile Ronald made his way to the Priory Hospital outside Binson, all unfamiliar territory to him. There he was brought up to date on Grace's whereabouts and spent some time trying to reach her through the Red Cross connections. Finally, he stayed the night at Binson, as it was going to be quite impossible to get back to Paris.

He did, however, send a wire to their friend the Baroness, knowing that Grace would be sure to contact her if in Paris.

When Grace got to M. Boutiron's office, she was surprised to find the Baroness there as well, with Ronald's telegram! Of course, she was over the moon, wasted an hour trying to reach him by phone, eventually sending him a wire, urging him to get back as soon as possible. Which he did, but not until late that night.

A week in Paris, for two young newly-weds, separated by war for such long periods, should have been idyllic. In reality their time together was fragmented, and disrupted continually by Grace's commitments. What should have been a time of pleasure and excitement, was spoiled.

They tried to make the most of it, roaming around Paris, seeing the sights at their best, in glorious summer weather. They took a boat down the Seine, went shopping in the *chic* Paris boutiques. In drab khaki uniform she may have been, but it certainly didn't diminish Grace's feminine side. She records in her diary: *"Bought some shoes 65Frs a pair – awful – price, but they are pretty ones – also silk stockings & the dinkiest garters."*

There was afternoon tea at the fabulous Rumpelmeyers; then the equally famous Café de Paris at night – *"Weird place – awful women, full of English officers"* was Grace's comment. They walked for miles, happy to be together.

But these periods were interrupted and obstructed by Grace being called away constantly. She had to go to the de Dion works at Puteau with Mr Sawyer to deal with vehicle problems. Then there were interminable meetings at Red Cross Headquarters; separate meetings with M. Boutiron; there were FANYs up to collect goods; others departing on leave, returning from leave.

They went to another well known café for afternoon tea. It was not a happy experience. Grace wrote *"Rotten on Sundays. Waiter tried to cheat Ronald of 5 Frs. Failure!"*

After a bit Ronald was 'thoroughly fed up with Paris'. Towns were never really his 'thing', being much more at home in wide open spaces. Grace now had to return to Binson. She and Ronald would both much rather have gone off somewhere alone for the time that was left to them, but it just wasn't possible. Once again she was trapped in the manacles of duty. Ronald went with her.

On their first full day there, Grace was called away to Chalons to collect or change those so-necessary Passes. She went in the de Dion expecting a quick journey there and back, but almost inevitably the car broke down, and she had to hitch a lift back to Binson. She records she was "very cross and tired", no mood to be in on Ronald's last night of leave.

Her sadness and despondency at their flawed week together really began to show through at this point. She was downcast and wistful, filled with a feeling of helplessness, so alien to a woman of her character. *"Wandered about. Ronald's last night. Wish we could have had proper leave, right away from Corps and work."*

The following day Doris Allen drove them to Chateau Thierry. There they said their goodbyes – Ronald to return to his unit, Grace back to Binson. It affected her deeply. That night's diary entry was full of misery and sadness. *"So...till the next time. I am so tired, I wish we could be together really; endless partings, and giving up, and doing without, and endless females, and always worry.*

"And people are afraid to die!

"Why?"

There is an awful note of despair in those words, a heart-wrenching *cri de coeur*. Just how strained were those sunny days together, Grace recovering from illness, Ronald with the stress of going back to the hell of the Front Line? And just maybe, a touch of jealousy, hence her nebulous reference to 'endless females'. Ronald was a man of great charm, full of laughter and twinkling blue eyes.

For a few days she involved herself furiously unpacking stores of one sort or another, doing all sorts of physical tasks to get her mind off things. Then, once again into action.

She had been in talks with the French authorities, for the FANY to provide reliefs for the *Directrice* of a French Army canteen, Le Foyer de Soldats, at a place called Fismes. Relations with the French were at a high point, and Grace readily agreed to this new venture, thinking it was only to be for a month.

She decided to visit it, see for herself, and meet Miss Joseph who ran it, and who was due a month's leave. Setting out with the Russell-Allen sisters, Doris and Gerry, they made good time. Even at Binson there was the constant booming of the guns 20 miles away, and the sinister rumblings got a lot louder as they neared Fismes. There they met Miss Joseph, listened to what she had to say, had a leisurely look around, and approved of what they saw.

Leaving rather later than they intended, they decided to go via Ville en Tardenois, lost their way, and found themselves much nearer the Front than was healthy. It was getting dark, and soon they were taking turns to walk in front with a torch, as headlights were not permitted.

Passing through a completely strange village, they *"picked up a poor Poilu with a wounded head, walking to railhead for Epernay, but he was pretty far gone so we slung him aboard"*.

They drove on, not really clear where they were. There was a lot of artillery activity – "star shells everywhere and big flashes". They had no idea where they were, neither did their patient! Though she later tried to find that village again, Grace never did.

They finally managed to get home safely, and next day they were back to the 'unpacking' routine. However, the French confirmed the arrangement quite quickly, and would let Grace know when her girls were needed, a day or two before Miss Joseph departed on leave.

Time passed rapidly, with little of note happening. Grace

celebrated her 31st birthday. The staff gave her a "lovely silver Vanity Bag" and had planned a birthday picnic tea in the grounds of the Priory, but that fell through due to the funeral of a leading Pere Blanc. It was held in the Cloisters, instead, which later drew a gentle rebuke from the Father Superior about holding 'revelries' in the Priory!

Meanwhile there was plenty to do at Binson Hospital. Grace was constantly on the lookout for anything that would entertain the recovering wounded. On a visit to a local Mayor with food and clothing collected for the poor of the town, there was a military band playing nearby. She talked her way into meeting with the C.O. of the Regiment, the 147th Infantry, and asked him if his band would play at the hospital. He agreed immediately, and Grace invited him and his officers to come along to tea at the same time.

Shortly after that, she had the personal satisfaction of being informed officially that Queen Alexandra of the Belgians "had been pleased to accept her gift of her book, Nursing Adventures".

That very day, she received a phone call from the French authorities that the FANY were to take over the *Foyer de Soldats* at Fismes in two days time. This was a particularly tense time in the French Army. Because of the dreadful losses incurred by abortive onslaughts against the German lines, the morale of both soldiers and civilians was at rock bottom and a number of mutinies had already taken place. In fact, there had been one at Fismes the previous Sunday, in which the men had locked up all their officers at gunpoint.

The paperwork for the temporary take-over of the *Foyer de Soldats* arrived, involving Grace in a frenzy of form-filling and letters to keep the Administrators happy. She finally set out for Fismes at about 5.30 p.m., getting there without any trouble. Leaving Andy Anderson, who was to be in charge, and a Mrs Wybrants, with Miss Joseph she set off back to Binson. She noted that she was held up by *"a terrible storm, had to sit in car for rain & hail & lightning. Heard thunderbolt, trees knocked down. Ran into a mutiny at Ville en Tardenois, men all drunk. Got home about 10"*. Such understatement of what must have been an exciting – and frightening – set of circumstances, was the normal FANY response.

Fismes was just 14 miles from the Front Line, and under almost continuous bombardment. Because of the way they carried on under fire daily, the French troops called them *Les Petites Soldats* for the bravery they displayed. It had always been busy, but Anderson and her girls greatly improved the place by the huge spring clean they gave it. Among the very large numbers of French troops they served, fresh from the Lines, they made a great name for themselves, and the Corps, even though only there for a month.

Soon after her return she was to have a good deal more to worry her. For a long time, since the war began, the FANY Corps had been a thorn in the side of the British Military Establishment because of their independence. Right from the start they had been told that there would never be women driving for the British Army. This had been the main aim of the Corps, but undeterred by the British attitude, they had carried on, driving for the Belgian and the French armies.

Finally, the fuse was lit in 1917, when the British Administration in Calais woke up to the fact that, in spite of all the obstacles and refusals they had constantly put in the way of the FANYs, here they were, in a large and important British Controlled sector, doing ALL the driving for ALL the hospitals in the area, Belgian, French AND British. They moved, loaded, unloaded, transferred, collected all wounded in the area. During the frequent and continued air raids on Calais, it was the FANY who turned out to pick up all casualties, civil and military, whatever nationality.

And yet they were still a volunteer, independent body, who ruled themselves. No matter how good they were, this was a state of affairs which, in the mind of the Military, could not be allowed to continue. In this, the Army were strongly backed by the British Red Cross (BRCS) who were not happy with the FANY Corps for much the same reasons. They were too independent. They should be either Red Cross or VAD.

Between them, the Army and the BRCS hatched a plan to abolish the Corps for good. If they cut off the head of the serpent, the rest would follow. They were in no doubt as to the identity of the 'Head' they were after. If they destroyed Mrs McDougall and her powerful and well organised Unit 5, attached to the Belgian Army, they had no doubt at all that they could get rid of the rest with little effort.

Grace had made a few enemies in her determined quest for expansion of the Corps, but she had also made a great many friends, some in high places. The whole episode is a bit misty – little appears in records – but somebody tipped Grace off about the plan while she was at Binson, soon after her trip back from Fismes.

She lost no time. Returning as quickly as she could to Calais, and to her Unit 5 Headquarters, she went straight to the General Commanding the Belgian section. He listened attentively, and swung into action.

Every FANY in Unit 5 was paraded in front of the Base Commandant, and his Chief of Staff, an aptly name Colonel Dieu-Donne. They were subjected to every step required by the Belgian Army to be enlisted – weighed, measured, photographed, and sworn in as *Soldats de la Corps de Transporte de l'Armee Belge*. They were then issued with the blue gorgets and silver badges of rank, as used in the Belgian Army.

The following day, as Grace had been tipped off they would, a delegation from the British Red Cross stormed into the Base, bent on eliminating the FANY. They were escorted to the Mess where they were met by the Base Commandant. He greeted them very courteously, and asked to what did he owe the honour of their visit.

He was told, rather bluntly, that they had come to tell the FANY that their services were no longer required, their passes would be withdrawn, and they would be sent home.

At this the Belgian General drew himself up. In the most dramatic tones he directed their attention to the fact that on this Base they were standing on Belgian soil, and the ladies in question were all Soldiers of the Belgian Army Transport Corps, over whom the BRCS had no jurisdiction.

The delegation was utterly poleaxed. It was game, set, and match to the FANY! Never again did the Establishment, either Civil or Military, try anything of that nature. And the FANYs in future worked under the auspices of the army, rather than the Red Cross.

There were those in the British administration who were not at all happy with this outcome. They sat and they brooded, and looked for revenge. It wasn't long before they got it.

CHAPTER 37

The Army's Revenge

The brush with the British Administration/Red Cross consortium came at a time when the FANY Corps' standing with the French was at its highest yet. The enormous contribution they were making in Calais dealing with the wounded was seen, recognized and appreciated. Night after night they were out during air raids – 193 unleashed on the port – in addition to their daytime chores, making them something of a legend. Even the rather dour and suspicious French civilians stood slightly in awe of these English *demoiselles*, watching, and exclaiming among themselves *"le bon DIEU protège les FANYs"*!

The hospital at Binson, under the energetic direction of Cole-Hamilton, was also earning passionate plaudits from all the French Top Brass who were constantly coming to inspect it.

Grace realised it was an ideal time to widen the scope of the FANY working for the French. Although they were running the hospital at Binson, there was not yet a Motor Convoy serving the French directly. All the work for them in Calais was carried out by FANY Unit 5, her own Belgian convoy.

Still deeply involved in overseeing the work being done in Calais and Binson, she nevertheless made time to draw up plans for a new convoy for the French. Mid-June 1917 she travelled to Paris. After a meeting with her old sparring partner, M. Boutiron, at the HQ of the French Red Cross, it was on to French Army HQ at rue Pinet, where she met a Captain Anjay. A long discussion about the employment of FANY drivers followed. The talks went well. Later Grace wrote down, in French, details of the plan, and the terms she envisaged in the contract.

The following day she was back again at rue Pinet, and gave Capt. Anjay the draft contract to read. He *"was fearfully keen, was all over it – asked me to rewrite it all in English, which I did in his office"*.

Leaving Paris on the night train to Calais, she arrived on the English convoy's doorstep at Gare Centrale early in the morning.

She writes: "*Surprised them all at the Gare! Saw cars etc. Franklin turned up in morning. Very much taken aback at seeing me – says she has at last got St. Omer.*" [New convoy for the British they had both been working towards.] That was great news after the long and protracted negotiations they had endured. In spite of everything, the British Administration was still allergic to women drivers.

On making her way up to her own HQ at the Belgian Convoy, there was more good news awaiting her – "*splendid report on Unit 5 from the Minister for War at Le Havre.*" At the time, Unit 5 was dealing with over 4000 casualties a month.

While there, she confirmed with the French that Unit 5 would do "*all the French work in future*" adding that "*arrangements have been made for petrol, and for a wonder everyone is satisfied*".

This was so typical of Grace, always several balls in the air at once, as she juggled her way along the path to FANY 'progression'. The Belgians were very happy to 'lend' their much enlarged convoy to the French. They were also, now, to provide transport for all the French Military Hospitals in the Calais area, as well as continuing to make their vehicles available to both French and Belgian civil authorities during air raids.

Grace was delighted at the progress: a new English convoy at St. Omer, and much wider responsibilities accorded to the Belgian convoy. The growing confidence being shown in the FANY began to produce more practical results, reflected by new equipment and better accommodation. Grace tells us in Five Years with the Allies: "*Six new GMC ambulances arrived from Le Havre, & a new barrack was erected for the new drivers, and I had a telephone put in my office.*" This last was something of a personal triumph, as telephones were in great demand and short supply. Everything seemed to be going well, and once more Grace, though anxiously awaiting news of her plan for the French convoy, was riding high.

Towards the end of July the news came through. Captain Anjay telephoned her inviting her to a further meeting in Paris. There she was told that, with minor adjustments, her plan for the first French convoy had been approved. It would be known as FANY Unit 6. Better than that, though, was the surprise location picked for them to operate in: Amiens. Grace wrote: "*An unexpected stroke of luck. Amiens is the largest French Hospital Centre, and this was a great honour."*

Under this Agreement the French Army supplied the FANY with vehicles, board and lodging, free rail travel, and later on, a Messing allowance, and even sheepskin coats to protect them against the freezing winter cold.

As usual wasting no time, Grace travelled down to Amiens that same evening. There she inspected the cars provided – Peugeots, Renaults and Panhards – and was not very impressed by their condition. Her contact was a Capt. Taffourman, and through him she arranged board and accommodation for the girls when they arrived. This really was an important breakthrough, and Taffourman turned out to be very helpful at all times.

Rushing back to her office in Calais, she got down to informing people of the development, deciding on commanders, arranging drivers. Binson itself was a major French enterprise, and now this convoy that was to work for them added a new dimension.

In the midst of all this activity, Grace became a fascinated spectator in a bizarre incident. A German submarine had come in too close to the shore at Wissant, near Calais, and was stranded on the beach when the tide went out.

A sentry at the camp of a Belgian cavalry regiment spotted it and raised the alarm. A troop of Lancers galloped out, surrounded the U-boat, calling on the crew to surrender. Which they did, after destroying all the ship's papers, and blowing a hole in the hull. The Commandant of the Guides Cavalry, a crack Belgian Regiment, knew Grace would relish the opportunity. She wrote later: *"Col. De Donne dashed in with his big Hispano-Suiza car, and took me out to see the Germans. We met the officer and his men being marched into Calais".* Apparently one of the prisoners made some remark about the Allies starving, and they were all marched to the nearest butcher's shop, and shown the array of meats and other foods on display!

Though enjoying her brief involvement in an event which must be unique in the annals of any navy or army, Grace had to get on. She desperately needed drivers for the new unit, with little time to spend recruiting them. London HQ apparently accepted the commitment without demur, as it involved no capital expenditure, vehicles and accommodation being supplied by the French.

Time was of the essence. There was less than a month to get it on the road. Drivers were the problem. The brief was for 20 drivers to be based at Amiens. The new Secretary in London, Irene Cowan, was desperately trying to speed the despatch of drivers to France, but encountered what was becoming, for some reason, standard stone-walling and delaying tactics by the London Committee of the French Red Cross (LCFRC). It was on this occasion that Cowan described Mrs Watson – a senior member of that organization, whom Grace admired – as thoroughly disagreeable, someone who did all she could to delay the process.

This all took much longer than anticipated, even after Grace's entry into the fray. FANY drivers already on active service were transferred into the new Unit 6. Doris Allen was put in overall command of French operations, while Joan Bowles took command of the Amiens Unit itself.

The convoy started work towards the end of August. Very short staffed they may have been, but being FANYs, they coped! Long hours, short breaks, single-mindedness and always cheerful, they won admiration and respect from all sides. Bowles was able to report that *"we never failed to send a car the moment a call came in"*.

The French doctors apparently laid bets on when the girls would give in, and no doubt that was partly responsible for their dogged determination to carry on.

There was another major difficulty. The male drivers and mechanics who were being replaced by the FANYs were angry. They simmered with resentment at their jobs being taken by women. Their vehicles were in pretty poor shape as it was, well below the standard accepted by the FANYs themselves. But the French drivers went further, and deliberately sabotaged the cars, in various ways. They would then stand back, smirking, with a 'now fix that' look on their faces.

However, the girls did *fix that*, usually making a better job of it than the former operators. This tended to make the French angrier still, especially when an officer rebuked one of them, suggesting he took lessons from the women.

Eventually the skill, ability, and constant cheerfulness of the FANYs won the day. Vastly impressed with the way the girls maintained the decrepit and worn out vehicles the French authorities were shamed into replacing them.

At last it all came together. The men's attitude changed; there was admiration for the work *'les FANYs'* were doing in difficult and dangerous circumstances; new FANY drivers began to arrive from England. The girls were doing an extraordinary amount of vital work for the large and scattered French hospital complex in and around Amiens.

It was too good to last.

It didn't.

Back in the rear echelons of the British Administration and Red Cross ranks, there were those who sulked and smarted. There was a perceived humiliation in the defeat they had suffered attempting to eliminate Grace and the FANY Belgian convoy. They began searching for loopholes – and found one.

With large organizations from three nations operating in a comparatively small area, there had to be clearly defined sectors of sovereignty. Amiens, close to the Front Line and in a restricted area, was located in the British sector, which housed one of the largest French Hospital Centres. British women drivers were not allowed to work for the British authorities there, it being so close to the Front Line, yet here were British FANYs driving for the French within that prohibited area. Outrageous. More heinous still was the fact that the French had not asked permission of the British before employing them.

This was just the loophole they had been seeking. It could not be tolerated. Those looking for vengeance had found a great pretext for indignation. The NIMBY factor! They couldn't stop the French employing British women, but could – and did – cry – *'not in my backyard'*.

The first intimation of trouble was a message from Joan Bowles in mid-September informing Grace that the French had not applied for authority for the FANYs to work in the British sector.

Grace went straight off to the Base Headquarters in Calais, even though it was a Sunday. There she eventually saw the Chief Intelligence Officer, with no result. Despite her follow-up efforts, a few days later she was to record *"Gt. flap at Amiens. Letter from Bowles they are leaving for Villers-Cotterets. She is delighted."*

Next morning Grace headed for Amiens, noting laconically *"Good run, barring three burst tyres!"*.

There, getting no satisfactory answers to what was going on, and after two days of fruitless enquiries, she headed for Paris, and spent the whole day at the Ministry of War arguing her case. The French were sympathetic, but it was all in vain. The British were apparently quite adamant. The FANY must move out of Amiens.

Leaving Paris at 10 p.m. she headed back to Amiens. She was not in a happy frame of mind. The high hopes she had had for this first major French motor convoy appeared to have gone up in smoke. The time Unit 6 had spent at Amiens was a mere six weeks, but once again the girls had displayed those most valued and enduring attributes – courage, competence and good humour. They would be remembered for that.

The establishment blimps at the British H.Q. had had their revenge, but in reality had won nothing. Only contempt. At least the convoy lived on, at Villers-Cotterets in the Marne Valley. Her lips tightened as she determined it would not just stop there. She would make sure it expanded again into a major force.

Arriving at the house that had so recently been their quarters, she found it locked and deserted. Unit 6 had finally departed.

By now it was well past midnight. Angry, frustrated and weary, she broke in and spent the rest of the night there.

Grace

Six of the FANY contingent

The Grave at Boulogne Cemetery of
Grace's older brother Charles

Her younger brother Billy's grave
at Armentieres Cemetery

Grace and comrades

Unit 5 FANYs

FANYs of Unit 5 driving for Belgian War Office

FANYs with the Queen

HM Queen Elisabeth of Belgium

Grace in 1914

Charlie died of Wounds 22-5-1915

Billy killed in action 25-1-1916

Grace's husband Capt Ronald McDougall

CHAPTER 38

Trouble In The Marne Valley

She woke refreshed, but still not happy. Bitterly disappointed that the French had been unable to change the minds of their British counterparts, and furious with the British for the stand they had taken, she reluctantly adjusted to the situation. So often there were these minor spats between the Allies, as she knew only too well. She had to return to Calais.

At least Unit 6 was still up and running albeit on a reduced scale at Villers-Cotterets. Grace determined that she would return as soon as possible to put pressure on the French locally and get things sorted out. This she was good at, and knew it.

In Calais she wasted no time in clearing the paperwork that had built up in her absence. Topping up with money, she noted in her diary on an optimistic note: "Got petrol etc, ready to start."

It wasn't to be. As so often in the past, the war intervened, this time uncomfortably close! The Germans launched a major air offensive on the Channel Ports.

Next day her diary records: *"Awful bomb raid started – fell all around our Mess, before we could move."* The bombs rained down hour after hour, falling on The Citadel, the French Barracks, the Railway Station.

Telephone lines were down all over, and a messenger on a bicycle struggled through the rubbled streets to ask the FANY to turn out. They responded immediately, already expecting the summons to duty. It was all hands to the pumps as their battered old vehicles drove into town. In the smoke and destruction, all thoughts of Unit 6 faded.

At the Place de L'Armée – *"Lots of dead & wounded,"* Grace wrote. She recognized that the immediate need lay here – now – in Calais. She revelled in the excitement of it all. What she didn't know then was that the air assault would continue day after day, night after night. Brief but graphic details appear in her diary at the time.

"Rue d'Havre, 2 cellars smashed – 19 people inside, one woman saw

husband & both ch. killed one a baby."

Again, *"Woman dug out at 3.30 a.m. gave her our Sal Volatile!"*

Even when the raids temporarily died away, there was much work to be done: casualties to be transferred between hospitals; medical staff and supplies to be moved around; the dead transported to morgues. All this through streets often blocked with bomb debris.

After one all-night session with their ambulances, Grace and her teams got back to their Mess, bone weary and looking for sleep. *"5 a.m. got home,"* she records, then *"early evac. (all cars but 2) at 5.45!"* – which meant rushing out to transfer wounded from an incoming hospital train to various hospitals in Calais. Once again they answered the call, *"finally getting to bed around 8 o/c, slept till 12"*. And so it went on. Grace set out to try to obtain sandbags to help protect their quarters against the bombs. She had no success. *"Tried place after place, all red tape. Another alarm at night."*

It was a testing time for all of them. The following night: *"Raids began at 8.30 went on till 1 a.m. Lay down drest* (sic) *and slept till 7."* Then more air raids at 12.30. *"Fire alarms, shrapnel everywhere."*

There was more to come, even as October arrived and the raids were easing off. Sadly she recalls for that night: *"Raiders. One woman – 2 children killed by shell at 1.30 in Rue Gambetta. Night alarm."*

Then began the grim task of burying the dead. It was war, and the FANY had to turn their hands to anything. Hearses were in such short supply that Grace was approached by the authorities, asking if they would help out by lending their ambulances. She readily agreed, and three Panhard ambulances were allocated, each carrying three coffins. Once again the FANY drivers won admiration for their skill in handling their makeshift hearses at a walking speed, keeping pace with the mourners – no mean feat with the cars of that time.

More than 40 people were buried that day. Everyone hoped that the bad weather had brought an end to the raids, but that evening the skies cleared and the bombers returned. *"Awful noise at night. Heavy firing. Bombs on gunners."*

It really was the last throw for the time being. Winter weather closed in, and Grace recorded on October 3rd: *"Rain & wind. Everybody hopes to sleep tonight."*

They did, thankfully.

Next morning, a FANY driver, Faulder, attached to UNIT 6 at Villers-Cotterets, arrived with an urgent message from Bowles. The unit had had a nightmarish journey from Amiens to Villers-Cotterets, relieved only by the unstinting assistance given them by the locally based Scottish Women's Advance Hospital Unit (SWAHU) who looked after them for the few days before they were found a billet by the French.

This turned out to be a disused Pork Butcher's shop, filthy, cramped, smelly, and utterly unsuitable. Not only was there a total lack of furniture, but by all accounts there was also a ghost which groaned frequently, and played the cello as well! The local French authority, it seemed, were not prepared to do anything about it. A billet was a billet. *Voila!*

The girls were also upset that the amount of work they were being given was nothing like what they were used to.

Once again, on getting the news from Faulder, Grace was furious with the French. Where her girls were concerned she was fiercely protective. During her campaign in Paris against the French giving way to British demands so easily, she understood she might lose the battle, and so had got an undertaking from the French that if they had to move, her girls would be properly looked after, fed and housed. This was like a red rag to a bull. The following day she swept into action. She headed for Villers-Cotterets.

Just before leaving, she received a phone call from the British Consul-General in Calais, to tell her he was recommending her for the OBE (Order of the British Empire). Thanking him, she pointed out she was on the verge of leaving to sort out an urgent problem, and would get back to him sometime. Whether she did is not recorded, but the recommendation was apparently not implemented.

Things didn't go smoothly. Grace herself had a hellish journey, having decided to go via Amiens to have yet another discussion – for want of a better word – with the French Medical Authorities based there. This, she felt, went well. She left them in no doubt that her girls must be properly housed, and given more work to do. She was told they were being transferred to Chateau Thierry, a bigger and busier centre, where there was a large clearing hospital.

In a happier frame of mind she set off for Villers-Cotterets and Unit 6 only to have her car break down at Compiegne. There three French mechanics worked on it continuously, but even so it wasn't ready until midnight. It was an example of Grace's single-mindedness that she set out immediately. Unfortunately she took the wrong road and got stuck in deep mud. Walking to the nearest town, Pierrefonds, and arriving around 2.30 a.m., weary and very fed up, she telephoned one of her many contacts, a Capt Duhern – one can only imagine his feelings at being woken at that time of the morning – and was directed to a large Military Transport Centre in the town.

Duhern, Transport Admin Officer at French Area HQ, must have phoned the depot. Grace was immediately looked after – a truck drove her out to her vehicle, towed it out of the mud, and all the way to Villers-Cotterets, by early morning, worn out. To her initial dismay she found that Unit 6 had already left for Chateau Thierry. She was able to snatch a few hours' sleep, before meeting up with Duhern. They had a long discussion in the afternoon, in which Grace rammed home the message that a lot of things had to change, fast, not least the accommodation. Duhern assured her it was all in hand. Unit 6 was already settled in Chateau Thierry, and a good billet had been found for them there.

With her mind set at rest, Grace called on the Scottish Women's Hospital section to have tea with them and thank them for their recent help to her girls. Looking forward to a good night's sleep, before heading for Chateau Thierry, she was to be horribly disappointed. Her diary records: *"Awful night, no blankets slept in clothes & leather coat froze awake at 4 a.m. awful billet."* She doesn't reveal where she was billeted!

Later in the morning Capt. Duhern drove her to Chateau Thierry where she inspected the quarters allocated to Unit 6, and was disgusted. According to her diary, they were: *"Awful! Bare rooms big enough for 3, with straw! Went with him* (Duhern) *to Place* (local French HQ) *got furnished house – Fixed lunch at Hotel for all the others & got installed in house in afternoon"*. When she was in fighting mood, and where her girls were concerned, Grace took no prisoners. She was desperately sorry they had had to put up with the butcher's shop at Villers-Cotterets, while she was held up by the air raids on Calais. It wouldn't happen again if she could help it.

Now she was happy, getting this large furnished house and garden for them. Not only that, but the French came across with additional perks. Each girl would not only get rations, but an allowance for washing and Messing.

It was not all good news. The vehicles supplied by the French were decrepit, badly maintained and liable to fall apart at any time. Some would not even start. However, it wasn't the first time the FANY had been lumbered with this sort of car, and most were by now expert in coaxing the brutes to perform miracles.

With accommodation, allowances and vehicles agreed and provided by the French, Unit 6 started work promptly at 9 a.m. on October 8th in their new base, and were soon almost back to the frenetic regime they had gone through in those brief weeks at Amiens. Grace was there and watched with pride to see them get started again.

Basing herself temporarily at Chateau Thierry, she shuttled up and down the Marne Valley dealing with local French Medical Authorities. Whenever she felt she was getting bogged down by the locals, she would race up to Paris to the Rue Pinet HQ, or the Anglo French Red Cross, to get things sorted out.

Even with all the pressure she was under, she was never one to miss a bit of fun. While introducing Bowles to the Unit Books, she was told of a Fancy Dress Dinner to be held at Binson. She went along disguised as a French officer, and according to her diary: *"Nobody knew me!"* This was so typical of Grace who loved parties and dressing up.

Once Grace was satisfied that Unit 6 had settled in well at Chateau Thierry, and all was running smoothly, she began searching for further outlets in that French zone. Travelling down to Chalons sur Marne to meet with a Staff Captain responsible for transport in that area, she was delighted to be told by him that the FANY cars he inspected at Binson *"were the best kept of his Group"*. Never one to miss an opportunity she immediately came straight back with *"that was said everywhere of the FANYs!"*

A couple of days later a Staff Captain, le Lorrain, from the French HQ at Chalons, came down to Chateau Thierry to ask Grace why she had engaged 20 more drivers. She immediately told him of

her plans for expansion, the need for far greater coverage along the
Marne Valley, around 200 km. Such was her enthusiasm and powers
of persuasion that they agreed there and then to the idea of a new
unit to be based at Epernay, with sections at Chalons sur Marne, and
Bar-le-Duc further along the valley.

That same afternoon she drove down to Chalons, meeting again
with Capt le Lorrain and one of his colleagues, Capt. Mythereon.
"Measured huts," she noted. *"Huts for Eps (*Epernay*) fixed also – 10
cubicles & Messroom, new Mors cars. Waiting drivers now."*

Although some weeks would pass before the new Unit 7 moved
in to Epernay, Grace and the two Staff Captains had laid the
foundations for the project; all was ready for them. Her efforts had
paid off. She had yet another convoy for the French.

It was November by the time Unit 7 was operational, having
been welcomed with open arms by the staff of the major Clearing
Hospital at Epernay, and plied with flowers, cakes and champagne.

Between them, Units 6 & 7 had a very large stretch of territory
to cover, heavily militarised, and for that reason subject to constant
air raids. Their task was made still more difficult by one of the worst
winters on record, bitter cold, continual snow and ice, the most
appalling driving conditions.

Living conditions were no better. The cubicles were not insulated,
heaters didn't work properly, fuel was scarce.

Grace visited these widely-spaced units of hers as best she
could, despite the weather, doing what she could to get the French
to respond to the situation. They did try, but were in much the same
predicament themselves, at the mercy of the elements.

Back in Calais for a flying visit in November she was once again
involved in the air raids. *"Bombardment!"* she writes. *"17 wounded
6 killed we got them all – Moses & I were there first of anyone & had to
tie them up and sort them out."* Some gruesome details. *"I had to help
the Military Policemen lift a woman's body onto the stretcher & carry
the stretcher because her head was off and all the men round Eng. & Fr.
were afraid to touch her, poor soul. Awful night 1 Eng. Tommy killed & 1
wounded."*

The long winter dragged on, Grace shuttling back and forth
between her HQ in Calais, the large Hospital at Binson, and along the

Marne Valley keeping a special eye on her teams in Chateau Thierry, Chalons, Epernay and Bar-le-Duc. It was taxing for her, but even more tiring and dangerous for the FANYs out driving constantly in dreadful conditions.

It wasn't just the danger under their wheels they had to contend with, but the frequent and increasing air raids as German aircraft were improving all the time. There was little respite. Calais and Boulogne were prime targets, and had been for a long time – so much so that Grace and her girls were becoming almost blasé about them. There was a dugout close to Grace's office in Calais, and during air raids she and Marples would sit on the top step in the open listening for the phone to ring. One or other would then run across and answer it, triggering a call-out.

This was considered dangerous, and the Governor kindly offered to have a phone installed for them inside the dugout. Unfortunately this fell through, as the British Administration decided that the Belgian quota of phones in the area was complete!

The Belgian Area Commandant, General Clooten, an old comrade of Grace's from the early days in Ghent, then begged them to let him put men on duty instead "so that they could stay under cover". This was refused because the FANY decided *"we did a better job looking after casualties than men"*.

Shortly after, the British Base Commander wrote to the Belgian Commandant to say that British women drivers were **not** allowed out in air raids, and asking him to forbid it. This was forwarded to Grace marked "SEEN AND APPROVED". She gave it short shrift. Scribbling across it *"SEEN AND **NOT** APPROVED"*, she sent it back. No more was said.

The 3rd Battle of Ypres was in progress, and casualties were pouring in. Belgian Unit 5 was handling 6000 casualties a month. Similar numbers were flowing through Franklin's British Unit 3; Units 6 & 7 along the Marne were inundated with French wounded.

Pressures were enormous, and a small tragedy was waiting to happen. Shortly before Christmas, Baxter-Ellis ran into two men in a street, killing one. It was the first time anything like this had happened, and everyone felt it. Grace wrote: *"(Ellis) is in dreadful state of nerves, poor kid. Everyone upset."* The Court of Enquiry was held on

Christmas Eve and Ellis cleared of blame, but it must have had an effect on the Christmas celebrations.

They did their best. It was the last Christmas of the war, had they but known. All were war weary and saddened one way or another. Grace spent it in Calais. She wrote: *"Got 2 big turkeys from Boulogne. Big Mess dinner. Great success. Mess looked very pretty. Played games afterwards."* A brief, bald statement covering the sadness they all felt within themselves; recent events; separation from their families. But each of them, from veterans like Grace and Franklin to the rawest recruit to arrive, knew they were there by their own choice, and understood why they were giving up so much.

As yet another year of war drew to a close, there was a sense that the FANY had proved itself, virtually in the heat of battle; and among the girls a tremendous sense of comradeship and belonging, which they would never have experienced back home.

For Grace, and her old friend Cole-Hamilton who had supervised and run L'Hôpital Binson so successfully, 1918 was to bring an unpleasant shock with a bitter aftertaste.

But before that, Grace was to experience great personal sadness as an old comrade and staunch ally moved out of her life.

CHAPTER 39

Farewell To General Clooten

The King of the Belgians' annual Fete was celebrated towards the end of that year. It was tinged with sadness for Grace, as her old friend General Clooten was to be replaced as the Belgian Area Military Commander. There was a service in the Cathedral as part of the Fete, and Grace, who had had been given a prime seat, watched Clooten come in with the new General and a group of VIPs, and, she couldn't help but notice, *"came out first – all alone"*.

Later that afternoon he made a surprise visit to The Mess at Belgian FANY Unit 5. There he was welcomed by the FANYs, who knew how much he had helped them in so many ways. He made a long and moving speech thanking the FANY for all they had done for L'Armée Belge, and Belgium.

After lunch next day, Grace went up to General Clooten's house to say her personal goodbyes. It was most obviously an emotional meeting, a parting of great poignancy for her. From their first brief meetings in the chaotic time of siege and evacuation of Antwerp and Ghent in 1914, their relationship had grown with mutual respect. He had been commanding the Belgian 7th Division then, and when Grace returned from England, he was Commandant of the Belgian area of Calais.

There is a sense of grief and almost despondency at their farewell. She writes about it at some length in her diary. *"He was so kind and nice and is so sad about going."* He opened up his heart to her. *"He said he had been married very young – at 20, and his wife was 19 – but they were very much in love and were still, and they had always been together and now for 3 years he had to live alone. – He was very sad, and says he goes from here to – he knows not where, to live in hotels or rooms – alone."*

There is so much anguish and distress in the words of this tired old man, heavy responsibilities on his shoulders, unsure whether he will ever see again the wife he loves so much. Here they are, Belgian General and young Scots girl, in a foreign land, both separated from family and friends in their respective countries.

Grace continues: *"He said beautiful things about our work & what he thought of the FANY & then I cried & he cried & he kissed me on both cheeks – & I just squeezed his hand and pressed it to my lips and ran away with tears rolling down my cheeks & he stood with his eyes brimming over – Poor old Gen Clooten – I am so sorry for him – and he has been so very good to me always."*

As she was leaving the house, her old friend Colonel Dieu-Donne ran out to greet her and shake hands, but she couldn't face him just at that moment, writing, *"I made Marples drive off quickly"*.

And so they parted, each deeply saddened, to go their separate ways, their paths dictated by the immutable exigencies of war.

CHAPTER 40

The Unkindest Cut Of All

For months, as 1917 drew to a close, the hospital at Binson had gone from strength to strength. Cole-Hamilton and her team had done an amazing job. Now completely unrecognizable from the filthy, scruffy shambles the FANY had inherited from the French, it was held up as a role model for other French Military Hospitals.

Inspections by French Medical Brass-hats were frequent, and were routinely accompanied by plaudits and congratulations.

The hospital was an inspiration, the staffing exemplary, and the French were apparently delighted. So much so, that at the end of 1917 Grace was informed that the SSBM – the French Red Cross – had decided that Binson would become a major medical centre for the area, or Triage, as they called it. This was a great boost to FANY morale, and a landmark in their approval ratings from the French.

Their representatives met with Grace and Coley in January 1918, asking for a significant increase in personnel. Grace, full of excitement, and delighted at the turn of events, at once set off for London to arrange recruitment.

Ten days later a brief, matter-of-fact letter to the FANY was handed to Cole-Hamilton. In it they were bluntly informed, that in view of the proposed expansion, the French Red Cross, the SSBM, had decided to take over the whole project themselves, and staff it with French nurses. The FANY were given a month to organise their departure!

And that was that.

After all the praise they had received this was a doubly unexpected blow, well below the belt. It was hard to take after all the effort they had put in, not to mention money, and supplying so much new equipment – beds, bedding, medical supplies of all kinds.

Every FANY who had been involved was not only shaken to the core, but furious with the French for the way it was done. It was just another of the unfathomable decisions for which the French had become notorious among the Allies. Perhaps their strong sense of national pride had been dented by the transformation at Binson.

Whatever their reasons, without discussing the matter with anybody concerned, doctors, orderlies, patients – let alone the FANY themselves – the decision was made. It was not up for discussion. French nurses would be taking over. When the French patients were informed, there was genuine shock and disappointment, many of them begging the FANY to stay.

Perhaps one of the saddest consequences was the departure of Coley. She took the sudden, abrupt change of direction as a direct slur against her personally, and her management of the hospital. She also felt it was a direct affront to the FANY Corps itself, of which she was very proud.

One month after being handed the curt little note, she handed over the keys to a token delegation of French nurses, and departed, not only from Binson, but from the FANY Corps itself.

Before she left, both she and Grace were Guests of Honour at a dinner given by the French doctors at the hospital. The doctors and patients clubbed together to present the Corps with a magnificent silver tea service. Grace and Coley were both presented with silver medals by the SSBM, as a mark of appreciation for all they had done.

By now Grace was used to projects closing as situations changed, but found it hard to forgive the French for this stab in the back, as she regarded it. However, she shrugged it off, and as usual concentrated on finding new outlets for her girls. She was able to expand Units 6 and 7 along the Marne, and during December had laid the foundations for a new unit, Unit 9, at Chalons sur Marne.

However, as a result of this much increased FANY commitment to the French convoys, the French introduced some changes to their administration. They insisted on a complicated system of attachments to what they called Sections Sanitaires, with a French Officer in charge of each section. They also wanted a FANY officer in overall charge of all FANYs working for the French, with whom they could deal directly. Grace and Franklin were asked to nominate someone.

Grace was an obvious candidate, and very tempted. She told her children in later years how she went through a deal of soul-searching. There would be greater scope with the French, but she still felt immense loyalty to the Belgians, who had done so much for them.

"It was the Belgians that gave me my chance, & accepted the FANY in 1914, when neither the British nor the French would place us. I had shared their retreat and their struggle, and longed to be with them in their hour of triumph."

And that was her decision, despite Doris Allen writing to her: *"We shall all be delighted if you come to the French. You have worked long and hard enough for the Belgians, and I don't think you need mind leaving them now. You cannot possibly do more for them than you have done."*

Grace finally remained committed to the Belgians, and it was Doris Allen herself that both Franklin and Grace confirmed as head of the French sections.

She was shortly to be stretched to the limit, as the German Army broke through along the Marne Valley, in their final great offensive of the War. Allen and her teams were to become involved in the frenzied evacuation of hospital after hospital in the path of the German successes.

Parallel with these changes, a proposal for a new British convoy came to fruition. It had been launched some time before by Franklin and Grace, for a new convoy to be established near British Army HQ at St. Omer.

The negotiations, as usual, had been protracted, complicated, difficult, and involved overcoming many deeply entrenched objections to women doing men's jobs – this in spite of the freely acknowledged success of the FANY convoy, Unit 3, in Calais.

Finally agreement had been reached, and the new Unit 8, St. Omer, was established. Its commander was an amateur ex-racing driver, Muriel Thompson. This convoy adopted as its emblem a 'tail-in-the-air' red herring, as a result of speech made by Surgeon General Woodhouse to a group of FANYs. Commenting on their strong independence as a distinct unit, yet working for and under such a variety of larger official military organisations, he told them: *"'Pon my soul! You are neither fish, flesh nor fowl; but, if I may say so, you are thundering good red herring!"*

And thus they remained.

A new Unit serving their own men, close to British Army HQ – Franklin and Grace and everyone else agreed it had to be really good. Drivers were hand-picked from among the girls with hard-earned experience in the heavily bombed streets and docks of Calais. They were determined not to be found wanting. Nor were they, when sorely tested just weeks later.

While all this was going on, yet another readjustment was inflicted by the BRCS – a sensible one, as it happened. In the same way as the French had insisted that a senior FANY be appointed in overall command of all French-attached FANYs, so the BRCS demanded a FANY 'Supremo' for all those working for the British Army, through them.

There was one obvious candidate – Lillian Franklin. She had long, hard experience running Lamarck hospital in beleaguered Calais, then so successfully commanding the first FANY ambulance convoy for the British, Unit 3. She was particularly remembered for her conspicuous bravery when the ammunition dump at Audruicq was blown up. She was unanimously elected by a committee of senior FANYs. Her group was known as FANY (English Section).

It was the turn of the Corps to make some administrative changes themselves. The French and Belgian Convoys were banded together under the title of FANY (Allied Section), and another obvious leader was ready and waiting – Grace.

From then on, Grace and Franklin were officially Co-Commandants of the Corps. There were changes, too, at HQ in London, designed to deal with the new Field arrangement. Janette Lean, who had resigned after losing her battle with Grace almost a year before, now returned as Secretary (English Section). 'Andy' Anderson, who had so distinguished herself running the Foyer de Soldats at Fismes, then as Quartermaster at newly-acquired Binson Hospital, took on the post of Secretary (Allied Section).

On this new solid foundation, the Corps entered 1918, the final year of the war, ready for anything. It was just as well, because in that first half of the year ahead they would face the most desperate, dangerous and stretching time they were ever likely to experience.

CHAPTER 41

The Beginning Of The End

That winter of 1917/1918 was bitter and unrelenting. Month after month of ice, frost and snow, roads like broken glass, pitted with shell holes. In all the FANY convoys attached to the Allies, the girls worked on under incredibly difficult conditions, ferrying the wounded and sick pouring in from the Front to base hospitals or to evacuation trains. When not doing that they were delivering Medical Staff and supplies wherever needed.

Things were bad enough. They suddenly got worse.

It was a grim time for the Allies. The French had suffered enormous casualties, leading to disillusion and mutiny in their armies. The British to the north were considerably under strength, and, additionally, had taken over 67 kilometres of the French line. A lot of this consisted of trenches well below standard, just as the FANY had found their French vehicles to be largely unserviceable.

Then, on 21st of March, Germany launched a massive offensive. It was a last attempt to shatter Allied resistance and defeat them. That morning, three million shells hit the British trenches in front of Amiens. By the day's end there were 17000 new casualties to deal with. The effect on the FANY's workload was immense and immediate. Wounded poured in throughout the day, swamping all facilities for dealing with them. The English and Belgian convoys in Calais were stretched beyond the limit.

That offensive fortunately didn't last, and petered out around Amiens three weeks later. One reason given was that the German troops couldn't be stopped from over-eating and drinking from the huge stocks they looted from captured British stores!

After a pause to regroup, the Germans struck again, this time against the French along the Marne. Again they were initially successful, and hospital after hospital had to be evacuated in their path, wounded driven to waiting trains and barges.

Horrified by their experiences, and although still heavily involved in Calais with the Belgian Convoy, Grace did what she could in encouraging and supporting the French Convoys by visiting them as often as possible.

These trips were not without their hazards. On one trip, Grace, driven by Marples, was on her way to visit one of the French units. Two men stopped their car and made to attack them. One was a Belgian soldier, one a civilian, who leapt onto the car. Quick-thinking Marples picked up a tyre lever lying on the floor and passed it to Grace. She didn't hesitate. Swinging the lever with all her might, she cracked the nearest man over the head. He fell back, Marples accelerated away, and the incident was over.

It wasn't the first time Grace had dealt with this kind of problem. In June 1917 a similar event had taken place, returning from a visit to Reims. Passing through Ville en Tardenois, just a few days before the French troops there mutinied, a drunk French soldier leapt onto her car. Grace made short of it in her diary that night, adding: *"Most objectionable, I hit him off."* She went on: *"Belgians never did that sort of thing."* Sadly she was now apparently proved wrong.

The remainder of the visit passed without incident. She was able to see at first hand just what the convoys were having to deal with, and the stress they were working under.

The main burden, however, lay on Doris Allen and her teams. The following weeks saw them operating along roads clogged with retreating soldiers, walking wounded and civilian refugees. It was hellish. In her diary Doris recorded:

"The wounded are pouring in, in all sorts of conveyances. Hundreds waiting to be received, situation appalling, not enough staff to deal with them…wounded lying all over the ground. It was simply ghastly. Ambulances waiting to be unloaded, sometimes fifty at a time."

Unit 6 had to leave Chateau Thierry in a hurry. It was chaotic. The FANY coped as best they could, even going that extra mile as usual when they felt it was in the interests of the wounded. At Epernay, when all the staff at the main evacuation hospital moved out at short notice, half of the FANY convoy decided to stay on, under dangerous conditions, until the following day, to evacuate any late arrivals who might be brought in during the night.

At last this German advance, too, was held, surprisingly by the Americans. They had finally agreed to become involved. For months their Commanding General, Pershing, had obstinately resisted calls from Allied Chiefs, insisting that that they would only enter the fray as a self-contained Army, under their own commanders. However, as the situation became more desperate Pershing consented to assisting the French.

He positioned some of his machine-gun Battalions across the Marne Valley around Chateau Thierry. They held the German advance, and broke it, just short of the town.

Grace and her driver, young Moses, along with Joan Bowles Commanding Unit 6 had a brief – and amusing in retrospect – encounter near there, with the Americans. On their way to Toul to call on a detached FANY Unit, they took a wrong turning, ending up much too close to the Front for comfort. Having driven for miles through empty countryside, they stopped to try to check where they were.

Grace takes up the story in 'Five Years with the Allies':

The road went on for miles and the Renault was going splendidly. Once Bowles and I got down by the roadside and still no sign of life – no sign of anyone. Suddenly I saw men's heads. I got quite a shock, and we all looked. Hidden in the fields cut deep in the earth were trenches filled with American soldiers. We cheerfully waved to them, and remarked they must be supports. Then we saw more trenches and more heads and still the truth did not dawn on us. Suddenly the Renault swerved and Moses jumped, for a furious soldier had leapt on us from nowhere, his rifle with bayonet at the charge. "Halt," he screamed, "Halt!" He poured forth a volley of language; we could not follow a word. Then a Corporal dashed out. "What are you doing here? Show us your papers. What is the Word?"

He threatened us with his gun and an officer now plunged at us with a revolver levelled at our heads. The road was right on top of a trench that stretched along on either side.

"What are you doing?" the officer hissed at us.

By this time I was off the car beside him. "What's the matter?" I asked, "We are going to Toul."

"You are putting all our lives in danger," he said quite angrily. "Standing here in the open talking to you – don't you see you are going straight to the German lines?" – he pointed ahead – "They are not three kilometres away, you can see them. They can see us."

"We must go back," I said, utterly taken aback.

"No, no. You can't turn the car. All right, men, go back to your places," he said to the other two soldiers. "They're not spies." And to us: "There is a path on the left a few yards along, it turns suddenly down this side of the little hill there." He pointed to a rise in the ground. "It is your only chance, there is no road."

He vanished into his trench.

Moses looked at me, her lips smiling in spite of herself. "Oh Mrs Mac, if we'd gone into the German lines with the Renault, what would the Belgians have said?"

I was in no mood for joking now. I realised what utter fools we were – that camouflaged, deserted road, that absolute absence of life. The trenches of Americans – and we had not guessed! At that moment there was a shrill screaming sound, and a tree on the roadside not far ahead swayed stupidly and rolled over on its side, across the road.

"Shall I turn, Mac?" Moses gasped.

"No," I shouted, "drive like hell, watch for the turn off."

The Renault went all out.

"HERE, MOSES. LOOK!"

Another shell came screaming along the road. The Germans had seen us, they must have been puzzled as to what we were doing, heading straight for them. The car swayed and shook on one wheel. Moses turned a white face to me.

"Oh Mac. I nearly turned her over. I was past it when you called."

I had only just seen the footpath in time. We were sheltered now, by a grassy hillock, and we heard a shell scream but we were safe. I think it was too sudden to realise it. I know my thoughts went to the car. The Belgians had let me take it as it was the fastest in the garage: if I had lost it to the Germans? – It was unthinkable!

We were driving through masses of Americans lying on the ground waiting to go up when darkness came. They eyed us with wonder. We did not stop, saw a road, and got onto it, and passed an American burial ground.

The three of them finally got to Toul, had some lunch with the small group of the French convoy, and then travelled on to Chalons sur Marne where they caught up with Unit 9, rushed off their feet as were they all.

Once the German advance was stopped, the casualty flow stemmed. The Marne Valley Units, pretty well exhausted, were given a much-needed – and appreciated – two weeks' rest at Connautre, well south of the fighting line. Here they were accommodated, to their great amusement, in a German POW hut, surrounded by barbed wire, which they considered gave it 'an air of great distinction'. They were all able to relax, and meet up again with old friends from Binson, as Grace and others came to join them for brief periods.

Always full of admiration for her FANYs, Grace wrote of these Units:

"The girls were wonderful from start to finish, the comradeship & affection & loyalty to their officers & pride in their Corps. I speak for all the French and Belgian Units & I feel certain the English Units were the same, for they were all FANY."

She was absolutely right.

The English convoy came under tremendous pressure when another phase of the German offensive was launched. Aimed initially at Ypres, and Hazebruck which wasn't far from St. Omer, the major British communications centre, its immediate success meant the urgent evacuation of all hospitals in that area.

Unit 8, the newly formed convoy near St. Omer, found themselves driving day and night under almost continual bombardment, dealing not only with military casualties, but civilian, too.

Once they were called to an exploding ammunition dump. They arrived, to find the place littered with dead and wounded. The girls coped magnificently. All day they worked quietly and competently, as the explosions continued, collecting the wounded, loading them into their ambulances, delivering them, and returning for more.

It turned out to be a memorable day indeed for the Corps. Not only did they earn unstinted praise from all the Army personnel who were there, but no fewer than 16 Military Medals for their bravery and devotion to duty, to boot!

Because it was an almost unprecedented number of recommendations, every single one was closely scrutinized, checked and re-checked, and each and every one was found to be truly merited.

It is worthy of note, that the British Army awarded these 16 decorations for bravery to an unofficial and independent group of ladies in uniform, with whom they had been at loggerheads since war broke out.

A far cry, indeed, from the jibes levelled against them not so very long before, of 'soft white hands' and 'go home and knit'.

CHAPTER 42

Plus Ça Change…

There seemed to be no end to the carnage. Month after month from that first hammer blow against the British at the end of March, the Germans attacked. April, May, June and early July saw massive offensives launched desperately at different sections of the Allied lines. Each *sortis* achieved initial success, and though all were finally held it was at dreadful cost. It was a crucial moment in our history, and the time chosen by Field Marshal Haig to issue his 'backs to the wall, fight to the last man' order.

Wherever the FANY operated they were faced time and again with hospital evacuations and patients rushed from place to place. In Calais itself, sick and wounded continued to pour in by the thousand. But slowly the mood was changing. Every enemy effort had been blunted and held. Realization was dawning, difficult to accept at first, that the tide *was* turning.

The Americans – who had declared war on Germany in April 1917 – had still taken very little part in the conflict. But the sheer numbers of them pouring into France – almost two million – and the huge industrial capacity of the USA, gave everybody renewed hope and confidence. At long last a faint light had appeared at the end of the long, dreary tunnel.

At the same time, a different emotion manifested itself among our two European Allies. Belgian and French resentment grew suddenly among their higher ranks at the parties and impromptu dances that had become such a feature of out-of-the-line and off duty activities in the makeshift British Officers' Messes.

The FANY, too, were delighted to seize any opportunity to dance and laugh and unwind. They worked long hours often under awful conditions, and it was their way of relaxing. Back home their lives revolved around parties, dinners and dances. They were natural-born hostesses and 'mixers'. Wherever they were in France their Messes became a beacon of hospitality in the black darkness of war.

Pressure was put upon Grace by local French and Belgian

commanders to stop the merrymaking and dancing. *"If half of your country was occupied by the enemy"* was the case they made, *"would you be behaving like this?"*

It put Grace in a very awkward position. Throughout her time with the FANY she had encouraged everything like that, seeing it as a great morale-booster for her girls. In 'Five Years with the Allies' she explained her quandary and how she dealt with it. Once again she was able to draw on her occasional gift for diplomacy, when it was needed. *"I explained to the Belgian General my position and that the girls could not see why they should not dance. I told him I understood and sympathised with the French and Belgian point of view, but the girls were hard workers and keen as nails on their jobs and dancing freshened them up!"*

Nothing further was said, and Grace never mentioned it again.

There were more pressing things happening, wiping away thoughts of that nature. The light at the end of the tunnel was bigger and brighter. The tide had really turned.

At the end of July the French launched a massive counter attack at Compiegne, and on 8th August the British did the same east of Amiens. It was the start of the road to peace, but every inch of it would be hard fought, all the way.

Back in Calais, Grace had much to cope with herself. Air raids on the port were almost a nightly occurrence, but 4th August saw a brief respite. A service was held in the Cathedral to mark the start of the war, four long years before. It was packed with troops of all nationalities. Grace wrote: *"I used to love the Te Deum. Not merely from the religious point of view, but for the music & the great building filled with all these men in uniform of all countries."*

In a moment of introspection, she went on: *"I was proud of being a solitary woman among these rows of Generals and Colonels. I hated it at first from sheer shyness"* [which doesn't sound like Grace] *"but afterwards loved it as a tribute to the FANY"* [which is more in character].

The following day casualty loads were larger. With only two ambulances in service, 70 wounded had to be transferred to another hospital at Guemps. This meant long hours driving back and forth, helping to load and unload the patients.

The Germans kept up their pressure on the Channel Ports. Air raids were frequent, the bombing heavy. Aeroplanes had advanced considerably since 1914, and were keen to prove their mettle.

Grace goes into some detail describing a week soon after that Cathedral service. It was nothing special, just fairly typical of what went on, but gives an indication of how the FANYs coped.

On Sunday 11th August Grace became heavily engaged in the series of raids that lay ahead, She recorded it almost as 'A Week in the Life of a FANY in Calais' at that time.

That Sunday night, a major strike set three large depots on fire. *"What a ghastly night it was,"* she wrote. *"Ten cars out all night."* Between them they picked up dozens of dead and wounded – English, French and Belgian soldiers – taking them to hospitals, Aid Centres or mortuaries as necessary.

A submarine base was hit, and many civilian workers, too, had to be tended to and transported to suitable medical centres.

A large French military hospital in rue Leveux was badly damaged. The elderly Chief Medical Officer, a Monsieur Flambert, popular with all the FANYs, was killed as he stepped out of his dugout. Grace knew him well, and by coincidence had just arrived at the hospital gates with an ambulance full of wounded, when the bomb fell. *"The crash was tremendous,"* she remembers. They had no idea what had happened inside. *"We rang & rang the bell & kicked the doors and at last took the wounded elsewhere."*

Later that night the British Base Commandant came to ask for the help of the Unit's cars, but they were all out already. The English depot had been bombed, and according to Grace, was a 'complete shambles'. *"Our boots were drenched with blood,"* she adds.

That whole dreadful night took on a surreal air. *"At 4 a.m. we sat on a bench outside the Mess and watched the flames raging in the wood yard. It was a curious sight, and over our heads wheeled flocks of birds, white in the reflected glow and uttering shrill cries. Once in the flaming sky we saw a German 'plane with all the searchlights chasing it, and we could have sworn we saw a black thing fall from it. We thought it was a parachute, but it may have been merely our excitement."*

It must have been an incredible sight, illustrating so clearly the huge leap these girls had made voluntarily, from comfortable, affluent drawing rooms back home, to sitting on a bench amid raging fires, in war-torn Calais, 'boots drenched in blood'; this blessed relaxation from hours of driving, saving lives, rescuing wounded soldiers and civilians alike. The feeling of relief and satisfaction can be imagined, and above all, the great awareness of comradeship which had developed among these young ladies, binding them together forever. Grace herself revelled in it.

Later that day the girls were able to take stock, and note the date, August 12, open day for grouse shooting. In normal times many of these girls would be elegantly presented guests or hostesses at great country estates in Scotland. But this was war and, instead, they themselves were under fire in drab uniforms, weary from long hours of toil, far removed from the familiar scenes of home.

That night the bombers returned; 4.30 a.m. and two cars were sent to Boulevard Gambetta to pick up casualties; 5.15 and Grace went with a British Army truck to an underground hospital, to collect a shell-shocked soldier, because the driver didn't know the way; 6 o'clock, Grace and O'Neil set off to partly re-opened Leveux Hospital with French civilian wounded.

Eight o'clock, and Grace offered the hospital two cars to replace their damaged ones. The offer was gratefully received, and Marples and Moses took over duty there. They had been up all night, but remained on duty until six that evening.

During that afternoon a trainload of 180 wounded arrived. As usual, the FANY were ready and waiting, transferring them to hospitals, boats and trains. Hour after hour of helping, lifting, carrying.

Seven p.m. and Moses was sent to Gravelines to pick up two more patients and bring them back to Calais.

Then – "that night we slept!".

There was a sense of heartfelt relief in those few brief words.

It didn't last.

Next morning it was *"early evacuation as usual at 5 a.m.. Bond and Barron on duty all day, other cars called out as required. No let up. Back to reality. Again!"*.

On that Tuesday Grace received a letter of thanks from the Calais Governor, General Ditte, for the bravery of the FANY drivers.

He began with *"les plus grands services"* over the years they had been operating there. He went on: *"Day and night they maintained with tireless devotion the movement of wounded Belgian, English and French soldiers. Their good sense, like their calm, was always much admired by everyone."* There was much more.

This was just one of many such eulogies delivered by French and Belgian dignitaries and Brass-hats. While appreciating the intent, the girls tended to receive the flowery phrases with amused embarrassment.

After passing the letter on to her FANYs, it was back to work, little or no time to think about it. The week was moving on: *"Five a.m. Thursday morning, more evacuations, but fewer today, only two cars needed."*

A short time later, though, a trainload of 140 casualties arrived, and it was once again all hands to the pumps! The large hospital at Port de Gravelines had been bombed. Again. This time five killed, 15 wounded. *"The mad officer,"* Grace writes, *"who couldn't get on the train the night before this, and his three orderlies, were killed."* That night still more bombs fell on Calais.

With her FANYs constantly out during these frantic air raids, Grace always worried about them. All of them, whatever their convoy, whichever the hospital.

"I was haunted day and night," she wrote, *"by the thought of any of the girls getting killed. I felt terribly the burden of responsibility."* The pressures and stresses of her role were getting to her.

Friday, the week drawing to a close, saw the funeral of the *Medecin Chef,* Chief Medical Officer in Calais, killed a few days earlier at Leveux Hospital. In Grace's words, he was *"given an immense funeral"*. The wreath presented by the FANY Corps was given pride of place. *"A kindly thought of the French to show the appreciation of our work."*

Funerals or not, work was always waiting. Four wounded French soldiers on stretchers needed immediate transfer. Grace herself, with an old FANY friend, Bond, were available and delivered the patients to the new centre, in the brand new GMC Ambulance presented to the FANY by the City of Aberdeen. This was something that made Grace really proud.

And so it went on, days and nights of hazardous duties for them all. Just another average week amid years of suffering. But now there was a new spirit of hope and anticipation spreading through the Allied Forces, as they battled their way steadily onwards, gradually pushing back the enemy.

The long dark days of stagnation were over. With her comrades in the English and French convoys, Grace hoped she would soon be on the road to victory with her Belgian convoy. As she herself had said, *"I had shared their retreat and struggle, and longed to be with them in their hour of triumph."*

She would not have much longer to wait. Her hour of triumph was waiting, but some dreadful times lay ahead, that would stretch both Grace and her girls to the limits of their endurance.

CHAPTER 43

"Comes Slowly, Flooding In, The Main"

The slow, dawning hope that the tide of this dreadful war was changing for the better became reality when the British unleashed a massive offensive against the Germans on August 8th 1918. Supported by ANZACS and Canadians, it swept across the long–stagnant No Man's Land, throwing the enemy back eight miles – a huge distance in those days of static trench warfare.

It was a time of one-liner quotes from the Generals of both sides, following Haig's famous 'Backs to the Wall' *cri de coeur* in March. Now his German counterpart, Ludendorff, dubbed this British attack *'the Black Day of the German Army in the War'*. Not to be outdone, the French went on the offensive with Marshal Foch declaring *'Tout le Monde a la Bataille!'*.

The initial surge forward couldn't be maintained. To counter the Allied attacks the Germans resorted to indiscriminate use of poison gas, and the FANY were suddenly under the most appalling pressure as hundreds of gassed soldiers poured in daily from the Front Lines. Not only were many of these wretched victims blinded, but their faces were paralysed.

The Medical Services were once more swamped, unable to cope with the sheer numbers. The unfortunate men lay about largely unattended. Desperate French Medical Officers begged the FANY to help them nurse and tend these casualties. With the same dedication which had earned them such praise in the past, the girls did just that. After a full day of driving, starting at 4 a.m. until evening, they then worked through the night doing what they could for these shattered men.

Grace felt terribly for her girls working such long hours under horrific conditions, herself putting in exhausting hours supporting and encouraging them as much as possible. Luckily, her second in command in Unit 5, O'Neil Power, was always a tower of strength, allowing Grace to get away as often as she could to travel around visiting the French convoys, and do the same for them.

It was a long journey for her from Calais, looping around behind Amiens, and along the Marne Valley, but she loved every moment of it, feeling part of this great movement. It gave her, too, the chance to pass through and see many of her old friends with Unit 8. It was, of course, Boss Franklin's convoy, but they both shared the same enormous pride and pleasure in directly serving their own British Tommies, something especially dear to all the FANYs.

This Convoy itself was stretched to the limit, following up behind the British advance. History has largely ignored the tremendous achievements of the British Army in the last 100 days of the war, probably due to the huge panorama of the overall picture, advancing Allied forces stretching hundreds of miles eastwards from the Channel Ports. By this time the average age of the British army was barely 18. They suffered dreadful losses, over 300,000, as they moved inexorably forward, smashing their way through the formidable Hindenburg Line by the end of September. At the same time they inflicted more casualties on the enemy, and took more prisoners, than the French, Belgian and American armies combined.

It was this endless stream of wounded that fell so heavily on the shoulders of the two English convoys at first, down from the Front Lines, through temporary holding hospitals, and on to Calais, to be shipped home on the constant flow of Hospital Ships plying back and forth across the Channel. Both Units, 3 and 8, led by the fearless Franklin and her officers, coped, but only by ignoring clocks, working long, long hours, snatching sleep where they could. Like all the FANY units at this time, it was sheer determination not to be beaten that kept them going.

Through that month of August the Germans kept up their aerial bombardment of the Channel Ports, Calais in particular. It was part of their last desperate throw, but seemed never-ending in its intensity.

There was occasional relief. On the 20th the British 8th Corps, in spite of the Army's ongoing offensives, found time to hold a Horse Show, just seven miles from the Front Line. Anything of this nature acted as a great morale booster to the troops.

Grace received an official invitation, and took along her three stalwarts, O'Neil, Moses and Marples. The Grand Stand was decorated, she remembers, with pink velvet hangings borrowed from the French racecourse at Bethune. One of the special presentations was a "wonderful old-time carriage complete with four horses, and postillions, made out of gun carriages".

There were many Top Brass present, including Generals Plumer and Horne among others. *"Had the Germans put a shell into the Tea Enclosure,"* writes Grace, *"half the Headquarters staff of the BEF would have gone west."* Adding wryly, *"and with them our humble selves!"* However, it was a splendid day, all went well, and all felt better for the break.

Then it was back to work.

A few days later in the midst of a normal day for them – 200 wounded being evacuated from the holding hospitals, 240 new patients arriving by train from the battlefields – Grace received a telegram from Sezanne informing her that one of her French convoy FANYs, Shaw, had died from dysentery. It was something she dreaded, a possibility constantly bedevilling Grace's thoughts. Shaw was the only FANY to die on Active Service, but it made it no easier to bear. She looked on each of them as her own, and constantly worried about them. The death affected her greatly.

The funeral was scheduled two days later, and handing over to O'Neill once more, Grace set off for Sezanne. She got to Paris with no trouble, but there her car broke down and she was quite unable to raise the spare part needed. Finally, the Americans came to her rescue, with their usual generosity, providing her with a car, driver and officer escort all the way there and back. To her eternal regret, she was too late for the funeral itself.

The French had been incredibly supportive, providing a room draped all in white, with greenery collected by some of their men sent into the hills to gather it. Doris Allen, in charge of the French section, wrote, *"the effect was beautiful, making a lovely little chapel to which Shaw was brought, covered with the Union Jack"*. The French buried her with full military honours, saluted at the end by an Officers' Firing Party.

Returning to Calais shortly after, she was happily surprised to find that Ronald had got leave, and was waiting for her. She persuaded him to take her back to Scotland – *"away from everyone"* – possibly a reference to his family with whom there was often some sort of friction. There they had an idyllic couple of weeks.

Later, in retrospect, she looked on the unexpected break as an Act of Providence, happily unaware as she was at the time of the enormous pressures she would be under in the weeks ahead. She was just so happy to be together again with her husband in her beloved Scotland. Settling for The Trossachs, they tramped together across the hills and the heather. At other times she sat and read and relaxed, while Ronald indulged his passion for fishing.

Her mood of supreme contentment was reflected in her memoirs. *"Only the Scottish people,"* she wrote, *"realise what it is to be exiled from their moors year after year. My heart was hungry for my own country and the kindly folk up North."* It is probable that when she came to write about this in 'Five years with the Allies" she was strongly influenced by her years of what she looked upon as exile, in Southern Rhodesia, after the war.

While she was relaxing on leave in Scotland, her second in command O'Neil, she acknowledges, *"had her hands full at a critical time".* The Allied offensives and German counter-attacks were in full swing. Casualties poured in day and night, and the bombing raids continued. Cars and ambulances were often out of action, as base workshops were denuded of drivers and mechanics, sent to the Front Lines to maintain the vital flow of essential ammunition and weapons to the fighting men.

It was a desperate time, but O'Neil, with the help of old hands like Wood and Clayton and Marples, managed, as Grace had every confidence she would. One of the girls, Barron, had to be sent to a hospital in England after a bad accident while driving in an air raid. So it went on, but the FANYs, as ever, managed.

Grace and Ronald's leave raced by, and at the end of September she landed back in Boulogne, bringing with her a new driver. The shortage of cars being acute, and not knowing she wasn't alone, O'Neil had sent a motorcyclist with sidecar, to drive her back to the Mess at Calais.

It was late, and as Grace noted, *"I could not leave her* [the new driver] *to fend for herself at that time of night,"* so Grace sent her back in the sidecar, making her own way to Calais.

She arrived early by train, bracing herself mentally for whatever lay ahead. She thought she was ready. She had followed the news daily in the papers. The British Army was hammering at the Hindenburg Line. The French, Belgians and Americans – the latter now involved in the conflict – had launched offensives in the Argonne and Flanders.

She realised things would be bad.

They were worse.

CHAPTER 44

"... Heart And Nerve And Sinew"

She was plunged immediately into almost chaotic conditions. The Colonel in charge of L'Hôpital de Passage, Unit 5's base clearing hospital, was desperately trying to find beds for the wounded now pouring in; 500 were needed straight away. Fortunately the Colonel had already made various contacts, and it wasn't long before the beds were available.

Once that had been organised, Grace's team went into action, transferring 250 to the Cavalry School at Guines, about 20 miles away. That done, 250 more were collected from L'Hôpital de Passage, and put on a train for Rouen. Bearing in mind that most ambulances only carried four stretcher cases – some only two – transfers took a long time, and stretcher cases had to be handled with particular care. 'Sitters' as the girls referred to the walking wounded, could be fitted in, around eight in the back, and two more squeezed in beside the driver!

That day, Grace's first back at work, the girls had lunch standing up, at 3 o'clock in the afternoon. Then every available vehicle was out again until after 9 o'clock. The FANYs had dinner and a brief rest, until the first trainload of wounded – 550 of them – steamed in at midnight, to be cleared by 2.30 in the morning.

Forty-five minutes later another arrived, 130 stretcher cases, and 180 'sitters'. Cleared by 6.45, all drivers dropped onto beds, again, fully dressed, until 8 o'clock, then they were back behind the wheel – patient transfers, moving doctors and nurses, delivering equipment and stores. Moses spent all morning transporting coffins from one hospital to another!

During that afternoon further clearances had to be made to outlying hospitals and centres, then more trainloads of wounded came in; and just as they finished the last one they were told another was on the way. The girls lay down on their beds, fully dressed. Thankfully the train was late arriving and they were able to sleep until early morning.

That crisis over, Grace joined General Viban in a renewed search for empty beds in the area. The situation was getting desperate, more trainloads on the way.

From the British Assistant Director of Medical Services (ADMS) they obtained an abandoned WAAC (Women's Army Auxiliary Corps) camp. The French Governor General Ditte provided a disused aeroplane hangar. Then Grace remembered the YMCA. They were very helpful and produced a huge marquee, large enough to take around 300 beds. A FANY car was sent immediately to collect it, *"and we had it up by 2 p.m.!"*. The YMCA were also able to offer a house with 150 beds.

The FANY vehicles swept into action. Beds and equipment had to be organised and transported; 150 stretcher cases were collected from Gravelines, a further 60 from Soupriantes. The first train of the night arrived around 7 p.m. with 400 patients, and the YMCA 'auxiliary' hospital was ready by 8 o'clock. 'A damn close-run thing' as Wellington would have said.

The need for bed space was increasingly urgent. A French Mortar Camp was taken over. Another train in at 2.45 in the morning, 430 casualties. Things began to grind to a halt. Eight local hospitals were full to capacity. Wounded lay suffering patiently, while Grace and the Senior Medical officers struggled to clear the log jam.

They managed to get space from Belgian Aviation at Beaumarais, some miles away. As soon as this was confirmed, Grace's girls swung into action again, transferring 200 cases from local hospitals at Soupriantes and Gravelines out to Beaumarais. They were then free to move 100 waiting new arrivals to the now empty beds at these hospitals.

They finished this task at 7 o'clock, just in time for the French hospital's early morning evacuation. There was a frantic rush to move the 150 stretcher cases to the further-out hospitals, using four cars promised previously.

Yet again, a hurried, standing-up breakfast, then off to the hospitals at Soupriantes and Gravelines to fetch 200 stretcher cases back to L'Hôpital de Passage for the next train out going south.

A quick lunch, then rounding up another 270 men for Vival and Gravelines to fill the outgoing train. Mid-afternoon saw the minor hospitals being emptied, and by 5 o'clock they were left with 240 casualties to be reorganised, with temporary beds to be found for the less badly wounded.

In spite of short-term evacuation of the smaller makeshift hospitals, they still had to be staffed, even minimally, by doctors and nurses, all in short supply. Doing this left the major L'Hôpital de Passage with just the senior Colonel in charge and one doctor.

The strain was beginning to tell. Grace scribbled in her diary: *"Life is turning into a nightmare of endless trains."*

Though there was a brief respite in the trainloads of wounded, the vehicles were constantly in use transporting all manner of stores and equipment needed to replace the inevitable shortages caused by the huge, unexpected demand. The never-ending stream of shattered bodies and minds continued to flood in from the battle areas.

Grace's diary records, for Sunday 29th, with a touch of tongue-in-cheek – *"Now, 5.30 p.m. there is a temporary lull. 'All is quiet on the FANY Front!'"*

Not for long!

Forty officers for immediate transfer to Paris.

She goes on: *"Monday 30th. Train arrived 64 stretcher cases 95 sitters."*

An evacuation train ready to go just as another one, loaded with wounded, arrives.

"All cars hard at work until 11 p.m.."

At 11.30 Grace sent all the girls to lie down. She and O'Neil tried to get the 'books' straight, weary though they were. In three days of frenetic activity they had drawn 4,900 litres of petrol. Only 90 litres were unaccounted for. Not bad, considering the conditions and extreme pressures they had all been under.

And so it went on, the dreadful cost of winning a war mounting day by day.

At 12.30 another trainload of casualties arrived. Cleared by 2.30, yet another pulled in at 2.45. Unloaded and sorted by 5.30 a.m. still another of this endless stream of trains full of suffering men arrived.

The offloading went on until 8.30, and Henri, the FANY's cook, came to them, full of sympathy and admiration, loaded with prodigious quantities of sandwiches, neatly wrapped and packaged for the girls.

"I pushed them into the girls' pockets," wrote Grace, *"as they drove up, loaded and set off again."*

Three hundred men to be fetched from Soupriantes, Gravelines and Vival, and sent south. *"Always, beds must be emptied to be ready for new arrivals."*

Grace was now becoming more worried still about her girls, the long, backbreaking hours they were working. She had already sought help from PARC, the central transport depot of drivers' pool, repairs etc but had been turned down. Long hours were nothing new to the FANY, but Grace could see no let up in the immediate future.

"The girls were wonderful," she wrote, *"but were feeling the strain; they had been driving three days and two nights with about three hours' sleep."*

She went to General d'Orgo and explained that the Corps of Transport (CTC) must lend them at least half a dozen drivers, so that the girls could catch up with eight hours' sleep.

The General's response was swift and practical. That night six CTC drivers reported to Grace for duty.

Grace had also criticised the largest of the Calais hospitals for refusing to modify their waiting facilities and thus wasting valuable time, with patients suffering as a result. She put forward her own solution to the problem, based on bitter recent experience. That too, was swiftly taken care of, with no apparent hostility on the part of the hospital concerned. Its Quartermaster paid them a visit, armed with packets of chocolates for everyone, and arranged for a large jug of drinking chocolate to be delivered every day.

However, it wasn't all sweetness and light. With extra drivers on hand, Grace organised her girls into two shifts. One was given time off for a good long sleep, after which they would take over and allow the second lot a good rest. Human nature and pride being what they are, there was an immediate outcry. The first shift were absolutely livid at being picked to go first, and angry at CTC men driving THEIR cars while THEY slept.

The only way that Grace finally got the matter settled was to pull rank and *order* them to bed.

The General rounded things off nicely, by arranging for three teams of three mechanics, from PARC, to each give one of the vehicles a full service every night, a job the FANY had been trying to do themselves whenever they could snatch a few minutes. This was far more satisfactory from all points of view. The concentrated mileage of day and night use had put tremendous strain on the vehicles, many of which were five or six years old.

The condensed entries from Grace's diaries and writing paint the truest picture of the huge pressures, night after night, day after day.

"Always Guemps and Guines, and the new hospitals, always trains. Always evacuations. A French & a Belgian train arriving one before the other was over, and we finished both at midnight. Evacuation 12.30 ended 3.30 – train at 4.15 finished 7.20: 200 stretchers, 340 sitters. Ten cars for Guemps. Evacuation from smaller hospitals. 10.30 p.m. train of 260 cases. A train 9.30 p.m., and 12.30 a.m. Guemps for 11 cars between 3.30 a.m. & 7.30 a.m.. Other 3 cars for Guemps after breakfast. Evacuation 200 men between lunch and 3.30. French evacuation at noon. Then four cars for Guemps, one for Guines, eight for nearer places, also cars for Beaumarais & Sangatte, then a train at 7.15 p.m. with 300."

These terse, graphic entries by Grace drive home the enormous, ever-present demands laid on the shoulders of these young girls, pushing them to the limit.

This was a brief synopsis of what Grace describes as *"the story of ten days that stand out in my memory"*.

She mentions others. Farrar, who fell asleep at the wheel of an ambulance, with four stretcher cases inside. *"Fortunately she was on the side of the road away from the canal!"* McDowall, seriously ill, and rushed to a VAD hospital. O'Brien and Calder, struck down by the flu. *"One of them in the danger ward. That added to my worries, I had little time to go and get news of them."*

It was a bad time for them all – wounded, Medical Staff, FANYs, everybody involved. Nothing had prepared them for those scenes of trauma and strain.

If that were possible, there was even worse to come.

CHAPTER 45

"And So Hold On..."

It was called Spanish Flu!

Locally it was referred to by the FANYs as Flanders Grippe. No matter its name, it was deadly, a killer, at its peak more deadly than bullets or bombs. The hospital trains pouring into Calais and other centres now carried more sick than wounded. Numbers rose horrifically.

No longer were the casualties only from among the fighting men at the front. Spanish Flu knew no boundaries. It spread everywhere. As the trainloads of patients increased, the numbers of doctors, nurses, carers way down the line dwindled, as they too succumbed to this dread infection, a virus which defied the best that medical science could do to defeat it.

The FANYs were no exception. Many of them were struck down with it, wherever they were.

As soon as it began to take hold, Grace took what little action she could to fight it. She bought tonic for all her girls, and insisted they take it, though the virus being what it was, any effect was probably in the mind rather than medicinal. Her more practical, and likely successful approach was, she remembers to *"dash in and spray all the cubicles and Mess Rooms with disinfectant"* in between the trainloads of sick and wounded being cleared.

She writes of the flu cases being absolutely ghastly, streaming in by the hundreds every day. It so weakened the men they died in the trains on the way. They died where they were, lying hunched up on platforms waiting to be loaded into cars or trains to be moved on to hospitals. *"Died,"* wrote Grace, *"within hope of Peace. It was cruelly hard."*

The work was both heartbreaking and backbreaking, often short-staffed as the girls went down with the bug themselves. Not just the girls. During these *'nightmare days'* as Grace called them, both the Colonel in charge of l'Hôpital de Passage, and the only resident doctor, were taken ill and had to get hospital treatment themselves.

The Colonel was so upset, he sent for Grace and apologised profusely from his stretcher, for leaving her on her own!

This put Grace in something of a predicament. On the one hand she had no official status, apart from commanding the FANYs of Belgian Unit 5. On the other, such were the chaotic circumstances brought about by the epidemic, she was the only person with any authority who knew what was required. It had always been the Colonel's job to make up the trainloads for the South, a vitally important job, to clear local hospitals, making room for the new arrivals who needed immediate attention.

The watchword, the key phrase in use at all times, was – 'the lines must be kept clear!'.

Happily, there was someone else who knew a great deal about the operation – the Head Clerk, Jules. Unassuming and, more often than not, totally ignored, he just quietly carried out the Colonel's instructions. Writing about him, Grace noted: *"Jules was a treasure, fat and podgy and pimply and we had laughed at him."* But no more. He was a huge help to her, and she freely admitted that she could not have got by without him.

Working together for the first time, Grace and Jules looked at the figures – 600 on the way, sick and wounded. It was a daunting thought. What if she got it all wrong? What if….? She pushed the unease to the back of her mind. She looked at Jules. *"He pursed his lips and shook his head."*

Between them they 'made up' the next train for the South. Jules knew this part of the routine from following the Colonel's orders for so long. He and Grace sent the orders out to the various hospitals in the area. Somehow they had to send 600 patients away to make room for the 600 new arrivals en route.

There were off-the-cuff decisions to be made. Some patients were too far away to collect in time. Grace managed to make up numbers from a train recently arrived, men considered able to make the onward journey immediately. They *had* to send 600 men away. They sweated at the thought.

There was another hitch. What Grace hadn't known was that every trainload of Belgian wounded travelling on French railways was charged £200. Requisitions were presented by the French railway official – somebody had to sign it before he would allow the train to proceed. Again, Grace and Jules exchanged glances, eyebrows raised.

By this time Grace was beginning to enjoy herself, a happy mood of recklessness. If there was a comeback later she would deal with it then. She took the requisition, looked the official in the eye, and signed it. Red tape – to hell with it. *'The lines must be kept clear.'*

On one occasion Grace, worn out, was persuaded by Marples to go and get some sleep. There was a train due at 3 a.m. but she could deal with that. Unfortunately, in the early hours she was woken by a fuming Marples, because the French sergeant in charge of the train would only take orders or a signature from an officer. *"So,"* wrote Grace, *"I put my coat on over my pyjamas and sallied forth!"*

She recalls, too, *"another long, endless day running into evening and night"*. In despair she sent a telegram to Commandant Bemmelmanns, her boss at Belgian HQ in Le Havre. They must have help, she pleaded.

That evening Bemmelmanns turned up himself, smiling but firm, and worked like a Trojan all night helping the depleted FANY section to load and unload sick and wounded, always cheerful, always supportive. When the trainloads were finished, he got onto PARC transport and demanded trucks to carry the patients to the outlying hospitals. Within a short time several of these arrived, each with wooden seats for 20 men. Loaded with waiting 'sitters' they set off, saving the FANY drivers hours of driving out and back, out and back, and allowing them to get some much needed rest.

Jules and Grace between them, with the support of Bemmelmanns, kept the flow going, the lines clear. Calais was the only section not to break down under the strain. The Belgian Minister for War sent his personal congratulations, as did the British Base Commander. And his French counterpart.

Grace herself was unstinting in her praise for the *'seventeen girls of mine who never faltered, never let us down'*. They kept Calais clear, though many at times were ill themselves. During these eight crucial days they cleared no fewer than 10,070 sick and wounded through the system.

She was full of heartfelt affection and admiration for the FANYs of her Belgian Convoy. *"There may be other* wars, *we pray not,"* she wrote, *"but there will never be other girls like these."* She went on to recount all they had been through in these past years – bombing, violence, death, destruction. The job, for them, at that time, had subsided into *"an endless procession of trains & stretchers of wounded & flu-stricken men, and they carried on, managing to smile, however tired they were."*

She loved these girl of hers, and was so proud of them, so fearful for their safety. Listing the seventeen names in her memoirs, she added: *"There is a statue in Calais called 'The Brave Boys of Calais'."* She goes on to suggest that if a millionaire had some money to spare, he *"could do worse"* than have a similar monument erected, with a FANY on top and an ambulance carved in stone beneath, entitled 'The Khaki Girls of Calais'!

Alas, it never was…

CHAPTER 46

Back To Bruges With The Belgians

A week or so into October the stream of casualties began to dwindle. More FANY drivers had arrived from England, lifting the burden of work for those already there. Further north there were signs that the Germans would be making a major withdrawal. Belgian cavalry had broken through in a battle south of Bruges.

But for Grace and her girls another grim week lay ahead, even with more hands to deal with it. *"From the 13th to the 19th,"* she noted, *"the cars were going all day and half the night."* Trainloads of 700 then 550 to start with. From Tuesday to Thursday evening 3,100 casualties passed through. Sounding a note of almost despair Grace wrote in diary: *"Shall we ever sleep all night again?"*

The Germans pulled out of Bruges on October 20th. Knowing how much Grace wanted to go back into Belgium with a victorious Belgian Army, General d'Orgo, Belgian Area Commander, sent for her and offered her a seat in his car. She accepted with delight.

But as she climbed into the car, it was surrounded by elderly Belgian officers, all desperate to return. Grace could see how sad they all looked – *"tears on their war-torn faces"* was how she put it. They had been in exile for four long years, their wives and children were in the city, and they were frantic with the desire to return.

"They looked at me with hostile eyes, those old Colonels who had hitherto spoilt me with their courtesy and consideration."

It was an unequal battle, doomed from the moment she studied these old faces. She spoke to General d'Orgo, offering to give up her seat. Perhaps he would give her the necessary Pass, and she could follow up in her own car?

His relief was almost tangible. The Pass was signed and in her hands in minutes. Three of the old soldiers squeezed into her space, unthinkable with a woman. Lined faces, happy now, beamed at her through the windows. She waved to them, and went off to collect her dependable old Unic that she had brought to Calais so long ago.

She and Marples set off in pouring rain. They headed for

Dixmude first, eager to visit the old Front Line *'poste de secours'* they had known in those reckless, hectic months of 1914.

The roads were worse than ever, from time to time barred by sentries when bridges were down or unsafe, or roads impassable. In the wastes of the old No Man's Land it was dreary and empty, not a soul in sight for long periods. Once, lost, and at a crossroads, they both thought they saw a nun standing along the road to their right. Turning, they drove to where they had seen her – not a sign of anyone. Unable to turn at that point, they decided to keep straight on. They later learned that had they carried on along their first route, they would have almost certainly been killed at a booby-trapped bridge further ahead. Grace never forgot the experience, nor understood it.

They finally hit a main road into Bruges, well maintained, and with signs in German – 'Nach Bruges' being what they wanted.

The town was swarming with people, shouting, cheering, singing. The Grande Place was a mass of Belgian flags, and people celebrating the departures of *'les sales Boches'*.

Their Unic was suddenly surrounded by crowds of laughing, happy women and children. Grace remembers: *"They were clinging to our hands, patting our cheeks, kissing us, sobbing and smiling together."* It was a wonderful feeling, especially for Grace back once more on Belgian soil after so long, among people she loved.

They joined the crowds to watch regiments of the Belgian Army march in, accompanied by a military band. By that time it was getting late, they found a hotel. While banging on the door trying to get in, Marples spotted a man leaping into the Unic. She hurled herself at him and struggled. Grace rushed across and hit him over the head; he broke free and ran off down the street. The Porter who finally opened the hotel door explained there were still many Germans trapped in Bruges, which was why the door was kept shut.

They had had a good day, and it ended better than expected. Grace scribbled in her diary: *"That night we dined on beefsteak and potatoes and slept peacefully on a soft mattress."* They had thought they would be sleeping in the Unic and eating stale sandwiches.

Next day she contacted General d'Orgo and obtained requisition orders to inspect any suitable buildings which would serve as

Quarters for the FANY section which was to be based in Bruges. She finally settled on an almost deserted Convent. There was a large dormitory with 20 cubicles well built, and a lavatory at the far end, with three smaller rooms which would do very well as a Mess, an office and a spare bedroom. It had been occupied by German troops, and she was amused to see notices hanging everywhere – 'GOTT STRAFE ENGLAND'. She wanted one for a souvenir, and was disappointed to find they had all been cleared away when she got back!

Once her selection was approved, it was time to head back to Calais. They decided to go via Ostend, and call in to see the huge German gun at Couckelaere, used to bombard Dunkirk, 30 miles away.

"The barrel was so long," noted Grace, *"that seven or eight men could sit astride it; the cement flooring was as wide as a dance floor."* The enormous, empty shell cases were lying about, and never one to miss an opportunity, she took one. *"I have it still,"* she wrote much later. *"My sister uses it as an umbrella stand!"*

Back in Calais the workload had become very much less – plenty during the day, but quiet nights. Orders came through, at last, for Unit 5 to be ready to leave Calais, accompanied by yet another letter of thanks from the Belgian Minister for War. On the night of October 26th fresh orders arrived, five ambulances to proceed to Bruges the next day. It was Bond's birthday party, which ended abruptly, as they all trooped off to the garage to select which vehicles they would take.

For Grace it was *"one of the worst moments I had – Bruges, I long to take the cars up myself. Only those who have been out there could ever understand the lure of the Front, after all, to be O.C. has its drawbacks. It was my place to stay behind."*

She sent her faithful O'Neil in charge. So it was, by coincidence, that four years to the day that Grace took the first FANY Convoy across the Channel, the first FANY unit went into liberated Belgium. Grace's one regret was that she was not leading it.

CHAPTER 47

Grace Returns To Ghent

Still more new drivers arrived from England, requested six weeks earlier to staff the new section of Unit 5, to be stationed at La Panne. Things had moved on rapidly since its conception, and now it would not be based there.

However, the extra hands and vehicles were very useful in reducing the workload in Calais, especially since the despatch of five cars and drivers to Bruges. There was a feeling of excitement in the air in the expectation of moving up shortly nearer to the Front Line.

In the meantime, when two new girls arrived, in an effort to break them in to this new environment, they were sent to Valloires to collect wounded for Couchil-de-Temple, a journey of about 340 kilometres. Alarm bells began to ring in Grace's head when they hadn't returned by 10 o'clock the next night.

Taking the old Ford and a Belgian sergeant, she set out to search for them. It was fortunate she did. Two hours later, at a level crossing, they came upon a dreadful accident in which a British soldier had just lost both his legs, and was in a parlous state; no transport, and miles from anywhere. Grace and her Sergeant leapt down and applied first aid as best they could under the circumstances. Some of the men with him knew of a Canadian Military Hospital three miles off, and Grace drove him there immediately. The doctors there rallied round, and "were splendid" Grace records. She remained for some time, and they told her they thought he would survive.

She got back to Calais about 3 a.m. leaving her search for the missing drivers till the next day, only to find they had already returned, by a different route.

The Colonel, now fully recovered from his bout of flu, had just been on a visit to Bruges. He told Grace he thought she should go up there at once to sort a few things out. The girls there were not happy, *"were sleeping on stretchers on the floor, and there were no supplies to be had"*.

This, of course, was grist to Grace's mill. Putting McDowall in charge at Calais until Moses' return in a day or two, she took three cars and drivers and headed for Bruges. At the time she was suffering from a bout of flu herself, but *"simply dared not give in at such a time of confusion"*. The long day in the open and her faith in her favourite jollop, Easton Syrup, which she carried with her *"cured me, for by the time we reached Bruges about 7 o'clock, I felt fit again"*.

She had long accepted that if anything could go wrong, it would. It did. On arrival she found that one of their number, another new driver, who spoke no French, had somehow got separated, and was lost. She grabbed a cup of coffee, called for a car, and set out with Bond to find the missing driver. Eventually they did, broken down, stuck in mud, weary and worried and fed up. A passing carload of American naval officers stopped, were able to fix it, and she got to Bruges safely.

To her dismay, Grace found that morale was at a very low ebb. Their quarters were intensely cold, they didn't have enough blankets, and heating arrangements were sadly lacking. On top of that they were missing the friendly and familiar surroundings of Calais, where they had spent so much time in very comfortable, specially built housing. There was also very little work to keep them busy, take their minds off things, and give them the job satisfaction they had become used to.

Grace went into action again, and was able to sort out the accommodation problems in a very short time, but the question of work was different. It was also vital. It kept the adrenaline flowing, the excitement level high, the satisfaction of winning. She told General d'Orgo of the situation, and he promised to do what he could.

Returning to Calais on November 6th she found herself with a lot of office work to sort out and get through. Rumours of peace abounded, and there were one or two false alarms. In fact, by the 10th the stories were so strong, and the atmosphere so explosive, that there was a big peace celebration. Ships sounded sirens, church bells rang, trains blew their whistles; it was pandemonium. A huge bonfire was set alight in the park. Unit 3 entered into the spirit of things. Boss Franklin wrote in the FANY Gazette: *"British, French and Belgians, attracted by the glare, all came and sang National Anthems, cheering wildly, while Mrs McDougall and one or two of her girls came up and joined in."*

Later that day Grace took five cars and headed for Bruges once again. They all congregated in a warm little café, *"sitting restlessly discussing the rumours that flew about, the troops under orders to advance on Ghent next day"*.

Seeing their khaki uniforms, strangers kept coming up to them and asking, "Peace? Is it true?" Grace notes in her diary: *"We went 'home' thoughtfully – if it was peace? but it was late & we were tired, more tired with four years of war than we knew. We could not begin to reconstruct the world, so we slept!"*

Morning brought peace!

"There was no rejoicing, a sort of startled unbelief, staring at each other's faces we could not understand the meaning of it."

Grace thought about things fast and furiously. Remembering the frantic period of four years ago, buses packed with wounded soldiers, pulling out of a dark and freezing Ghent, she knew what she had to do. The memory of it had remained with her ever since. She couldn't resist. Peace meant another sort of freedom. She must go back, would go back, right away. She selected a car, and four good friends to go with her. The excitement was infectious.

O'Neil, definitely; McDowall as driver, two others, and old Alphonse their Orderly, whose wife and children he had left in Ghent so long ago. He was wild with excitement, laughing and crying at the same time. Would his family still be there? He was desperate to find out.

They set out in the highest of spirits. The roads were crowded and unfamiliar. A mass of troops was marching towards Ghent. They moved to one side to let the car past, amid cheers and waves. Again, German signs everywhere – 'Links', 'Rechts', 'Achtung', 'nach Ghent'. This was the stuff of dreams, Grace's dreams. She waxed lyrical. *"Regiment after regiment. Sturdy, war-torn little Belgians going back to your own country, to your own homes. Your exile is ended, your torment of separation is ended."*

She became more thrilled when she realised some of the troops were comrades from regiments they had worked with in the dark days of 1914, *"with whose doctors we served at Oostkerke, Caeskirk, Loo and Forthem. They will not forget, and nor shall we, that we stood beside their dying and their dead in the Battle of the Yser"*.

These were the kind of memories that stayed with her all her life, which probably helped her through the difficult years that lay ahead.

Driving into Ghent itself they met the same storm of celebrations they had witnessed in Bruges: crowds out in their thousands waving flags, cheering. It was slow progress. At one point an elderly man pushed out of the crowd, throwing himself at Grace, wreathed in smiles, grabbing her hand, kissing her cheek. *"Madamoiselle,"* he shouted, *"don't you recognize me? I carried one end of the stretcher with the dying Englishman – you had the other end, in 1914!"*

Grace peered at him more closely, and recognised him behind his white beard as one of the stretcher bearers. She was thrilled to see him, even though she hadn't been too impressed at the time with his skill as a bearer.

They drove on, to the Maison St Pierre Convent where the final evacuation took place. The nuns were delighted to welcome her again; the old Mother Superior had died, however.

Anxious to find out about the man who took her across the Frontier into Holland, Monsieur de Weert, she discovered to her dismay that he had been selected as a useful hostage, if required, and taken to Germany some months before. He had not been heard of since. She was much saddened by the news, as he was the man to whom she largely owed her freedom.

Determined to see as much as possible, Grace drove to the cemetery where Foote and Brand had been laid to rest. Rough wooden crosses were now in place to mark their graves.

The stolen day out was closing fast; they headed back to Bruges. It had been a unique experience for all of them, especially nostalgic for Grace.

The following day, she and O'Neil drove back to Calais where the Belgian Base Headquarters were to hold a farewell banquet for 300 Allied officers in the area. Grace, O'Neil and Moses would be the only ladies present.

General d'Orgo presided over the feast, General Ditte on one side, Grace on the other. The British Base Commander sat beside Ditte.

The banquet was a great success. Grace was very amused, but discreetly so, at all the flowery speeches praising one another's contribution to the struggle, and how supportive they had all been. First it was the Belgians expressing their sorrow at parting from their French and British friends and Allies. Then the French Governor saying how he would miss the departing Belgians, and thanking them for all they had done. Finally, the British Base Commander praising both the French and Belgians for their great co-operation in the past years, and acknowledging the great Entente Cordiale between them all. After which all three National Anthems were played.

The truth was that they had all been at each other's throats a great deal of the time. The French, deeply suspicious of the British in every way, and continually maligning the Belgians, resenting their presence in their country. The French themselves were constantly making problems for all their Allies, objecting to almost every suggestion made; while the British got up everyone's noses with a lofty contempt for everyone not British.

The three girls derived great amusement from the speeches. And no doubt it was general amongst most of those there. Not that it mattered much then. The war was over; there was much wine at the tables – it was in great demand, everyone was in a jubilant mood, rifts were being healed.

Soon after the official speeches had ended, Grace recalls: *"Both General d'Orgo and General Ditte looked at me, and said, 'It is your turn, Madame, to speak' and before I could protest, General d'Orgo had rung his little bell for silence, and announced 'Madame McDougall will now speak'."*

Shaken slightly by this sudden and unexpected summons, she rose to her feet among encouraging cheers, and started off in her fluent but sometimes erratic French. She followed the general pattern of previous speakers, saying how proud she was to be going back into Belgium with her Belgian comrades, but sorry to be leaving France. Unfortunately, thinking in English and speaking in French, she made her 'howler' as she called it. Paying tribute to the French Governor of Calais for the help and support over the last four years, she added: *"General Ditte a été toujours notre bon ami."*

This perfectly reasonable English phrase apparently had another connotation in French, meaning lover rather than friend, which she suddenly realised to her horror. She remembers in her memoirs: *"I stopped dead, blushed crimson, and in a moment the room was in an uproar."*

Quickly excusing herself *"from more faux pas in a foreign language"*, she sat down, still embarrassed. Then, as the cheers and laughter subsided, the band, which had played the national anthems of each of the previous speakers, launched into Rule Britannia, and the four were presented with *"wonderful bouquets of flowers"*. All was well.

Within a few days the Belgians had departed, and only Grace and Moses were left to close up shop. It was a dismal prospect: cold, wet weather, empty Mess full of memories, and the debris and junk of years to clear away. Out of the blue, a motor-cycle courier arrived with a message from Brussels for Grace. It read: *"Chère Madame, if you wish to assist in the event of which we have spoken, you must leave at once for Bruxelles. Even tonight may be too late."*

Grace knew immediately what the carefully worded message meant. The King and Queen of Belgium were returning to their Capital, after their four years of self-imposed exile at La Panne.

She and Moses reacted quickly, packing a few clothes and setting off in the Unic. Stopping at a hotel in Bruges for dinner, they met up with an officer of the Guides whom they knew well. He, too, was headed for Brussels, and asked if he could travel with them. They were only too glad to agree. It was a miserable, stormy night, and *"they crept into Brussels at 3 a.m."*.

Finding a hotel, she and Moses dropped into bed, quite exhausted, to be wakened next morning by a maid with a message from the Guides officer. He was at the Ministry of War, and had seats for them to view the Royal Parade, but they must get there fast. They did!

There were troops from all the Allies at the march past, including Italians, Portuguese and Americans. The focus of all the thousands who turned out to watch was on the King and his Queen, on horseback, side by side. Behind them rode their three children, and as a wonderful gesture of gratitude to the British, the son of our own Monarch, the young Duke of York, rode with them. The celebrations went on far into the night, Grace and Moses joining in happily. The partying went on for three days.

Grace was disappointed that the British missed a great propaganda opportunity. The Americans had large numbers of film crews with their army, recording everything that was happening. They cleverly combined the pictures of some of the actions the Americans took part in, with previously recorded film. In a very short time, 'newsreels' were made available to the few cinemas all over Belgium and France, desperate for films to show. In Brussels, Moses and Grace were invited to one such showing. She was horrified. *"Picture after picture of supplies leaving America – fish, meat, butter, sugar, everything on an enormous scale. American guns, American shells, American vehicles. Then American troops in France, American regiments, American artillery, and crowning insult, British tanks –* the Americans didn't have any *– driven by our Army Service Corps men, and on the step of each tank an American soldier waving a little American flag."*

There is no doubt in Grace's mind: they won the propaganda war.

The film ended with a shot of a small American cemetery, each grave with a Stars and Stripes flag attached to it.

When asked afterwards what she thought of it by the cinema manager with an officer from the American film section beside him, Grace suggested there was something they had forgotten to include. *"Give the people some idea of the truth. Show them pictures of the huge British and French cemeteries, then show the pictures of your American graves."*

The next day Grace and Moses went to Bruges, where she was told by General d'Orgo to go to Germany, to visit the HQ of the Army of Occupation, and decide whether the FANY Belgian Convoy should join them, or stay in Brussels with the Ministry of War.

It was a very relaxed time. She set off with her comrades of old, Wood and McDowall. The Belgian Army of Occupation HQ was in a dreary industrial town, Krefeld. There she presented her credentials to an elderly Colonel, who appeared to have no knowledge of, or interest in, the FANY Corps.

It didn't take any of them long to decide to reject the Army of Occupation and remain in Brussels with the Ministry of War. Before they left they heard that a detachment of the Guides were quite near, at a small village called Weyberg.

They could not resist the opportunity, made their way there, received a warm welcome, and stayed several days as guests of the Regiment. Regretfully tearing themselves away, they headed back to Bruges, via Brussels. There, Grace made her report, and registered her decision to stay with the Ministry of War.

When they finally got back to Bruges, there was a letter from England waiting for Grace telling her that her mother was not well. With the pressures of the war lifted, her decision was much easier to make. She packed immediately, drove to Boulogne, and went home on leave.

Christmas wasn't far off, but, as the days went by, and her mother slowly recovered her health, she was torn between staying on and the *"frantic letters from Bruges that my presence was urgently required"*. The girls were becoming bored, some very disenchanted with peace-time service, and wanting to be released.

She chose to stay on until Christmas was over, her mother back on her feet, and with *'strangely heavy heart'* set off again for Belgium.

CHAPTER 48

From Bruges To Brussels

Grace arrived back in France on New Year's Eve, crossing the Channel with Dancer, a Canadian girl who had joined the FANY in November.

They were disappointed there was no transport to meet them, but things had moved very rapidly since the Armistice, and most of the Corps were now 'up country' following hard on the heels of the advancing Allied armies into northern France, Belgium and Germany itself.

Unit 5, Grace's Belgian convoy, had settled into Bruges. The RTO at Boulogne fixed them up with Travel Orders, advising them to go via Paris and Brussels, the main line routes being more reliable.

She remembers, ruefully, spending New Year's Eve in the train, arriving in a changed and crowded Paris. *"We got into a taxi at 6 a.m., hungry and tired, and at 8 a.m. were still in the taxi having been turned away from 22 hotels – all full up."*

Finally, remembering the address of an American Major she knew, they drove there, and after much ringing of the doorbell, she recalls *"a strange figure appeared clad in a long, loose garment – an American nightshirt"*. Never having seen one before she could scarcely contain her giggles, which made her feel slightly better after all she had been through in the past 24 hours.

The Major let out a muffled curse – he later insisted it was an apology – and vanished, returning shortly more suitably attired to usher the two girls in. Things then improved. After a hot bath and breakfast, the Major sent his Orderly out to find them a hotel. Successful, the girls spent that night in comfort, and travelled to Brussels the following day.

By now, still only weeks after the conflict had finally ended, there was a wonderful spirit of relaxed camaraderie everywhere. Grace's companion, Dancer, met up with four American officers about to drive to Bruges, who immediately offered them a lift. Grace remembers vividly: *"They all came from Texas, and they all had broken noses – whether this is coincidence, or a characteristic of Texas I do not know!"*

Although Grace had not been away all that long, changes had inevitably taken place, with more under way. Already some of her girls had moved on or gone home to England.

To her dismay – and sadness – O'Neil Power, her second in command and long time friend, left within two days. Her mother's health had suddenly deteriorated. During all those difficult and dangerous months – years – in Calais, when Grace herself was so often away, O'Neil had held the fort, loyal, supportive and efficient. In Grace's own words, *"O'Neil had been my right hand"*.

This was a scenario being faced by many millions as men and women of all services went home. Friendships forged and tested in the white heat of conflict were now being further tested by separation, as old comrades said their farewells and headed homewards.

One of Grace's favourite girls, the young, attractive, adventurous Moses had already left. It was she who joked 'what would the Belgians have said if she had driven into the German lines', after so nearly doing so. Joining the American Red Cross in Paris, she was shortly after dispatched to Albania, where her work became legendary. Grace wrote: *"She made history, young as she was, and was adored by all the rough mountaineers who called her 'the Duchess'."* Her other claim to fame was the raising of the first troop of Albanian Boy Scouts!

Grace bemoans the fact that *"three stout veterans were lost to me"*. The last was the redoubtable Marples, another long-time friend, whose quick-wittedness in passing her a tyre lever when threatened by two deserters had got them out of a tight spot. Torn between a desire to stay on, and an invitation to go and join up with Moses in Albania, she couldn't resist the challenge, and off she went.

Never one to resist a challenge herself, Grace quite understood their position.

Others began to drift away. *"The thrill of Active Service was over,"* she wrote. But there was still work to be done. Duty called.

The Minister for War in Brussels summoned Grace to a discussion about the future. *"He begged me to stay on for a few months."*

The whole service was in a bit of a mess. Men were desperate for leave, to be again with their families from whom they had been separated for so long. If Unit 5 would stay a bit longer, based in Brussels, they would *"render an inestimable service to Belgium"*. A great deal of driving would be involved, the Minister explained, and after years of driving cars and ambulances under difficult and dangerous conditions, who better to carry out this work but the FANY Corps?

Grace carried the word back to Bruges, and in spite of some girls already having left, there were still many eager and willing to stay on in Belgium, and fill the breach.

After carefully assessing the situation in Bruges, Grace wrote to the Ministry of War to tell them that two cars were all that were needed there, and two of her girls had volunteered to stay on and drive them. The remainder were ready to move to Brussels and carry out any tasks that were allocated to them.

To her frustration, there was no response to her letter, and after a suitable time Grace took matters into her own hands. Dealing with Officialdom and Red Tape were almost second nature to her now.

Leaving two cars and drivers as specified in her letter to the Ministry, she packed up the remainder of the convoy and headed for Brussels. It was still early in the year, bitter weather still prevailing. With her own brand of wry humour she records: *"The roads were white with snow, and we arrived blue with cold!"*

As expected, accommodation was in short supply, but after resorting to a 'hotel tout' as Grace put it, they got rooms at a small place behind the main railway station.

While her party settled in, Grace lost no time in making her way to the War Ministry. There she confronted a very surprised Commandant Bemmelmanns, her contact.

"I was thickly coated with snow and ice," she wrote, *"when I entered his office, and told him we had come and required work and quarters at once. He was quite upset, poor man, but I was firm."* One can only imagine his feelings on being suddenly confronted by this snow-sprinkled Amazon.

Then came the ultimatum. Pulling no punches she told him bluntly that his Minister for War, personally, had begged them to stay on, and they must either give us work or let us demobilize.

It was a gamble – demobilization was the last thing she wanted for herself or her FANYs. Fortunately, her ploy succeeded, but only after an anxious wait of three days.

When the word finally came through they were ordered to report to the big Military Transport Centre at Cinquantiere Park. Here they were to be based for their remaining few months.

Grace's second in command was now Mary Baxter-Ellis. The two of them had gone together on that momentous fund-raising Blitzkrieg in the North of England and Scotland to finance the newly acquired FANY Hospital at Porte à Binson. They made a good team then, and still did.

As usual, minor problems arose. One of the girls, Cameron, was anxious to visit her husband, who was C.O. of a Canadian Regiment now in Belgium.

Grace agreed immediately, but then went down with a peculiar kind of 'snow sickness' as it was called, collapsing whenever she got out of bed, and was laid up, for some days. Once again the stresses and pressures she had been under for so long were catching up with her. The poky hotel they were still living in had no such thing as room service, or even its own dining facilities. For meals, they were dependent on a small café below the hotel.

Each day, Baxter-Ellis took the girls down to the Transport Centre where they were allotted their jobs for the day. This mostly involved driving senior Military officers from place to place in Brussels, or much further afield, all over Belgium, France and into Germany itself. It was an entirely new routine from what they had been used to for so long, and they became very involved, determined to maintain their reputation.

Once Grace recovered, however, she asked for news of Cameron. In all the excitement she had been overlooked. Nobody had thought to ask Cameron where her husband was stationed. Eventually the British Consul found the name of the village for them. Now seriously alarmed Grace set out to trace her.

She finally made contact with Colonel Cameron. On the night following her visit, he was driving her back to Brussels in the regimental carriage, when the horses bolted. In the ensuing crash his wife had broken her ankle badly, been taken to the nearest British

Military Hospital, then evacuated to England for specialist treatment. The mystery was solved but they had lost yet another of their number. At least she was safe, but in true FANY fashion the others shrugged it off, kept in touch now they knew where she was, and got on with the job!

However, the situation was not ideal. One part of the promise made by the War Ministry was being fulfilled: they had been given work. Proper quarters were still missing. Having put 'snow sickness' and Cameron's adventures behind her, Grace was free to concentrate on that aspect.

It didn't take her long to get things up and running. A visit to the War Ministry produced a new contact, a young Belgian Air Force Lieutenant Bonnevie, who was delighted to work with these attractive young English ladies, and help them in every way possible. In no time he was able to acquire a really good billet for them, a large house at 13 Rue de la Limite. It had been occupied by German officers and was in excellent condition.

With Bonnevie's help they settled in quickly. He arranged for three German POWs to be allocated as their Orderlies, living in servants' quarters on the top floor of the house. He also arranged for Grace to be issued with a revolver, and each evening around 10 o'clock, Baxter-Ellis solemnly got it out and marched the men up to their quarters, locking them in for the night!

This show of force was apparently more theatrical than a necessity, for as Grace recorded in her memoirs, the 'prisoners' *"became very attached to us, and even begged us to take them to England when we left!"*.

Once the girls had put the finishing touches to the decorations, their Mess became a *"centre of much fun and gaiety"*.

Indulging in her penchant for hyperbole, Grace wrote:

"So now began our life in Brussels. Nobody thought ahead, we all revelled in the present, in the freedom from strain, the knowledge that the dance of death had ended. We were perhaps a trifle unbalanced, a little distraught after years of exhaustion, years of living on nerves, and will power; and who was to blame us for snatching at life and love? All the things of which war had deprived us?"

CHAPTER 49

Revelry To Tragedy

Invitations poured in.

During their stay in Bruges, the Unit had had very little in the way of entertainment, apart from the Victory Ball, and invitations to occasional dances at one or other of the airfields around the town.

But now their lives were filled with luncheons, dinners, receptions, dances. Life was filled with fun and laughter. According to Grace, *"we all went dancing mad"*.

Apart from restaurants, Messes, private houses, there were Night Clubs, too, of which Grace remembers, *"the less said the better"*. Not as bad as it sounds. The FANY maintained their strict rules of propriety – they never went out except in pairs at least, and always with a suitable man or men. These unwritten rules that governed their behaviour were respected and followed to the letter.

Every Sunday evening there was always an 'At Home' in their Mess at rue Limite, and it became a Mecca for officers of all the Allied forces – mostly Belgian and British. It *"became quite a fashionable stunt to come to the Fannies' Sunday Evenings"*. They got ices and orangeade from the best *patisseries* in town, and frequently held dances until early Monday mornings, for which they hired a pianist for 30 francs a night.

Grace herself took on the job of Mess Secretary to start off with, a job made easier by her access to the Officers' Canteen as it was called. There she was able to purchase quality Dry Champagne at 14 francs a bottle, and unlimited quantities of red Rhine wine at just 1 franc a bottle. These last came from a huge stock laid down for the German Army based around Brussels.

An additional and very useful perk, with the help of Lt Bonnevie, was access to the large 'liberated' German aerodrome outside Brussels. *"Here were left,"* writes Grace, *"thousands of gallons of petrol that were seized upon with great rejoicing."*

The Belgian population were determined to repay what they saw as a debt of gratitude to those who had delivered them from the

German oppression. Many of the wealthy especially welcomed the FANY, a unique organization of young ladies in British uniforms, not bound by the arbitrary disciplines of military service, and on a social par with them. They were women doing men's jobs with enormous confidence and professionalism, yet remaining glamorous, fun loving and feminine.

They threw their homes open to them in generous hospitality – and forgave unintended indiscretions. At the palatial home of Comtesse Paula de Liedenkirk, Grace and some of her FANYs caused a certain degree of consternation by preparing to smoke in the drawing-room. Unheard of behaviour before the war! Grace wrote wryly: *"So much for our barrack room manners!"*

And so the 'fun and gaiety' continued, from mansions in Brussels to chateaux in the country. She remembers a dinner given by the 51st Scottish Territorial Division at the Chateau of the Comte de Lichterveldt. The old Scottish Colonel in charge arranged for the Pipe Major to play in the background, as the guests worked their way through the magnificent banquet. She said: *"Never have I seen such expressions of polite endurance on the faces of the Belgian guests."*

There was so much going on, so many things to do. They frequently went to the Opera, and there were a few cinemas, still in their infancy. The other great love of the FANYs was riding, and here again doors were flung open for them. The Commandant of the Belgian Army Cavalry School gave them carte blanche, lent them horses whenever asked for, he or his officers escorting them to all the best places to ride. It was an idyllic period – Grace recalls glorious gallops in the woods round about.

It wasn't all play, though, there was much work to be done. Apart from long hours acting as drivers to the Top Brass and senior politicians in and around Brussels, they frequently had to be away from base for days at a time as Generals and Ministers went on tours of inspection or attended conferences as far afield as Paris, Lille, the Channel Ports, Arras, Luxembourg.

When they weren't motoring all over Flanders and beyond, they were much involved with their ambulances, transporting sick and wounded from place to place, especially ex-POWs who were frequently found wandering along roads, often near to collapse, after walking out of their camps when the German guards fled.

Grace vividly remembers one horrendous trip taking doctors and medical staff to a Russian POW camp. The guards had disappeared overnight, taking all available food and provisions with them, leaving behind a motley collection of starving, ill, Russian prisoners, always singled out for the harshest treatment by the Germans. It obviously affected her deeply, and she wrote about this episode: *"Dear God! That was Hell let loose on earth. These starved, emaciated, wolfish creatures were animals, not human beings & their cries & gestures and bestial ways made the girls turn sick."*

The climax came when one of the girls, finding it impossible to contemplate eating her sandwiches in front of these 'hunger-driven souls', threw her food to them without thinking. In the resulting uproar and scrabbling by these wretches, she had to be rescued by the doctors, and officers in charge.

They never went back, but never forgot the scene.

There were happier memories for the FANY. When the body of Nurse Edith Cavell was being repatriated to England, they were chosen to mount a Guard of Honour at the Gare du Nord station. This British nurse had been in charge of the Berkendael Institute in Brussels. After the German occupation she stayed on and became involved in helping over 200 Allied soldiers to escape from Belgium. She was long under suspicion, largely through a couple of English soldiers leaving their hiding place at the Institute against orders, going to a local Café, and getting drunk. Her days were numbered.

Finally she was arrested. The only evidence against her was a postcard from a British escapee back in England, thanking her for helping him escape. This was a particularly stupid thing to have done, but it was enough. After nine weeks in solitary confinement, the Germans shot her. The story went around the world and did enormous harm to Germany's standing.

In 1919 her body was exhumed from an unmarked grave at the Brussels prison. Her funeral procession wound through the streets of the city, escorted by British troops all the way. At the Gare du Nord an altar had been set up inside the station, and there the FANYs of Unit 5 proudly mounted a Guard of Honour round her coffin, while a brief service was held, and the time came for it to be placed on the special train.

Of this, Grace wrote: *"Ten of the girls hoisted the coffin onto their shoulders and carried it to the train that steamed off for Ostend and the boat to England."*

This sombre but uplifting event over, the parties, dinners, hospitality went on as before. Grace met up with the couple on whom she had been billeted in those far off days of 1914, went to stay with them in their house in the Ardennes.

So it went on. Had she looked back on past experience, she might have realised that the bubble had to burst sometime. But such was the continuing and contagious euphoria of Peace – all thoughts of that nature were banished.

One night in April the Coldstream Guards stationed at Namur held a magnificent Dinner and Ball for Grace and her FANYs. They pulled out all the stops to make it something really special.

She recalls: *"It was a wonderful night, we danced the soles off our shoes. We all enjoyed every minute of it."*

At five o'clock in the morning they arrived back at their Mess, flushed, happy, the excitement and exhilaration of the last few hours still paramount.

Mary Baxter-Ellis, Grace's second in command, was, to their surprise, waiting for them, fully dressed, a strained expression on her face. Making Grace sit down she handed her a telegram. It was from Grace's sister. It read simply:

"Mother dying. Come home at once. Isabel"

CHAPTER 50

Too Late

Grace was tough, resilient. She was used to moving fast when she had to. Baxter-Ellis had checked: there was a train leaving for Ostend at 6 a.m. and Grace was dressed in her uniform, packed and on that train.

There was a long lonely journey ahead, no way of making contact with those at home, her thoughts running riot, hoping for the best, fearing the worst.

At Ostend she went straight to the Commodore in command of shipping, and he got her onto the first available boat. Even so, it was 8 o'clock that night when she reached Dover. Seething with impatience she managed to hire a taxi, but only as far as Folkestone. Her mother had been moved to Worthing a month before. At Folkestone she had to organise another taxi to Worthing.

It was 4 a.m. by the time she arrived at the house. She rushed to the door: *"I rang and rang and there was no reply."* By then, after nearly 24 hours of travelling, scared of what she might find, weary and hungry, she was beside herself with worry.

"I called and got no answer. I ran round the house demented and saw lights in a ground floor room." One can only imagine her state of mind, maybe a bit unhinged. Desperate. She wrote: *"I tried to get in, knocked on the window, my heart was thumping."*

She could see light through the drawn blinds, but could hear nothing from inside the house. *"At last, half crazed, I got a knife from the driver and forced a front window and climbed in."*

Everything was horribly quiet, she remembered, and she could hear her heart beating. It was then that she began to accept her worst fears. A door in the passageway had light shining through the edges, a key in the lock. She opened it gently. It was a moment she would always remember. *"My mother, my dear, dear mother, and the candles burning round her and flowers on her breast."*

She could not remember how long she knelt there, before dragging herself to her feet and going in search of others. At last she found her sister and nephew and a nurse upstairs, could never understand how it was they had not heard her at the door.

The next few days passed in a haze, the local minister, visitors, undertakers. It was a sad and sombre time for them. Then, from Worthing, a long, slow, melancholy train journey up to Aberdeen, and the service and burial.

Grace recalls: *"A cold, grey day up there when we laid her to rest – and that night I took the train back to London."*

She was physically and mentally worn out. The stress of command through four years of war had left its mark, pulled her right down. It was a month before she returned to Brussels. On the surface she was back to her old confident, ebullient self, but her physical health beneath it all was seriously undermined.

A month later, in June 1919, after discussions with the girls of Unit 5, they decided to ask for demobilization. The decision was taken largely because of the number of ex-servicemen now looking for jobs to support themselves and their families. All the girls felt the same. Here they were, thirty of them, holding jobs that could and should be for the demobbed Belgian soldiers. After clearing it with FANY HQ, Grace sent in an official demand for demobilization.

It was accepted with reluctance.

But it was not quite the end.

The Grande Finale organised by the Belgian Government was about to follow, and FANY Unit 5, Corps de Transporte Belgique, was an essential part of it.

CHAPTER 51
Grande Finale

The Peace Conference being held in Paris was attended by journalists from all parts of the world. The Belgian Government arranged for around 100 of them to take part in a spectacular tour, to show them the damage the Germans had inflicted on the country. They invited the remaining girls of FANY Unit 5 to accompany them as a gesture of gratitude for all they had done. It was launched on June 6th with a Banquet given by the Mayor and Corporation of Dunkirk, which had suffered so much.

Grace had pride of place next to the Mayor, basking in the reflected glory. She was in her element. Not only that, she had been allocated a car with the Belgian Lieutenant in charge of all the male drivers involved, with an Army Sergeant as chauffeur! The procession of pressmen and photographers went everywhere – to Dinant, to Namur, to Charleroi, to Louvain, to Malines – so many ruined towns and villages and war zones occupied by the hated Boches.

Everywhere they went they were welcomed with crowds and cheers, with a special reception laid on at Liege.

"The crowds were enormous," Grace wrote, *"for miles before we went into the town & they lined the streets."* Among the cars near the front of the motorcade, Grace in her khaki uniform, officers' bars, medals, and a sergeant driver, caused quite a stir. People couldn't place what she was doing there – nor the other FANYs further back. Grace recalls: *"The schoolchildren threw us flowers and kisses and cheered. In Liege a woman presented me with a handsome bouquet of flowers, everyone yelled with joy at our imposing procession."*

At the Reception Room at Liege, old Major General Jacques *"embraced me, and recalled our friendship on the Yser Front in 1914".*

From Liege the column moved on to Spa through more cheering crowds, to a huge banquet organised and served by local women in national costumes.

At the feast, General Jacques had reserved a place beside him for

Grace. At the end, when the time came for toasts, he stood up and raised his glass. *"To Their Majesties King Leopold and Queen Elisabeth."* After the Royal Toast was drunk, he added another, *"and to Lieutenant Madame McDougall who has been with us since 1914, first at Antwerp, and then in our trenches on the Yser".*

It must have been a wonderful moment for Grace, bringing back so many memories, and being so publicly recognised for all she had done. Many of the men who had been in the retreat from Antwerp to the Yser left their seats and crowded round Grace, shaking her hand and kissing her cheek.

"It was my little hour of triumph," she wrote, *"and dear old General Jacques beamed at me over his glass – pleased and proud."*

It was the high-point of the tour for her. Back in Brussels the journalists not only made flowery speeches, but presented each of the girls with a little gold pendant inscribed with their name and the date, 6th-16th June 1919.

Later she was presented to Cardinal Mercier, who thanked her *"in his soft, flowing voice for what I had done for his country".* This meant so much to her, with her religious upbringing in Aberdeen, and her time spent at a Belgian convent before the war.

There was more to come. Her Majesty Queen Elisabeth of Belgium commanded their attendance for Tea at the Palace, to say her farewells to her *"Petites FANYs"* as she always called them. She had a very high regard for them, never failing to acknowledge any of them if ever their paths crossed while out in public.

She was a perfect hostess, putting them all at their ease, chatting to all of them. When tea was over, she invited them into her garden for official photographs, afterwards producing her own camera and taking snapshots of the group for herself. Her final act was to present Grace with a signed photograph of herself, in a silver frame, a treasured possession. Of the gathering, Grace wrote: *"That was the Grande Finale."*

It was.

The girls were all given a month's pay, and railway passes to wherever they wished. Grace, with friends Wood, Fergie and Morgan headed for Xamtem, where Belgium's crack cavalry regiment, the Guides, were stationed. The FANYs had had a long association with these men since 1914, and had been the first British back into Bruges, marching alongside them.

Grace remembers: *"We spent a wonderful week with them – it was summertime and we were in the highest of spirits. They were, as always, very perfect hosts, and it was sadly we left them."*

They were almost at the end of the road, but still managed to find their way into sticky and tricky situations. Driving to Dusseldorf after leaving the Guides, they ran into a kind of stand-off between Allied troops and Germans in the city, apparently refusing entry. French artillery was lined up, ranged on the town, with Belgian infantry in reserve. French sentries were guarding the bridge when Grace and her companions, still in uniform, left the car and approached.

According to Grace the sentries *"mistook me for the Queen of the Belgians, presented arms and gave me a Royal Salute, and let me pass. Two French Generals hurried from the other side to meet us, bowing, saluting showing us their arrangements. They escorted me to the place where the German barriers were and walked back with me across the bridge to our car, and stood bare-headed till I got in. We thought it prudent to move on – we realised their error, we wondered if they ever did?".*

From there, the four drove on to Cologne where they received a welcome from ex-FANY Decima Moore, who had organised and was running a wonderful Leave Centre Club for Allied servicemen. They had lunch with Decima and a General Levy.

After that it was back to Brussels for the last farewells. Even that was not to go according to plan. Arriving back in their old Mess, the few remaining girls had gone to a ball at the Rue de Loi, leaving a message that the others were to follow. It seemed like a fitting end to their demob tour. They all got dressed up and headed for the party. But – as she reached the front door of the house, Grace was suddenly hit by appalling pain in her side, and would have collapsed, if it hadn't been for Wood.

They sent for a taxi and Wood took her back to the Mess. It seems her old enemy appendicitis had struck again. Two doctors arrived *"and I had gallons of morphia but nothing seemed to help"*. The next day she was urged to have her appendix out once and for all. This was followed by a message from the Queen's doctor Neuman that she should immediately go to the Berkendael Institute. This was the medical clinic built up so effectively by Edith Cavell, and now run by the Matron she had trained to take over.

Grace was there for three weeks. Ronald, already demobbed, had come over as soon as he heard of her illness. She was, she recorded, *"thoroughly spoilt and made a fuss of – the nurses extraordinarily kind and sweet"*.

There were flowers galore, visitors flocked to see her, and *"handsome young men helped my husband carry me downstairs into the garden!"*.

In spite of her comfort and cosseting, her husband's presence, and blessed relief from the pain of her appendix, it was an upsetting and depressing time for her. Not only did she miss taking part in the Victory Parade through London – something she would have dearly loved – she also missed the first FANY reunion dinner, sending a telegram of good wishes instead. Most disappointing of all she had to turn down the Royal Command to attend the Garden Party at Buckingham Palace, when leading FANYs were introduced to the King and Queen, thus missing another potential high-point in her life.

Though physically improving, the reaction to her recent experiences set in and took hold. The hectic euphoria of the aftermath of war; her mother's death; the end of her life with the FANY Corps she loved; the parting from friends and comrades; the prospect of a future thousands of miles from the world she knew, in an alien country – all these accumulated, her nerves went to pieces, and she fell apart emotionally.

Friends took her and Ronald to Luxemburg where, amid idyllic surroundings she rested and recovered while Ronald fussed over her and fished. From there they moved to Zoute, the Chateau Roumont, a centre of hospitality and fun when Unit 5 first moved to Brussels.

By then Ronald, always something of a rover, was itching to get back to Scotland and join his older sister, Mabel, with whom he was very close. Because of the bond between them Mabel had come to resent Grace taking such a large part in her brother's life, an attitude that lasted throughout their lives.

Eventually, with Grace feeling very much better, Ronald took off for Scotland. Grace, still under doctor's orders not to exert herself, stayed behind.

By September she was fully recovered and back in Brussels. The Belgian War office loaned her the use of a lorry and driver to take her to Calais. There she collected the last of her belongings, abandoned almost a year before, in the hurry to join the triumphal return to Belgium.

Calais was being presented with the coveted Croix de Guerre in recognition of the suffering it had undergone through the years of conflict. Grace wrote: *"It was a great moment to be there."* It must also have been a sad one, for her, on the verge of leaving, perhaps forever, with so many memories of her times there – dangers, happiness, comradeship, challenges, friendships.

From Calais she was driven back to Ostend, again a place of memories. There she met up with another FANY, Stubbs, with whom she would cross to England. The ship's Captain was under orders from the Belgian War Ministry to provide Grace with a cabin.

"Someone gave me a bouquet of flowers, people kissed me and patted my hands, and with misty eyes and a strange tightening of my heart I watched the coastline recede; Belgium – the Belgian Army – what hopes and fears and suffering we had shared."

This was September, the same month in which, five long years ago, Grace had arrived in Belgium, alone and untested. Since then she had experienced the hell of an unspeakably dreadful war. She had plumbed the depths of despair; climbed the peaks of success. Tragedy and triumph had become part and parcel of her life. Those years had taken from her a sister, two brothers and her mother.

She stood at the door of a new life, one she looked upon with both anticipation and dread. A woman who loved adventure, she had little idea of the emptiness and loneliness of the life that lay ahead. She also loved her family, friends, the social whirl, dancing, gaiety, and was desperately sad at the thought of leaving these behind, perhaps forever.

Her own words underline the extent of her feelings.

"The boat bore me inexorably to the doom that awaited; the doom that was spoken of almost at once, as my husband greeted me at Victoria Station.

'We sail for Rhodesia in three weeks!'"

EPILOGUE

It was a hectic three weeks – seeing as many friends and relatives as possible, shopping, arranging finance. During this frantic period the Corps held a farewell dinner for Grace and Ronald. Speeches were made, plaudits and congratulations passed round. Grace thanked all those who had supported her so well, helped her through difficult times and built the FANY into the great Corps it was.

She and her husband were presented with a magnificent dark oak canteen of silver, the night ending in fond farewells and tears as old comrades parted, and Grace was made an Honorary Officer and Life Member of the Corps in recognition of her outstanding contribution over the years.

The remaining days rushed by. Family and friends travelled to Southampton to see them off. *"To Rhodesia,"* wrote Grace, unable to resist hyperbole, *"far away from friends and comrades; to loneliness and a country that knew not war, nor the Gods of war, nor the brave glory of after-battle wine, the flushed, recounting faces!"*

This was written in retrospect after years spent in Rhodesia. She felt that her life was ended, after *"five crowded years of youth and life and love and death"*.

During three uncomfortable and crowded weeks on the ship, Grace's old adventurous spirit reasserted itself, along with her steadfast optimism and confidence. The lure of the challenges ahead had displaced the wrench of leaving behind her life in England.

They spent a hectic week or two in Cape Town, Ronald happily showing her around many of his old haunts; sightseeing along the wide-curving Bay of Good Hope; savouring afresh the wondrous views from the top of Table Mountain. Both of them relaxed and happy, it was the honeymoon they had never managed back in 1915.

Then came the long, winding, fascinating three day train journey, across the Kalahari Desert, through the Hex River Mountains, over the Transvaal border and on to Bulawayo. Grace was intrigued to learn that it translated into 'the Place of Execution'. As far as their dreams of farming success was concerned, it became only too relevant.

Ronald, impatient to set up as a farmer, and confident in his knowledge of the land, jumped in and bought the first farm offered to him, without even going to see it. The '40' miles to it turned out to be double that, and the 'good roads' were little more than rough tracks most of the way.

No records remain regarding their subsequent problems, but in 1926 Grace published a novel about an ex-FANY who goes to farm in Rhodesia with her ex-army husband. Most of the adventures experienced by the heroine of the book as a FANY are Grace's real-life episodes and incidents; and it is probable that what happened to the heroine trying to come to terms with the hard, rough life on the farm, also set near Bulawyo, were those of Grace herself.

She often told her family how difficult it was, how lonely and isolated the farm, Infiningwe, was, miles from the nearest white neighbour. Dealing with the locals was a nightmare until she picked up enough of the *lingua franca,* known as Kitchen Kaffir, to converse with them. Ronald was out all day looking after his cattle, and checking that the local 'boys' were feeding and watering them properly.

But she was a fighter, and struggled on, gradually winning through, becoming fluent in Kitchen Kaffir, training the 'boys' to her ways. One particular incident she liked to recount raised her standing considerably among the locals. She had been giving the kitchen servants a dressing down for breaking crockery, when she dropped a glass on the stone floor. Wide grins appeared instantly on their faces. But, instead of shattering as it should have, it bounced. Always a fast thinker, she seized the opportunity. *"There,"* she said, *"if you're going to drop something, that's the way to do it."* Apparently grins faded, mouths dropped open, and thereafter she was regarded with some awe!

The servants lived well away from the farmhouse, with their families, in their own huts, or *kaias.* This was standard practice in or out of towns. One of the first things old hands impressed upon newcomers was the constant mantra 'Never let a Kaffir into your home after sundown'"!

One thing Grace never got used to was the lavatory, a small wooden hut well away from the house itself. There were no such things as drains. The door had holes drilled in it, to let in some light, and give someone already inside a view of anyone else approaching. Small children were called *piccanninis,* and as this was a small hut, it was known as a *piccannini kaia.* Kitchen Kaffir was very basic. Within, spiders or other unpleasant creatures lurked. One never went to the 'PK', as it was euphemistically called, after dark.

During her first year on the farm she became pregnant. She was seldom able to get into town, but when she did her doctor was not happy with her condition. Shortly before the baby was due, the doctor sent a note to tell her she must come into Bulawayo to have the child. Putting it off to the last moment, she had a dreadful 80-mile trek in an ox-wagon, over tracks worse than any she had experienced in France. She told her family later that she really thought she was going to die, that it was a pain-filled nightmare journey, jolted and jarred at every bump.

It was all worth it with the birth of a sturdy young son, whom she desperately wanted, calling him Charles Ronald after the two men she loved more than any others – her father and her husband.

Back home on the farm, life was now still more difficult, though the Africans were far more helpful and amenable than they had been before now that Grace had wee Ronald, as he was known, to look after.

To complete her joy, delight and pride in young Ronald, Grace received a letter from the Belgian Queen, Elisabeth, agreeing to become his Godmother. She had sent the request off with some trepidation to the Palace, asking if the Queen would grant her the honour. After weeks of suspense, as mail boats chugged across oceans, the Queen agreed. Grace was over the moon.

The next three years were difficult and Spartan, Grace's loneliness was somewhat assuaged by having her baby son to look after. Towards the end of 1923 she became pregnant again, and decided that this time she would not go through the awful experience she had had with Charles Ronald. She still had some money left, the farm was just about breaking even, and in Spring 1924 she returned home, where on 9th May she gave birth at Selling, in Kent, to a daughter, Rona Grace.

Again, it was a difficult birth, and luckily her cousin Elizabeth,

with whom she had weathered her illness back in 1916, was there
for her once more. Now with two young children to care for, Grace
realised she had to be fully recovered and ready. The thought of
going back to that hard unrelenting slog in Rhodesia was daunting.

The months went by. Baby Rona was happy and healthy, Ronald
bright and talkative. Grace felt she needed more time to bolster
her resolve. She visited family and friends, proud to show off her
children, and met up again with old comrades from the war. It
was a wonderful time of relaxation and happiness for her, back in
civilization.

To complete her return to normality, she determined to go
once more to Belgium, which remained so deeply etched into her
memories. This was, perhaps, the best decision she could have made,
and there is no doubt it buoyed up her spirits and helped her to face
the difficulties that inevitably lay ahead. She loved Belgium, cared
passionately for the Queen, and admired and respected her for the
manner in which she had conducted herself during the war.

She writes about her visit at some length in her memoirs. Arriving
in Brussels with Ronald and Rona, she *"was astonished and touched to
find that they still remembered me and still showed their appreciation of
the little I was able to do for their Army"*.

No doubt tears were shed, too, when *"on the morning after my
arrival dear old General Clooten waited upon me with an enormous
bouquet of flowers"*. She was so delighted, felt so honoured that he
should have come to see her, and so soon.

Grace had written to the Palace to inform them of her intended
visit, no doubt in the hope the Queen would give her an audience.
She did, sending for both her and young Ronald, who was fascinated
by the soldiers on guard outside, and the rows of footmen lining the
corridors inside. Grace noted that when they reached her *"the Queen
herself, so dainty and exquisite"*- held his attention.

Like any mother, Grace had been anxious to ensure his good
behaviour at the Palace. He had admired a toy fire engine in a
shop window, and Grace told him that if he was very good at his
Godmother's, Mummy might get it for him.

At the Palace the Queen knelt on the floor with Ronald to help
unwrap and show him a wonderful model village she had got for him,

a variety of hand crafted and painted houses, cottages, churches, taverns and a village hall. It was to become a treasured possession for years. However, after thanking her politely for it, he then said in his clear, little voice: *"But Mummy, what about my fire engine?"*

The Queen, with children of her own *"didn't mind a bit"*. It was a measure of her understanding and generosity that Grace recalls: *"On Christmas Eve an enormous box tied with ribbon was brought to our Hotel, and proved to be a monster Fire Engine with ten Firemen in leather coats and helmets, complete with axes at their belts, and escape ladders and hosepipes. I don't think any small boy had such a wonderful Fairy Godmother!"*

Finally, to her amazement, the day before she was due to leave the Hotel and return to England, an Officer was sent from the Ministry of War to tell the management that *"they must not overcharge me, and must remember that I had served with the Belgian Army"*.

Her confidence and self-esteem were now fully restored by these unexpected but welcome tributes from her past. They gave her the will and determination to return to that lonely, faraway farm in Rhodesia. A new year – she would make it a new start.

Unfortunately, things began to go badly wrong that year, with the start of a severe drought throughout the area. It lasted over three heartbreaking years. All the cattle died, and there was no insurance against that sort of natural disaster. The family, almost bankrupt, and by then with another son, Desmond, packed up and moved into Bulawayo.

Ronald managed to get a job as a surveyor with Rhodesian Railways, not particularly well-paid, but by this time he was into his fifties, and not in a position to pick and choose. It also involved a good deal of travelling up and down the line which ran through Umtali on the Portuguese East (Mozambique) frontier to the port of Beira, Rhodesia's main outlet to the sea. There he had an office where he spent much of his time. His other base was a permanent tented camp in the bush just over the frontier in Mozambique itself, staffed by a dozen Africans, from where he carried out inspection tours of the hundreds of miles of line in his care.

After two years he and Grace moved to Umtali, a much smaller town than Bulawayo, but a lot closer to Beira, which meant that he was away from home much less. Grace now settled into the life of a colonial wife, and hated it. On the farm there was a physical loneliness, but here it was a loneliness of mind. In later years she confided in her daughter a great deal, who, in an article for The Guardian newspaper wrote: *"My mother hated golf, tennis drinking and the total cultural desert that was Rhodesian town life."* In one of her mother's diaries was this entry: *"Conversation consisted of a string of utter inanities interspersed with vicious gossip."* It was not a happy time for her. Now there was no motor car for her, no horses, no money.

Her life before Rhodesia had been one of adventure, comfort when she wanted it, social esteem, parties, discussions, riding. In Rhodesia she found it suffocating, and did her best to moderate this by using all the natural gifts she possessed – organising, writing, acting.

Having successfully broken into print with a second book, a novel titled The Golden Bowl, she began work on her war memoirs, using the material and diaries she had kept so diligently. This went a long way to alleviating the unhappiness she was experiencing. Called 'Five Years with the Allies', it covered those years very comprehensively. Unable to find a publisher for it, far too late for the post-war spate of books of that genre, she lodged it with the Imperial War Museum, where it has since become a valuable source of information for later historians writing about women at war.

As well as writing her memoirs, she took up freelance journalism, writing for the Cape Times, Rhodesian Advertiser and other papers. Regaining some of her energy and drive, she became President of the Ex-Services Association in Umtali, and also a prominent member of the Women's Institute (WI), being elected Convener of the Standing Committee for Peace for the Federation of Rhodesian Women's Institutes. She put her considerable acting talents to work organising an Amateur Dramatic Society, putting on plays which became very popular in the town.

In 1934 she even tried to raise a Rhodesian FANY contingent, but on running the idea past FANY HQ in London, it was vetoed on the grounds of the political and racial problems experienced there.

This was probably just as well, as the following year Grace had to return to England for medical treatment. Her heart had been playing up for some time, and it was felt that the climate and height above sea level had something to do with it. Originally, it was only to be for a year, but other complications set in and her stay was extended. The children had come with her, as it would have been impossible for Ronald to keep them with him.

In spite of her health problems, however, she refused to slow down, enrolling for a year's course at the Bonar Law college. She was dismayed, too, to discover that the FANY were not represented at the Silver Jubilee Festival of Empire. She responded swiftly, successfully forming an Old Comrades' Association, which ensured the Corps' appearance at many events of national pageantry, including regular participation at the Armistice Parades.

With the threat of a possible war hanging in the air, Grace found time to join the St John Ambulance Brigade and renew her Certificate in First Aid, then enrolled in the national Air Raid Precautions (ARP) organization, run within the local councils.

At the same time, she resumed her journalism as best she could, being published in a variety of local and, occasionally, national newspapers. The Daily Sketch published a long piece about her with her photograph, headlined 'CALL TO BRITAIN'S WAR NURSES' with a sub-heading 'Leader Says She is not in a Position to Give Reasons'. There is no follow-up to this in any available records, so quite what she had in mind may never be known.

In the summer of 1937 Ronald came home on three months' home leave, coinciding with the school holidays. It was a very happy time, weeks of good weather spent up in Dinnet, Aberdeenshire, Grace's old stamping ground. He returned to Rhodesia, due to retire in 1940. The war intervened. Rhodesia Railways asked him to stay on for the duration, as, with all the younger men flocking to the Colours, there was nobody to take over from him.

In the months before war actually broke out, Grace approached FANY HQ with a view to rejoining as an active member of the Corps, but was rejected as being too old. It really was a forlorn hope. After all those years of absence she would have been hopelessly out of touch with people, systems, equipment – the whole set-up. It was a plan doomed to failure from the start, but she was nevertheless upset. Added to which, some of those now running the Corps had been antagonized while Grace was Commandant, during those wartime years in command, and would have made things very difficult indeed.

She was living in Dorset, and working for a national charity covering a large area, for which she had been provided with a car. However, after the 1940 debacle, petrol was only provided for essential purposes, and the job folded. She took various positions after that, all to do with providing services for the Forces, the WVS, YMCA and the like, running canteens, helping out on mobile tea vans.

Moving to London in 1941, she found herself once again crossing swords with the Establishment, but from a different position. She got a job with the War Office, in a department looking after officers' records. It was a fairly lowly clerical job, but Grace was happy to do it, as she felt she was helping the war effort, and working for the British Army, even if indirectly.

She was horrified and outraged at the behaviour of her colleagues at work, many of them at that time Civil Servants. They came to work where many of them read books, wrote letters, and some even knitted. They sat around long tables with the files in front of them, alternately working and relaxing. She couldn't believe it.

Unable to keep quiet, Grace told them in no uncertain terms what she thought of them. It didn't go down well. She herself was getting through file after file, working non-stop, until approached by the Union representative and told she was clearing far too many files and to *'cut down the numbers by at least half'*.

This she refused to do, again making her feelings very plain.

Shortly after, she was summoned to the office of the Civil Servant in charge of the department, who told her *'she was making waves unnecessarily, and she must learn to pull together'*. That didn't go down well. When she told him just what was going on, he apparently insisted she was exaggerating. Moved to another department, filing away letters and memos, she was again amongst women who were just *"Outright slackers"*. She could not take any more, and gave in her notice.

Fiercely patriotic she exploded at home. She could not understand how *"British people could behave like that"*. From then on she mostly worked in some of the many Forces Canteens run by the Salvation Army, or Toc H or the YMCA and others. Hard work though it was, with often inconvenient hours, she felt she was at least doing something directly for the Forces, with others who worked just as hard as her.

Throughout the war, Grace had to struggle to make ends meet. When it ended, so did the jobs she had been able to do. Ronald finally retired in 1945, but it was near the end of 1946 before he was able to get a passage home. Civilians were way down on the priority list. He came home, to Grace's relief and delight, but this was shortlived. A winter of food and fuel shortages and the sort of freezing conditions he hadn't experienced since WW1 was too much for him. He died from pneumonia, aged 72, in the February of 1947.

Grace remained in London until 1960, health now failing, then moved down to a flat in Bexhill-on-Sea, bought for her by her daughter Rona. She was comfortable and happy there, close to the sea.

This feeling of peace and contentment peaked when she was able to return to her beloved Aberdeenshire a few months before her death. Writing about it at length in a letter to Rona, it was obvious that the trip was a wonderful finale, a last high point towards the close of her life.

She was invited to stay in the Highlands with her nephew, the only son of her much-loved younger brother Billy. He pulled out all the stops, gave her a wonderful time. Also named Bill, he served through World War 2 in the Black Watch winning the coveted M.C. denied to his father.

He drove her the length and breadth of those Highlands she remembered so well, stopping to escort her round anywhere and everywhere she could remember from her youth. She ended a long letter to Rona about the trip: *"They say life completes a circle – mine has. I have been to all those places of early girlhood, and slept in my Aberdeen, only about 6 houses from the house I was born in."*

It was a letter shot through with excitement, enthusiasm, awakened memories, matching so well the wild exhilaration that coursed through her veins so many years before in the war-torn fields of France.

It was her final curtain call.

She was content and at peace with herself.

She passed away quietly after weeks in hospital, fighting to the last. It was fitting it should be the exact date on which she had enrolled in the FANY Corps way back in 1910, when it all began – 29th January. A Memorial Service was held for her, attended by a surprising number of people. FANY Headquarters sent three officers in uniform, a gracious and generous gesture that Grace would have appreciated.

In the small, quiet churchyard of Glen Tanar, by Dinnet, Aberdeenshire, at Grace's request, an Aberdeen granite plaque was installed on an outside wall of the old stone Chapel, overlooking the small cemetery, where so many of her forbears are buried.

It reads:

In Loving Memory of

GRACE ALEXANDRA McDOUGALL

1887 – 1963

Croix de Guerre,

Medaille d'Honneur de l'Ordre de Leopold II,

Medaille d'Honneur de la Couronne,

Medaille de la Reine Elisabeth,

Medaille de Secours des Blessés militaires,

Medaille des Epidemies

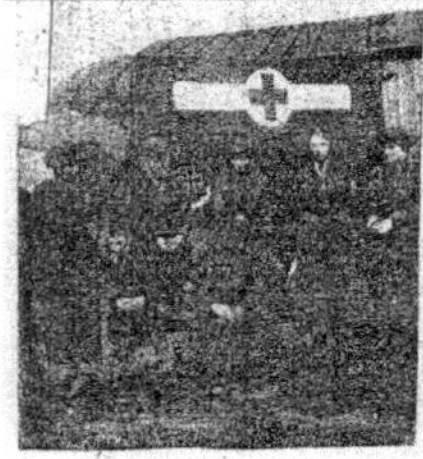

To Mrs McDougall
1st Lieutenant & O.C.
Allied Section F.A.N.Y.

With all good wishes for her happiness and as a token of our appreciation and friendship

Allen, D.E.R.	Cole-Hamilton, M.S.	Hunter, A.R.	Nocton, M.	Struthers, E
Allen, G.M.R.	Crisfield, M.	Hutchinson, S.	O'Conor, F.	Stubbs, M.
Anderson, G.	Crockett, L.	Joynson, B.	O'Neill-Power, V.	Swan, C
Ashdown, T.	Davidson, C.	Judge, P.	Peyton-Jones, G.G.	Sykes, A.
Bennett, P. Gasheton	Davis, W.	Lewis, J.M.	Pease, D.+E.	Sykes, M.
Berry, Nan	De la Mare, E.R.	Lindsay, S.	Pounds, E.	Thompson, D.
Blacker, W.	Dewar, A.C.K.	de Lisle, G.	Pace, H.	Thompson,
Bond, M.L	Dickie, E.	Lowson, N.F.	Reynard, H.M.	Thorp, L.
Bond, M.M.	Drabble, G.V.	MacKenzie, E.	Reynolds, G.J.	Tory, E.C
Bowen, Mrs	Edwards, S.	Marlowe, V.L.	Reynolds, D.P.	Trubridge,
Bowles, Mrs	Faulkner, E.	Marples, G.	Richardson, M.	Tupper, L.
Booker, E.	Frain, M.	Marshall, M.D	Richardson, G. Stewart	Walton, E.
Bradley, I.	Ford, H.	McClure, N.	Rivett, A.	Wicks, I
Brown, J. Monty	Franklin, L.M.	McDougall, M.	Robertson, M.	Williams, J
Brown, M.F.	Fraser, H.M.	McDowall, I.	Ravenscroft, ?	Walker, M.
Baker, Mrs	Goodliffe, W.	Morris, Mrs	Rothband, M.	
Bagnold, E.	Hall, M.C.A.	Morris, D.	Seymour, G.	
Cadell, M.	Hardman, E.M	Morris, P.	Spikins, K.	
Cluff, Nora	Holmes, V.	Morton, Mrs	Stisted, G.H.	
Cluff, Rev.	Hunter, D.E.	Moseley, R.G.	Stiven, B.M.	

Good wishes from FANY members

Grace with children

Grace centre with S Rhodesian Ex Services Contingent

The farmhouse at Infiningwe

Ronald Senior and Ronald Junior

Grace McDougall returned from Southern Rhodesia

Medals earned by Grace McDougall

Obituary

MRS. GRACE ASHLEY McDOUGALL

On 19th January, 1963, at St. Leonards-on-Sea, after illness gallantly endured, Grace (Ashley Smith), Ordre de la Couronne, Ordre de Leopold II (Belge), Mons Medal, 1914-18 Service Medal, Victory Medal, French Croix de Guerre (Silver Star), Medaille d'Honneur, Medaille des Epidemies, Medaille Secours des Blesses Militaires and (Belgian) Medaille de la Reine Elizabeth, widow of Ronald McDougall, Southern Rhodesia.

The following cutting is taken from *The Times* of 29th January, 1963: "Mrs. Grace Ashley McDougall, who died at the age of 76, was a very active member of the F.A.N.Y. Corps from 1910 to 1920. In September, 1914, she went alone to Antwerp, hoping to arrange for a unit to follow her to a hospital there. She drove an ambulance for the Belgian Army, and then escaped to England when the Germans overran Belgium. She returned to organise a unit for the Belgian hospital in Calais, starting on 27th October, 1914, and assisted in the foundation of other units for ambulance driving, welfare work and staff of a French Hospital at Binson.

"She was Commandant of the units of the F.A.N.Y. Corps, working for the Belgian and French Armies in the First World War, and was decorated for her work by the Belgian and French Governments".

The following is a cutting taken from the *Evening Standard*:— "First of the Many—The Women's Services in this country have lost one of their most intrepid pioneers. Mrs. Grace McDougall has died at St. Leonards at 76. In the first World War she was the first of the many. When war broke out she arrived alone in Antwerp, drove a Belgian ambulance, escaped through Holland when the German overran Belgium and got back to England.

"Within a few weeks she was back on the Continent with an ambulance bought with her own money, and a Red Cross Unit. Throughout the war she served with the First Aid Nursing Yeomanry"

Grace McDougall's F.A.N.Y. number was No. 3.